The People of the
Standing Stone

A volume in the series

Native Americans of the Northeast:
Culture, History, and the Contemporary

edited by Colin Calloway, Jean M. O'Brien-Kehoe,
and Barry O'Connell

THE PEOPLE OF THE STANDING STONE

*The Oneida Nation
from the Revolution through the
Era of Removal*

Karim M. Tiro

University of Massachusetts Press

AMHERST AND BOSTON

LC 2011014427
ISBN 978-1-55849890-7 (paper); 889-1 (library cloth)

Designed by Dennis Anderson
Set in Adobe Caslon Pro by Westchester Book
Printed and bound by Thomson-Shore, Inc.

Library of Congress Cataloging-in-Publication Data

Tiro, Karim M.
The people of the standing stone : the Oneida nation from the revolution through the era
of removal / Karim M. Tiro.
        p. cm.
Includes bibliographical references and index.
ISBN 978-1-55849-890-7 (pbk. : alk. paper)—
ISBN 978-1-55849-889-1 (library cloth : alk. paper)
1. Oneida Indians—History.   2. Oneida Indians—Government relations.
3. Oneida Indians—Relocation.   4. Indians of North America—History—Revolution,
1775–1783.   I. Title.
E99.O45T57 2011
974.7004'9755—dc22
                                        2011014427

British Library Cataloguing in Publication data are available.

For my mother,

Dora A. Tiro

Contents

Supplementary material available at scholarworks.umass.edu/umpress

Illustrations

Preface

AT THE BEGINNING of the twenty-first century, Indian claims to land and sovereign rights once again roil New York's political waters. None has generated more controversy than the Oneida nation's effort to recoup their 250,000-acre reservation in the center of the state, and their operation of a lucrative casino. Although similar developments bedevil states from Maine to California, the consternation seems greatest in the East. There, Indians were thought of as a "vanished race" whose continued existence was mostly in the form of artifacts buried in the ground. In the 1970s, however, eastern Natives forcefully asserted their presence and took up a prominent role in American Indian Movement activism. Natives posed hard questions about how Euro-Americans had acquired their land. Quite understandably, non-Indians responded with questions of their own. The first was, "Who are these people?" They wondered how Natives could really have survived for centuries in a Euro-American landscape of fields and factories. Because historians have traditionally paid attention to Natives only when they were physically resisting white expansion, nothing in the traditional historical narratives of the region provided satisfactory explanations. Native Americans, by asserting their rights, disturbed quiet land titles as well as settled histories and static conceptions of "Indian-ness" and ethnicity in general.

This book sheds light on these vexing issues by examining the history of the Oneidas during eight turbulent decades that began with the the American Revolution. In those years, the Oneidas weathered a trio of traumas: war, dispossession, and division. The Revolution devastated their villages, only to be followed by an invasion of white settlers who took control of

xi

nearly all their lands. Traditional subsistence practices became impossible to sustain as Euro-American settlements proliferated. The Iroquois Confederacy fractured and ceased to be politically effective. Between 1775 and 1850, the Oneidas went from being an autonomous, powerful people in their ancestral homeland to being residents of disparate, politically exclusive reservation communities as far as nine hundred miles apart and surrounded by whites. The Oneidas' physical, political, and emotional division persists to this day. But the distance traveled by the Oneidas during the three-quarters of a century examined here was not just geographic. Even those who remained in place were living in a world transformed. Culturally, ecologically, and demographically, their world changed more than at any time before or since. Oneidas of the post-Revolution generation were reluctant pioneers, undertaking more of the adaptations to colonized life than any other generation. Amid such wrenching change, maintaining continuity was itself a creative challenge. That process is at the heart of this book.

When the Oneidas appear in American history books, it is usually in relation to their loyalty to the Patriot cause. The Oneidas distinguished themselves as the United States' most important Indian allies. The character of this alliance, however, has been consistently misunderstood. Far too much emphasis has been placed on the influence of their missionary, Samuel Kirkland, and too little on the Oneidas' main concern, protecting their land. Rather than blindly following their Yankee minister, or being won over by Patriot ideology, the Oneidas correctly understood the strength of the revolutionary movement and the threat it posed to them. Historians have also interpreted the American Revolution as an "Iroquois civil war," but close examination of the Oneidas' activities suggests otherwise. Although the Oneidas fought earnestly for the Patriots, they consciously avoided taking the lives of Indians on the other side of the conflict. These courtesies were reciprocated.

Nevertheless, Oneida villages were devastated in the course of the conflict, and their population declined by nearly a quarter. The Oneidas' contributions to the cause of U.S. independence exceeded those of most Patriot communities. At the Battle of Oriskany, the Battle of Saratoga, and elsewhere, Oneida warriors and scouts were active on the Patriots' behalf. But neither their contributions nor their sacrifices translated into a durable sense of obligation on the part of the new nation. The Oneidas were dispossessed of nearly their entire land base within five years of the war's end. This and other postwar developments demonstrate clearly that the Revolution was, at least in part, a war of territorial expansion. The rush for lands in New York that followed the war's conclusion helps explain the Revolutionary motivations of rural Americans who made up the vast majority of Patriots, even though their more flamboyantly militant urban peers tend to overshadow them in the national memory.

Significantly, the Oneidas' lands were taken by the state of New York rather than the United States. That the Articles of Confederation and the Constitution entrusted Indian affairs to the national government did not preclude state activity in practice. Although scholarly studies of Indian law, policy, and treaty making almost invariably focus on the federal government, state governments have historically cast a longer and deeper shadow over the Oneidas and many other Indian nations. Even when the state's jurisdiction was of dubious legality, it posed a more immediate and potent threat to Indian rights and interests, representing as it did a local majority controlled only ineffectually by federal oversight. Settlers used the state to secure access to Indian land and ensured their ongoing prosperity through state-sponsored infrastructure projects such as the Erie Canal. The state was one of the pioneers' most useful implements.

The Oneidas' adaptation to the onrush of white settlement in central New York after the Revolution demonstrates that their survival was not really a matter of keeping inviolate as many elements of their traditional culture as possible. It was, more precisely, a process of engaging with aspects of the colonizers' culture and reshaping them to fit indigenous imperatives. In a bid to protect their territory and secure steady revenue to replace the faltering fur trade, Oneidas turned to leasing some of their land. They hoped this practice would satisfy Euro-Americans' demands and some of their own needs. The Oneidas were likewise prepared to conform to Euro-American practices of using written documents to enshrine all transactions. But titles, leases, and treaties were complex instruments even for whites, and translation of concepts, place-names, and mathematics made them particularly difficult for Natives to comprehend. Thus, the Oneidas placed great hope in finding an individual to broker their dealings with potential tenants or purchasers of land. They recruited a succession of candidates, including missionaries, traders, government officials, men who had grown up in their midst, and men who had married into their families. All of these men failed them not because they were particularly venal (although some were) but because they partook of the pervasive cultural supremacist ideology of the age, which held that Indians must ultimately surrender their lands and abandon their traditions.

Religion played an important role in the Oneidas' adaptation to their rapidly and radically changing world. Through Anthony F. C. Wallace's classic study of the Seneca prophet Handsome Lake, historians have become familiar with that Iroquois nation's religious revitalization. But the Seneca experience cannot stand for all Iroquois, let alone all Natives. The Oneidas exhibited only modest interest in the teachings of the Seneca prophet compared with their interest in Christianity. Consciously considering their fate in spiritual terms, the Oneidas exhibited a variety of beliefs and practices that defy the simplistic categories of "Christian" or "traditionalist." Most Oneidas engaged with Christianity to some degree to tap into its sources of power. They learned the terms and tenets of Euro-Americans' faith to better understand what they were up against, as well as to demonstrate its inadequacies and inappropriateness for Indians. The Oneidas did not, however, leave the engagement unchanged. At all points along the post-Revolution religious spectrum, their engagement with Christianity was conscious, urgent, creative, and resourceful.

In the nineteenth century, the Oneidas, like most other Natives in the eastern United States, faced a concerted effort to remove them to the West. The Oneida experience demonstrates that Indian removal was a national phenomenon and not just a problem that confronted Native Americans in the South. Because the removal issue is generally subordinated to the story of the coming of the Civil War, it is remembered only when it contributed to sectional tensions, such as during the debate over the Indian Removal Act. But like the Cherokee and other southern nations, the Oneidas and fellow Iroquois came under concerted pressure to leave shortly after the War of 1812 made removal seem a viable policy for dealing with Native Americans. The upshot of this pressure was the division of the Oneidas into two nations—one in New York, one in present-day Wisconsin—by 1838. Shortly thereafter, a third was created in Canada. This extraordinary result was brought about not through any successful effort to win the Oneidas over to the idea of removal but through sustained pressure by settlers, speculators, and the state of New York. The state made the most of factional divisions among the Oneidas to promote land sales, and in the 1840s even imposed severalty (the holding of land as private property) on them. Historians have demonstrated the devastating effects of dividing reservations into private parcels when the federal government did so throughout the West in the 1880s, but the Oneida experience preceded this action by decades.

Despite their division and dispossession, the Oneidas did not disappear. Like other Native peoples who had been demographically overwhelmed by white settlers, the Oneidas maintained a relatively inconspicuous existence on the margins of the dominant culture. Economically, they survived in niches such as performance, military service, handicraft peddling, and small-scale agriculture. Now largely landless, the Oneidas lacked anything that the dominant culture desired and were accordingly forgotten, even if they had not gone anywhere. Many Oneidas had already adopted European clothing and religious beliefs and they increasingly spoke English. To their Euro-American neighbors their becoming less visibly and audibly distinct meant that they had ceased to be Indians in any significant way. Despite all the pressure brought to bear on them, some two hundred Oneidas remained in the heart of their ancestral territory. They adopted elements of the dominant culture in such a way that their distinctiveness was always articulated, especially to themselves. In 1845, Henry Rowe Schoolcraft, the renowned ethnologist, was commissioned by New York State to execute a census of the Indian population. His tabulation of Oneida households reflects the persistence of extended families, traditional small-scale cultivation, and limited market involvement. His correspondence also reflects the Oneidas' suspicion of anyone remotely associated with the state.

In its general contours, the Oneidas' experience does not differ radically from that of most other eastern Indian peoples and should be seen as representative. The Oneidas are, however, better served than most by the documentary record. The light is relatively bright because of the presence of the missionary Samuel Kirkland. Kirkland began his mission before the Revolution and remained involved in Oneida affairs until his death in 1808. To be sure, Kirkland's large corpus of writings provides a Eurocentric view of Oneida life, tinctured heavily by New Light Calvinism and his need to appease his financial backers. But Kirkland's knowledge of the Oneida language allowed him to provide invaluable insights into Oneida life, as well as translations of Oneida speech. In part to demonstrate the difficulty of his task, he frequently quoted Natives who were critical of whites, including him.

Other fruitful sources on the history of the Oneidas include the extensive documentation generated by the thirty or so treaties and related negotiations during this period. In the Revolution's wake, the Oneidas were the new "eastern door" of the Iroquois, and treaty commissioners seeking land spent many days at Oneida before moving on. Their negotiations there were often the most protracted. After the treaties, surveyors produced field books that plotted lands to be distributed as well as compensation due Indian families. To the historian these field books also provide a record of changing Oneida land use practices and residence patterns. Annuity distribution records identify the leadership of various factions within the Oneida Nation at regular intervals. Receipts record who stayed where, drank what, and paid whom. Relatively few of the documents on which this study is based were written by the Oneidas themselves. Oral modes of communication predominated among them; only a handful of Oneidas during this period were literate. Nevertheless, the Oneidas were not silent in the face of land-grabbing or other insults offered by the people invading their territory, and their voices are partially audible through the minutes of treaties and other diplomatic encounters and petitions and remonstrances to provincial, state, and federal governments, as well as missionary societies and other potential allies. The Oneidas broadcast their grievances to Albany and Washington and Philadelphia, and their situation was discussed in capitals as distant as Paris and the Vatican. Taken together, these documents make up an uncommonly deep reservoir of data for the exploration of the onset of settler colonialism, as well as the Indians' varied adaptations.

My work here can contribute to a greater understanding of the experiences of the indigenous peoples who have seen Euro-American polities rise up all around them. In the present day, public discourse surrounding Natives' relationship to the towns, states, and nations that claim them as subjects has been marked by considerable acrimony. Indians' exemption from taxes, for example, has been decried as discriminatory. By probing the early phases of these relationships, I seek to add historical depth to these debates. An understanding of the history of the Oneidas' relationship to the settlers, state, and nation that surrounded them clarifies the origin and nature of the rights they assert. It also sheds light on the historical relationship between power and rights. Not all of the controversy pits Natives against their non-Indian neighbors. The Oneidas' experience of division and dispersal, at the individual and group levels, has left in its wake vexing questions about membership, governance, and the entitlement of various distinct groups to claim sovereign rights in, or compensation for, their aboriginal homeland. The Oneidas' troubles in this regard are hardly unique, and an exploration of their origins can place contemporary debates in historical context.

What this book should make unambiguously clear is that Natives were not merely passive victims of historical change. They analyzed their options, however narrow, and argued over the best strategy to promote the best interests of their communities. In the American Revolution, they had to decide whether to support Loyalists or Patriots, in what way, and to what extent. In the years that followed, they made similar choices with regard to myriad questions about such issues as religion, land use, and, relocation. The choices were never acceptable, and consensus was never achieved, but the people survived.

A FEW WORDS on terminology are in order. I use the terms *Indian* and *Native* interchangeably, acknowledging that they raise problems of historical accuracy and have been tainted by racist usage. I likewise employ the familiar *Iroquois* and *Six Nations* rather than the name often used by the people themselves, *Haudenosaunee*. I use *Iroquois League* when referring to the Six Nations' overarching symbolic structure and *Iroquois Confederacy* when referring to its practical, political dimension. I also employ *nation* and *tribe* interchangeably. Although both terms sometimes took on precise definitions in legal or scientific contexts, their meanings were always changing and continue to change. Both were common in the eighteenth and nineteenth centuries. Finally, in the text I discuss the problems with the factional designations *Christian* and *pagan*. Nevertheless, they are still useful because they were employed at the time and had clear historical significance, even if they did not accurately describe the factional conflict or the beliefs of the people to whom they referred. After the partition of the Oneida reservation in 1805, these parties became legally distinct, and so in discussion following that date their names are fully capitalized (e.g., "Pagan Party"). I have generally standardized the spelling of personal and place names throughout.

Acknowledgments

I HAVE TAKEN a good, long while to write *The People of the Standing Stone* and have accrued many professional and personal debts in the process. Richard Dunn and James H. Merrell guided me through the early stages of this project with patience, wisdom, and good humor. Richard Beeman, Nancy Farriss and Mike Zuckerman, were also very helpful. I had the benefit of a superb graduate cohort at the University of Pennsylvania, among whom I owe special thanks to Ed Baptist, Nicole Eustace, Laura Matthew, Liam Riordan, Randolph Scully, John Smolenski, and Kirsten Wood. The community of scholars at the McNeil Center for Early American Studies also helped get this project off the ground. I am grateful to have been in residence at the same time as Tom Humphrey, Kathleen DuVal, Rodney Hessinger, Jane Merritt, and Cynthia Van Zandt. I thank Dan Richter for facilitating my return for a stint as a postdoctoral associate.

The Conference on Iroquois Research provided a congenial atmosphere in which to discuss a wide array of issues. Over the years I benefited greatly from my conversations with Jack Campisi, Fred Muscavitch, Jon Parmenter, Christine Patrick, Bill Starna, and linguist extraordinaire Roy Wright, among many, many others. The Iroquois Conference would not be the same without the infectious, unruly enthusiasm of Laurence Hauptman. I thank him for introducing me to L. Gordon McLester III and for the invitations to participate in their series of Oneida history conferences in Wisconsin.

During several periods over the past decade, I have served as a historical consultant to the Oneida Indian Nation of New York. The Nation's staff historians, Anthony Wonderley and Jesse Bergevin, were always obliging. I was also consistently impressed by the knowledge of Oneida history of the Oneidas' attorneys. I particularly enjoyed and benefited from working with Jason Acton, John Donelkovich, John Druva, Tom Mason, Steve McSloy, and Michael Smith.

Historians understand that the documentary record does not maintain and organize itself. It requires careful custody to remain usable. Thus, I am grateful to all the librarians and archivists at the many institutions whose collections I have used. My research was aided very significantly by John Aubrey at the Newberry Library, David Fowler at the David Library of the American Revolution, Bill Gorman at the New York State Archives, and Frank Lorenz at Hamilton College. Historical study of New York State is in good hands with James Folts as the head of researcher services at the New York State Archives.

Fellow historians have contributed to this work as well. Research performed by Ginevra Crosignani, Kelly Hopkins, Kerry Oman, Helen Schwartz, and John Smolenski offered me new insights on Oneida and New York history. Tricia Barbagallo has been an invaluable consultant. Her tenacity as a researcher and her understanding of Albany's inner workings from the colonial period to the present are unmatched. Ed Countryman, Larry Hauptman, and Alan Taylor have shared sources with me and read this book in various stages of its creation. Like many others, I am deeply grateful for their extraordinary generosity toward younger scholars. I also thank the series editors, Colin Calloway, Jean O'Brien-Kehoe, and Barry O'Connell, for their counsel. Valerie Stoker also read the book and offered helpful advice for its improvement. Admittedly, I did not take all the advice given me. Errors of fact and interpretation, and all other shortcomings, remain my responsibility alone.

For more than a decade, the Xavier University history department has been a collegial and supportive environment. I thank my colleagues, as well as the dean of the College of Arts and Sciences, Janice Walker, for their consistent encouragement. Two students, Sarah Stuppi and Maura Kisseberth, provided assistance in the preparation of portions of the manuscript at different stages. In addition to Xavier University faculty development funds, this project has received financial support from the Andrew W. Mellon Foundation, the McNeil Center for Early American Studies, and the Pew Program in Religion and American History. Archival research was also supported by fellowships at the Newberry Library and the David Library of the American Revolution, a Larry J. Hackman Research Residency at the New York State Archives, and a Gest Fellowship at Haverford College.

Finally, I must acknowledge the publishers in whose pages some of the material that follows has already appeared. Chapter 3 is a revised version of my essay "The Dilemmas of Alliance: The Oneida Indian Nation in the American Revolution," in *War and Society in the American Revolution: Mobilization and Home Fronts,* edited by John P. Resch and Walter Sargent (Northern Illinois University Press, 2006). Part of that chapter also appeared in "A 'Civil' War? Rethinking Iroquois Participation in the American Revolution," *Explorations in Early American Culture* 4 (2000), and part of chapter 4 appeared in "'We Wish to Do You Good': The Quaker Mission to the Oneida Nation, 1790–1840," in *Journal of the Early Republic* 26 (2006), both published by University of Pennsylvania Press.

THE PEOPLE OF THE
STANDING STONE

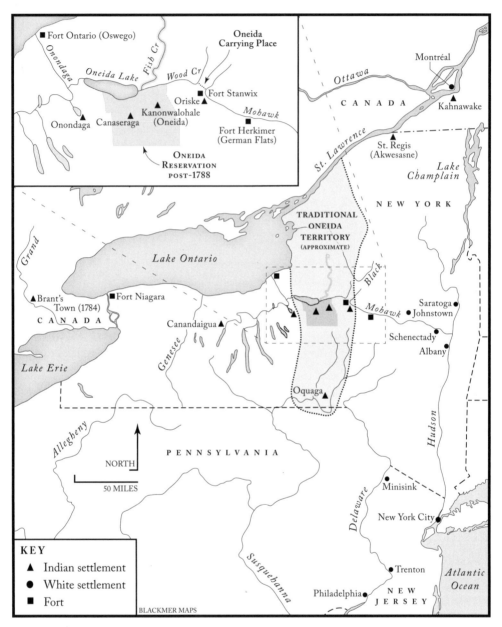

Fig. 1. Oneida territory in the later eighteenth century. Map by Kate Blackmer.

A Place and a People in a Time of Change

The Oneida Homeland in the 1760s

B Y 1765, over 130 years of direct contact with Europeans had wrought deep and disturbing changes in Oneida lives. Although the most devastating effects of imported diseases such as smallpox and influenza had passed, the Oneidas remained vulnerable, and their population of approximately one thousand was probably less than half their number at the time of contact. After more than a century of trade with whites, the Oneidas and the other five nations of the Iroquois League had shifted to European goods to fulfill the basic necessities. While deerskin remained the material of choice for moccasins and leggings, Indians had adopted European broadcloth and blankets for most of their clothing needs. Tools of wood, bone, and stone had been replaced by metal knives, axes, pots, pans, guns, and other implements of Euro-American manufacture. The supply of furs for trade and meat for subsistence depended on metal traps and firearms that required gunpowder and repair by a blacksmith. Tribal identity, however, continued to be based in the land. The Oneida landscape was a repository of their history, beliefs, and values. Specific locales were associated with stories of the creation of the world, right action, and history. Far more than a mere setting, their territory added meaning to their actions.[1]

The Oneida landscape was not inert, for the Iroquois endowed rocks, rivers, streams, mountains, and even the wind with personhood, the potential for independent action. Indeed, the Oneidas took their name, the People of the Standing Stone, from a certain rock they said followed them under its own power whenever they relocated their council fire. When placed in a tree, it was believed to improve their fortunes in war. Iroquois creation stories related that the world they inhabited sat atop a turtle's back. It grew through the agency of the muskrat and other swimmer people who had assembled it in the first instance for the benefit of Sky Woman, so that she might have a place to land when she fell from the Upper World. Because the land itself was a powerful, living being, stories of the creation could be related safely by storytellers only during winter nights, when the earth itself slept. But Oneidas were not always respectful. In 1744, the Oneida Shickellamy addressed a recalcitrant patch of frozen earth: "My Friend! I and my companion want to stay here to-night, and you must let me drive these stakes into the ground; so give way a little, or I will dig you out of the ground and throw you into the fire."[2]

Rivers, protecting hills, and a plenitude of game animals all attested to the activities of Sapling, the son of Sky Woman's daughter. Benevolent Sapling strove to make Iroquoia a more comfortable home for the mortal humans who would populate the creation. Mostly through his agency their landscape possessed all the necessary means of subsistence, while poison fruit, gnarled trees, and contrary currents all attested to the activities of his rival twin brother, Flint. Thus, features of the landscape could evoke narratives on the mythical world and social norms regarding proper conduct. Sodeahlowanake, meaning "thick-necked giant" (present-day Oxford, N.Y.), likely referred to the "Stonish Giants" who had threatened to destroy all the peoples of Iroquoia in the distant past, according to the nineteenth-century Tuscarora historian David Cusick, who had grown up among the Oneidas. Underscoring the belief that their world existed on a fragile plane between others, the Iroquois regarded caves, lakes, and mountains as places where contact with the supernatural was most likely to occur. Indeed, one white man who had grown up among the Oneidas recalled that they "used to show the precise spot of ground, a small hollow, where they said their ancestors came up."[3]

The Oneidas could traverse their lands from east to west in a day. The travel time from Kanonwalohale to the southern periphery was about two days; all the way to the northernmost reaches along the St. Lawrence would have been about three. The Oneida landscape was one of considerable topographical diversity. It included the plateau and rolling hills and mountains north of Oneida Lake and beyond, which they maintained as hunting and fishing territory; the fertile, level plain of the upper Mohawk River Valley, where most of their settlements were situated; and the hilly terrain of the Susquehanna drainage, where hunting and agriculture were practiced. The forest that blanketed the region was dominated by northern hardwoods, especially sugar maple and birch, with elm and red maple well represented in the Mohawk Valley. At the higher elevations, spruce and fir were preeminent. Passing through this landscape, one encountered evidence of human occupation, present and past. "We can trace the remains of orchards, and even of ancient clearings," some French visitors reported in 1793. Nathan Burchard, an attorney and surveyor who was well acquainted with the Oneidas, offered the members of the New-York Historical Society a verbal tour of the Oneida heartland in 1849. According to Burchard, "following the old Indian trail towards the North you come to an ancient . . . fortification." He described "the remains of old Indian cornfields," as well as "round cellars where Indians in olden times deposited and concealed their provisions from the Enemy," and stone heaps so "admirably piled" that "they show design and execution that must have come from hands skilled in manual labor." Burchard commented that pottery, arrowheads, tools, personal ornaments, and bones presented themselves to the "astonished ploughman" tilling lands that had belonged to the Oneidas. Others observed orchards, hunting camps, sugaring huts, brush fences, fishing weirs, and the occasional monument or earthwork.[4]

Kinship was the organizing principle of Iroquois society. The Six Nations formed an extended fictive family spanning the east-west axis of present-day New York State. Storytellers recounted how the Onondaga chief Thadodaho, amid the death and destruction of endemic warfare, learned the Condolence Ceremony from Hiawatha and the prophet Deganawidah. Spreading this Good News of Peace and Power, he ushered in peaceful relations between the nations by establishing the League Council. He also empowered its members to assuage one another's grief—which was understood to be the root of warfare—as kin. The nations were accordingly divided into moieties responsible for restoring one another's emotional equilibrium and spiritual power through condolence whenever necessary. The "older brothers" moiety comprised the Mohawks, Senecas, and Onondagas; the Oneidas, Cayugas, and, later, the Tuscaroras were counted as the "younger brothers." Some Iroquois expatriates in the valleys of the St. Lawrence and Ohio kept in touch with their kinfolk but no longer participated in the political confederacy.

Reciprocal actions of kin, such as the condolence, defined Iroquois social and spiritual life. They provided the paradigm for harmonious relations between humans and their other-than-human brothers, sisters, parents, and grandparents in the water, on land, in the sky, and beyond the sky. Ceremonies and rituals that enabled humans to communicate their appreciation for life and perpetuate their good fortune were considered gifts from the Sky World. For example, the annual Green Corn ceremony involved the entire community for four days of offering thanks before the harvest. Hunters likewise burned tobacco as an offering of thanks to animal grandfather spirits whenever they killed an animal.

The Iroquois understood their landscape through the metaphor of the longhouse, the traditional shelter inhabited by a matrilineage. Iroquois longhouses were divided sequentially into apartments, and Iroquois territory had a similar internal sequence. Located on either end, the Mohawks and Senecas were, respectively, the keepers of its eastern and western doors. As such, they managed Six Nations relations with the Iroquois' neighbors, English and Mahican, Shawnee and French. The Onondagas, located in the middle, were the keepers of the central hearth or Council Fire around which the decisions of the league were debated and agreed on. In the eighteenth century, the Oneidas and Cayugas played a forward role in managing relations with Native peoples along the Susquehanna and points south. Tribal territories were delimited by their customary hunting, gathering, and fishing needs. As Warren Johnson observed in 1761, "The Indians have particular Hunting Ground for Each Tribe, & never intrude upon One another's Places." They were, however, liable to adjustment. Even in treaties with Europeans, the Iroquois on occasion stipulated that they retained hunting privileges on lands they ceded.[5]

Although the territorial claims of the various nations were exclusive and stable, they were, in European terms, more akin to stewardship than ownership. All land was, like air and water, a gift from the Creator. Individuals and families could use the land as needed and possess the products of their labor as hunters and cultivators, but they could not privately own the land itself. The strength of the connection between a Native people and place was not diminished, however, because of the absence of a formal, proprietary deed. (As we will see, deeds had as much to do with ease of transfer as with absolute possession.) As Indians conceived of it, tribal stewardship existed for the benefit of descendants of the matrilineages whose membership defined the nation. The bones of ancestors were interred there and constituted a sacred link across the generations, reminding present occupants of their debt to those whose actions had sustained the animal population and the fertility of the land. It would not be inaccurate to say that the Oneidas felt that they belonged to this land as much as the land belonged to them. Through the reciprocal actions of the present generation, this link would be extended to generations yet unborn, "whose faces turn this way from beneath the ground." Thus, as the people defined the place, the place defined the people. Indeed, when the Tuscarora requested safe haven in Iroquoia on the basis of their Iroquoian origins, they made their case by demonstrating the similarities between their toponyms for given locales between the Carolinas and Canada. Whereas to most whites this was an empty land, a beckoning blank space on a map, to the Iroquois it was a named and settled land, densely peopled—though not exclusively by humans.[6]

The Forest

To the Oneidas, almost all of northeastern North America lay downriver. The Unadilla, Chenango, and Susquehanna Rivers flowed south into Chesapeake Bay; the Mohawk River flowed east to Albany, where it met the Hudson; and Wood Creek and Fish Creek flowed into Oneida Lake, which was in turn connected to Lake Ontario. The Black River flowed into Lake Ontario near the beginning of the St. Lawrence River. The Finger Lakes were connected to Oneida Lake by the Onondaga and Seneca Rivers. Most important, the connections that began with the meeting of the Mohawk and the Hudson created a nearly continuous waterway from the Atlantic to the Great Lakes—the only real break in the Appalachian spine between the St. Lawrence and Georgia. Indeed, Schoolcraft thought the Mohawk River's Indian name meant "river flowing through a mountain." The Oneidas controlled the most strategically crucial position along this passage: the short portage between Wood Creek and the Mohawk River known to whites as the Carrying Place.[7] This portage was the sole interruption of a water route (though a narrow and circuitous one) from the Atlantic to Lake Ontario.

The bodies of water that facilitated transportation were also an important source of food. It was customary for families to repair to lakeshores and riverbanks during the summer. To catch their fish, Iroquois men and women used a vast array of tools, including spears, nets, flares, hatchets, baited hooks and lines, weirs, dams, sluices, leisters, and tridents. The number of ways to catch a fish was exceeded only by the variety of fish available. In 1792, the Dutch scholar Francis Adrian Vanderkemp wrote:

> Never did I see yet a country, where all kind of fish was so abundant and good. . . . I salted within a short time of more than a dozen different species, the one contending with the other for the pre-eminence, the least of these affording a palatable food. *Salmon, pike, pickrel, cat-fish,* if well prepared, boiled or stewed, resembling the taste of the delicious Turbot, Otzwego Baas, an Epicurean morsel, *yellow perch, sunfish, tziob* [chub], three species of *Trout, River Lobsters, Turtle, Sword-fish,* and a *green coloured fish* of an exquisite taste, whitefish, &c., &c.[8]

Game, however, remained the principal source of protein for Oneidas in the mid-eighteenth century. In late fall and early winter, and again late in the winter, Oneida hunters ranged across the Susquehanna drainage and north to the St. Lawrence in search of white-tailed deer and other creatures. The first hunt coincided with the deer's rutting period. The final hunt, in March, took place when the deer had yarded, usually in oak-forested areas offering an abundance of acorns. The Oneidas hunted other, smaller game as well. James Smith, a Pennsylvanian who had been taken captive in Ohio by the Mohawks during the Seven Years' (or French and Indian) War, recalled "making and attending traps for catching raccoons, foxes, wildcats, &c." Fox traps were set "at the end of a hollow log, or opposite to a hole at the root of a hollow tree, and put venison on a stick for bait; we had it so set that when the fox took hold of the meat the trap fell." Among the losses claimed by the Oneidas during the Revolutionary War were a large number of steel traps as well as rifles. Despite unsustainable levels of hunting, fur-bearing game was still to be found in the forests of Iroquoia.[9]

In the Iroquois view, all hunting and fishing techniques, whether traditional or imported, would have been in vain had the hunter failed to perform the requisite preparatory and propitiatory rituals. The Iroquois could engage the animals' grandfather spirits (a spirit resembling the animal that directed its worldly underlings) through ritual and prayer. It was, they believed, only as a result of the benevolent interposition of these grandfather spirits that hunters could win over the spirits of their prey, thereby enabling the physical kill. The obligation of the hunter extended to the respectful treatment of animal carcasses and bones. Feeding them to dogs, for example, was prohibited, lest the animal's grandfather be alienated. Even insects could have such grandfathers. While camping at a thoroughly insect-infested spot in 1788, the missionary Samuel Kirkland wrote, "According to Indian tradition, the power that presides over that species of flies, resides near this Lake, & had appeared the shape of a moschetoe, of a monstrous size."[10]

However respectful of animals (and insects) this belief system was, it obscured the implications of hunting on the unprecedented scale brought on by European contact. The Indian hunters' careful observation of animal behavior leaves little doubt that they understood the short- and medium-term implications of overhunting animals, such as beavers, that had long reproductive cycles. The concept of extinction, however, was simply not congruent with a cosmology in which destruction and creation were alternating, rather than absolute, forces. In the Iroquois worldview, nothing that died could not return. Thus, Indian hunters did not believe it within their power to kill off a creature that existed in the spirit domain, or in the creation itself, which was a ritually recoverable, eternally returning event. The grandfathers could always restock the forests if they could be cajoled into doing so.

In the Native view, the declining game, like the other problems they faced, signaled a deficit of spiritual power rather than a specifically ecological problem. The lack of game was not a call to cease hunting activity. For Iroquois men to suspend the hunt would have been an abdication of their proper roles as men. Socially, the demonstration of hunting prowess was the most important part of establishing a man's credentials as a provider, and therefore in finding a mate. Hunting was crucial to reciprocal and complementary gender roles. Women gave life while men took it in an ongoing dialectic that ensured the well-being of the community. This relationship was symbolized in the wedding feast by the bride and groom's bringing corn and meat, respectively. Halting the hunt would have risked, rather than averted, further disequilibriation of their world. Thus, overhunting proceeded apace as pelts, though increasingly scarce, were still to be had in the forests of Iroquoia. Albany merchants continued to eagerly underwrite hunting expeditions, and still saw a substantial return.

The demonstration of martial prowess was another important path to prestige for young Iroquois men. Since the end of the Seven Years' War and peace with the Cherokees and Catawbas, many Oneida men had to settle for ritualized displays of strength and stamina. Continental Army captain Joseph Bloomfield watched Oneida warriors play "Ball, or what the Scot's call golf"—it was actually lacrosse—for high stakes before a large crowd in 1776. Count Paolo Andreani of Milan, visiting in 1790, observed that, at sporting events, "the women are present, and they proceed with horrible yells to incite the party by which they have interest." In addition to lacrosse, Andreani also took note of running and horsemanship competitions. By the late eighteenth century, horses had become an important way in which Oneida warriors asserted their status, and in which they invested substantial wealth.[11] By far the most impressive beasts introduced by Europeans, horses doubtless appeared spiritually powerful to the Iroquois. To capture one in the wild was a coup, because of the size and speed of the animal. Although not as well adapted to narrow, hilly, forested paths of the Northeast as they were to the Great Plains, horses nevertheless embodied central elements of Iroquois masculinity: physical strength and mobility.[12]

Guiding visitors through the woods was another way Oneida men supplemented their income. Travelers unfamiliar with the terrain might lose paths, which quickly grew impassable or invisible with brush and deadfall if not maintained. Alternatively, a multiplicity of paths sometimes made navigation difficult. According to Richard Smith, the going rate in 1769 was "a Dollar p[er] Horse the Trip that is one Day going & another in returning." But, he added, "the Oneidas and most other Indians are said to be extortionate and very apt to ask high Prices especially when they perceive a Necessity for their Assistance. Perhaps they learned this from the Dutch."[13] Spatially, hunting, warring, and guiding continued to take Oneida men out of the female domain of the village into the masculine domain of the forest, like the mythical twins, Sapling and Flint, ranging across the landscape in the story of the creation.

Burned-over Districts: Villages as Women's Space

Fire was used occasionally and extensively in the woods, but the village itself was defined by fire's abiding presence. Fire was used to clear brush and trees for settlement and was an almost permanent presence in the hearth.[14] Women's power and the norms of gender and familial reciprocity were nowhere more powerfully symbolized than in the pot of boiling corn mush soup hanging over the fire in the center of the house. Women bestowed the gift of life and they maintained it through further gifts derived from their village-centered planting, gathering, and cooking. Indeed, the senior woman of the household asserted control over the processing and distribution of the products of women's agriculture and foraging and the meat obtained by men's hunting as well. One's place within society was defined not by paternity but by the women who provided and sustained one's life. This system where social relations were mediated by exchange ensured a high degree of women's influence.

Women decided where villages would be located and when they would be moved. Women were best qualified to assess the productive capacities of a specific area, since they made greatest use of local resources such as reeds (for manufacturing bags and sieves), trees (for firewood, digging sticks, and baskets), berries, and nuts. Above all, they had to evaluate the fertility of the land, since they cultivated the crops that grew in and around villages. Iroquois traditions are replete with references to women's close relationship with the land. The central figure is that of Sky Woman's daughter, who despite having died during childbirth, continued to nourish humankind through the corn that grew from her breasts after her interment. The Corn Mother's story established an explicit connection between the fecundity of women's bodies and their role as cultivators of the earth, as well as an identity between human life, plant life, and the land. Iroquois women were careful to cultivate the soil in a manner that limited disruption or "injury"; wherever possible, the same small mounds were replanted year after year. Female kinship was extended to the vegetable world as well: the staples of corn, beans, and squash were called the "Three Sisters."[15] The Iroquois understood all power as multivalent, and women's productive powers were thought to reach a threatening pitch during menses and childbirth. During those times, women would repair to the outskirts of the village. Not coincidentally, on this periphery, the "Wood's Edge," the Iroquois defused the potential danger of outsiders by greeting them in ritual fashion.[16]

Throughout the season, women worked communally in bees to weed, tend, and harvest the crops. Visiting Oquaga in 1769, Richard Smith noted that "each house possesses a paltry Garden wherein they plant Corn, Beans, WaterMelons, Potatoes, Cucumbers, Muskmelons, Cabbage, French Turneps, some Apple Trees, Sallad, Parsnips, & other Plants." Despite Smith's dismissiveness, the land-intensive Iroquois agricultural complex was highly productive and stable. Beans returned nitrogen to the mounds they shared with corn stalks and that were surrounded by squash. The relationship between these three crops was symbiotic, maintaining soil fertility while producing foods high in protein and amino acids. Smith's observations of the garden were made before most of these vegetables had ripened; the comments of the soldiers who marched through Iroquoia during the Revolutionary War indicate quite clearly that the product of this agricultural complex was anything but "paltry."[17]

The possible culinary permutations of available ingredients were endless, and Iroquois women explored many of them. The metal implements they obtained through men's trade or diplomatic activities undoubtedly made this work easier. Kettles of tin and brass were common household items, according to an inventory of property destroyed at Kanonwalohale in the Revolutionary War. Kettles were particularly useful in gathering sap from trees and boiling it to prepare the Iroquois' preferred seasoning for their food. The decided preference for spoons over forks in the inventory, however, suggests continuity in their traditional soup- and stew-based cuisine.[18]

The productive activities of women elicited condemnations of "squaw drudgery" and male idleness from Europeans. Often this response reflected the white (usually male) observers' obliviousness to the power women held in Iroquois society, influenced by an underestimation of women's labor in their own culture. The twentieth-century Seneca ethnographer Arthur C. Parker, by contrast, describes women's work bees as "merry industrial gatherings," and his position is supported strongly for the Revolutionary era by the testimony of Scots-Irish captive-turned-Seneca Mary Jemison. Happiness aside, the real contrast between European and Indian women's status was that the latter more successfully claimed economic and political rights on the basis of their productive and distributive functions. Indeed, they established their ownership (such as it could be) of the land in the name of the clans they headed. This claim was passed down the maternal line from generation to generation.[19]

Politics

Although sachems, or peace chiefs, were men, the anthropologist Jack Campisi has noted that the institution of the sachemate was sanctioned by "a complex of myth and ceremony which gave legitimacy to the central role of women and support to the prominence of age." Women were the heads of the three Oneida clans (Turtle, Wolf, and Bear) and the matrilineages that comprised them. As such, the women controlled the tribe's nine league council titles. Clan matrons chose the men who would hold these titles and speak for them before the league. They reserved the right to remove them if dissatisfied with their service. Women's sanction of council meetings at the tribal and league levels was further symbolized by the provision of food: as the missionary Georg Loskiel noted, "Provisions must always be in plenty in the council-house; for eating and deliberating take their turns."[20] Likewise, women had considerable authority over decisions of peace and war. In particular, women determined when additional persons were needed for adoption, the acquisition of whom was a principal aim of Iroquois warfare. Women could enforce peace as well. Without their permission, as expressed materially in food supplies and moccasins, warriors were hard-pressed to go forth.

In addition to the sachems, other older, respected men constituted the village council. The traditional village leadership maintained its prestige through the redistribution (rather than accumulation) of goods. The ethic of reciprocity placed recipients under obligation to their benefactors, thereby securing their loyalty. Those who demonstrated liberality in their dealings with others—even to the point of self-impoverishment—established their right to a followership. Because persons were bound by ties of reciprocity through daily activities or more formal exchanges, gift giving constituted one of the strongest bonds of obligation a sachem could secure among his people. Since the goods on which the sachems depended were now obtained through diplomacy with outsiders (by the 1760s, this often meant the British superintendent of Indian affairs Sir William Johnson), it was in the chiefs' interest to maintain those peaceful relationships. But the stress on peace was ultimately rooted in league custom and ideology. The principal goal of the league as delineated in the Deganawidah Epic was to maintain peace and security, and the entire corpus of highly ritualized league protocol—of which exchange was a significant symbolic component—promoted the equanimity of all participants and good relations between them.

But peace generated its own discontents. It heightened a perennial tension between the sachems and the young men of the tribe, as the anthropologist Bruce Trigger notes, "[who] were anxious to win personal prestige and who viewed the efforts of council chiefs and older men to curtail warfare, not as prudence, but an effort to prevent them from challenging their elders."[21] In the era before European contact, the two groups had generally lived in tense equilibrium. By the mid-eighteenth century, however, the fur trade had tipped the peacetime balance of power away from the sachems and the women. The balance was undermined by a norm that Rev. John Ettwein described among the Delawares in 1772 and that applied to the Iroquois as well. Ettwein observed that "whoever shoots a deer, has for his private portion, the skins and inwards, the meat he must bring into camp for distribution." While the traditional prerogative of women to redistribute foodstuffs remained intact, the animal's meat was no longer its most valuable part. Indeed, Loskiel noted, "the flesh is left in the forest" because "their principal object in shooting them [nowadays] is their skin." With furs and skins regarded as the hunter's to dispose of, trade with whites allowed warriors unprecedented direct access to desired goods and potential gift-stuff to promote their own status and challenge the sachems and, indirectly, the women. The voice of the warriors' speaker grew more prominent in council as more warriors had more goods to distribute. Even the chief warriors, however, remained frustrated within the existing framework of Iroquois politics. They could not vote in confederacy councils, nor could they expect their nephews or sons to inherit their positions.[22]

Missionary activity amplified factionalism. The Presbyterian Samuel Kirkland (fig. 2) sought sachem approval when he initiated his mission among the Oneidas in 1766. But since Kirkland enjoyed only tepid support from Johnson and challenged the belief system that legitimated sachem authority,

D.C.Hinman. Sc.

SAMUEL KIRKLAND.

Fig. 2. Samuel Kirkland, portrait by Augustus Rockwell, ca. 1873. Courtesy of Emerson Gallery, Hamilton College.

the sachems remained aloof. Kirkland quickly shifted his attention to other men in the community. As Campisi has noted, the warriors saw in Kirkland's theology an alternative source of political legitimacy. Its emphasis on the individual, for example, justified defiance of matron or sachem authority. Also, the missionary himself was an additional alternative source of goods. Sir William cultivated the support of Isaac Dekayensese at Oquaga and others, but it was no secret he bestowed most of his largesse on the Mohawks among whom he and his many tenants lived. Kirkland brought the Oneidas modest quantities of cash, tools, and consumer goods he obtained from his backers, first Moor's Indian Charity School and later the Boston Board of the Society in Scotland for the Propagation of Christian Knowledge, as well as the Corporation of Harvard College. The Oneidas also saw Kirkland as a way to get something Johnson had denied them: a blacksmith. The absence of a blacksmith was something the Oneidas had complained about since at least 1764, but Johnson preferred to keep them reliant on services obtained in his district. Now they prevailed on the missionary to write directly to the governor for one. To the Oneidas' disappointment, the governor in turn consulted Johnson, who again withheld his blessing. Kirkland's challenge also galvanized opposition from the sachems, in addition to Johnson. Observing a pattern that would repeat many times in his career, Kirkland noted in April 1770, "My enemies increase w[it]h my Friends, as the design either meets with cordial reception or is rejected."[23]

Absorbing the Gospel

Although political considerations did influence individual Oneidas' receptivity to Christianity, they did not determine them. Facing a loss of control over their environment, and even over themselves through alcohol addiction, many Oneidas sought to restore equilibrium to their world by channeling power that the Europeans seemingly possessed. The Oneidas saw Kirkland in shamanic terms, as a ritual specialist whose function was to maintain a path. In Iroquois diplomatic parlance, the path and its condition, from clear and wide to obstructed and narrow, was a metaphor for the state of relations between peoples. In this instance, the path led to the Sky World inhabited by spirit beings, and baptism was the gateway. In 1772, Tagawaron, the pro-British chief, complained to Sir William Johnson about Kirkland's standards of baptismal instruction, which were higher than those of his Anglican counterparts. Tagawaron accused Kirkland of "shutt[in]g up the way [i.e., path] to Heavn, or mak[in]g it very narrow." The complaint was sufficiently damning that Kirkland could count "but a handful" of communicants by August of that year. Thus, baptism was important to the Oneidas at least as much because of its meaning in Native terms as its meaning in Christian terms. The purification symbolism of baptism was not lost, but more important was its signification of initiation or alliance. The Oneidas spoke of baptism as a ritual of alliance with a new guardian spirit: the "Heavenly Father" through whose hoped-for "mercy & protection . . . [our] warriors shall be preserved in their spr[in]g hunt." Alliance was a central value in Iroquois culture: it made strangers kin, and spiritual (and hence material) success was achieved through alliance with the spirits above and with the grandfathers of the game.[24] Indeed, the emphasis on alliance was so great that on a national level the Iroquois considered those who spurned their overtures legitimate targets for attack.

But Kirkland resisted much of the Oneidas' logic regarding baptism. "As to baptiz[in]g the child[re]n [of] drunkard[s], whoremongers, liars, thieves, profane, ignorant, foolish, I have no authority," he announced.[25] He was also perturbed by the Oneidas' practice of following the Christian ritual with feasting—another example of their religious eclecticism or syncretism. Feasts traditionally followed Native ceremonies that they considered analogous to baptism: for example, ceremonies performed to cure a sick individual or symbolically resurrect a dead chief through the installation of a successor. Kirkland noted with dismay that his Oneida flock insisted that feasting was an "essential part of the ordinance & without which it would avail nothing." They "practiced feasting at Baptisms," he explained, "& for the most part dance & frolick the whole night—even their head men & communicants would not only grace the feasts by their attendance, but bear a part in the songs & walk in the dance."[26]

While baptism and associated feasting became matters of contention, singing provided the most commodious convergence for Native and Christian religious practices. Singing circumvented the language barrier, at least in part. Kirkland had ridiculed the Jesuits' sophisticated use of image, song, and object as the "puppet-shows [of] the papists," but he devoted considerable time to translating hymns and psalms into Oneida, which the Indians merged with their indigenous singing traditions. The schoolteacher David Fowler, a Montauk Algonquian, had noted in 1765 that "they take great Pleasure in learning to sing," and when Ralph Wheelock visited the Oneidas in 1767 he was, he wrote, "Surprized at the Proficiency they have made at which they Sang Several Sacred Hymns in their own Language."[27] Since Indians already believed singing was spiritually efficacious, hymnody, like baptism, appealed to them. It offset some of the difficulties posed by a missionary who spoke stammeringly in a society ruled by suasion. From warriors' chants to women's corn-and-squash songs, Iroquois faith had never been silent in giving thanks to the spirits for protection and productivity. But above all, hymn singing tapped into the communal dimension of worship, which among the Iroquois was traditionally privileged over the personal, interiorized mode. Hymns made the community visible and audible to itself and strengthened communal solidarity.

In this way, Christianity spread but traditional religious ideology and patterns of social relations were not overturned. Continuity in Oneida life could be measured in the length of the litany of complaints the schoolteacher David Avery delivered to a group of Oneida communicants in 1772. To ensure that his audience received the full benefit of his opinion, Avery itemized his complaints, which were thirty in number. "Native deeproot Prejudice against ye Gospel," "Slight and Contempt of the Gospel," and "Heathenish Traditions" all indicated the continued vitality of indigenous religion. So, too, did their "Filthy dreams," a reference to the decidedly modern form of dream analysis the Iroquois practiced.[28] Under the heading of "idleness," Avery attacked the traditional gender division of labor and the value placed on leisure that limited Kirkland's agricultural reform program.

Relatively indulgent Native childrearing practices that had long been the bane of missionaries who sought to discipline the young were cited as a "want of Family government." Avery spoke of children "growing up in all kinds of Vice," exhibiting "disobedience to parents" and behaviors that "meet with little if any proper correction." The relative brittleness of Indian marriages was yet another perennial missionary complaint, and Avery demanded an end to "fornication-adultery," "quarreling of husbands & wives," and "covenant breaking—in ye married & church state." Undoubtedly breathless, the New Englander concluded, "Now, my brethren, . . . [y]ou know now just what I think about you." Two hundred years later, his bracingly frank though uncomprehending diatribe testifies to the perpetuation among the Oneida of many aspects of their traditional culture on the eve of the Revolution. The Oneidas engaged with Christianity, but they integrated it into an indigenous framework. This practice explains why, although Kirkland preached to audiences of up to four hundred every week, in 1769 he judged that only twenty-two individuals were sufficiently disabused of their traditional beliefs to have met his high standards for church membership.[29]

Patterns of Settlement

Iroquois settlement patterns reflected shifting social and political dynamics. During the mid-eighteenth century, the Oneidas inhabited five villages and several smaller settlements. Of these, Kanonwalohale ("skull impaled on a pole") was the largest and most prominent, containing about seven hundred persons, more than half the Oneida population.[30] It had been founded around 1746 and attained capital status, although the former principal village, Old Oneida, only about eight miles away, continued to be a political rival. Still farther to the east was Oriske, near Oriskany Creek and the Carrying Place. Canaseraga, about eleven miles west of Kanonwalohale, was populated primarily by Onondagas and Tuscaroras. Far to the south, along the Susquehanna, was Oquaga, where the Oneidas and other Iroquois coexisted with a host of refugees from Hudson Valley tribes, as well as Shawnees, Nanticokes, Conoys, Miamis, and Tutelos.[31]

By the mid-eighteenth century, Iroquois towns were, in the words of a nineteenth-century Tuscarora, settled "as butter is spread on bread." In 1769, Richard Smith offered this description of Oquaga: "15 or 16 big Houses on the East side and some on the West side of the Susquehanna. . . . There are some good Islands opposite to this Village which has a suburb over the River on the Western Side. . . . The Habitations here are placed straggling without any order on the Banks."[32] In its dispersal, this settlement pattern was a significant departure from that of the Oneidas when they were first recorded by Europeans. In 1634, the Dutch barber-surgeon Harmen Myndertsz Van den Bogaert paced the high wooden palisade that surrounded the sole Oneida village at the time. He counted 767 steps. (We can only imagine what the Oneidas made of his odd behavior.) He also counted the longhouses. There were sixty-six.[33] The palisade-and-longhouse pattern, however, was not a timeless norm. Villages circumscribed by aboriginal palisades were a strategic response to conflict and were used until European siegecraft rendered them obsolete.[34] By two recent estimates, a palisade of the sort described by Van den Bogaert required three thousand trees. Moreover, firewood, edible plants, and workable wood were just some of the local resources that were harvested intensively in the settlement area and were therefore more rapidly exhausted. Nearby arable land was quickly depleted, while repeated planting of the

same soil encouraged insects to take over. Dispersal alleviated these problems, enabling the Iroquois to take advantage of alluvial lands. The dispersed
and unfortified pattern of settlement also had the advantage of limiting
ecological pressures on the immediate area, thereby promoting settlement
longevity.[35]

Settlement in separate villages reduced political tensions as well. The
ideal of consensus discouraged management of durable local differences and
promoted faction, schism, and eventually relocation. However disruptive
the fissioning might have been, it eased tensions, facilitated decision making, and maintained the variety of viable political opinions and options.[36]
As among New England Puritans, who also valued consensus and were
distressed by its absence, dividing reestablished local uniformity and made
everyone a little more relaxed, at least for a while. In 1770, political differences determined who settled at Kanonwalohale under the leadership of
Tagawaron and at Old Oneida, where his counterpart, Conoghquieson, was
preeminent; the two settlements had differences that probably dated to their
original separation. According to Sir William Johnson, some Oneidas were
"disgusted" with both. He observed in 1758, "Many of our friend Indians
amongst the Six Nations who are disgusted with the ruleing Politics of their
People leave their Castles & go and settle at Oghquago." In that year he
noted that the Tuscaroras and Oneidas were "very much div'd amongst
themselves & that their intestine Broils took up all their attention."[37]

Liquor was also a significant issue. The mayhem attendant to alcohol
binges—or the irritating teetotalism of reformers—moved some to put distance between themselves and their compatriots.[38] Missionaries were often
prone to exaggeration, but their accounts of Oneida villages in the midst of
such events are consistently harrowing. Brawls were common and deaths
not unheard of. Stopping in an Indian town en route to Oquaga in 1753,
Gideon Hawley reported: "We soon saw the Indian women and their children skulking in the adjacent bushes, for fear of the intoxicated Indians,
who were drinking deeper. The women were secreting guns, hatchets, and
every deadly or dangerous weapon, that murder or harm might not be the
consequence."[39]

For his part, Kirkland discovered that drinking was not an exclusively
male pursuit. At Kanonwalohale one of his Oneida supporters informed
him of a three- or four-woman drinking party. In the presence of two or three
village leaders, Kirkland confronted them and poured their liquor on the
ground. An altercation ensued between Kirkland and one woman's husband.

Kirkland subdued the man, but then his wife entered and "raged with more Violence, began to strike & tried to bite like a dog." Kirkland subdued her as well but had to flee the village overnight for fear of retaliation. Such action marked the extreme of Kirkland's temperance activities, but the cooperation and thanks he received from other villagers demonstrates that the alcohol problem provided an opportunity for the missionary to gain a constituency. In a society that suffered from alcohol abuse but abhorred coercion, the arrival of a temperance-oriented outsider with no such qualms was a welcome development to some. On one Sunday in September 1774 Kirkland gave a sermon on alcohol use and noted the peculiar attentiveness of the audience. By contrast, he "had but few hearers," he said, when he discoursed on other matters that evening. Kirkland seems to have helped curb drinking at Kanonwalohale, making it a refuge for some from the other Oneida settlements, and probably driving the thirsty to the Carrying Place or Oquaga.[40]

Changing settlement patterns among the Oneidas were accompanied by changing architectural styles and materials. Richard Smith reported seeing houses "composed of clumsy hewn Timbers & hewn Boards or Planks," which were a departure from posts and bark. Oneida villages looked much like other Iroquois villages at the time, which is to say that they were beginning to look more and more like the villages of their Euro-American neighbors. Analyzing this convergence, Kurt Jordan has noted that "Six Nations peoples applied European techniques in the service of Iroquoian architectural principles."[41] As a result, although Kirkland's agricultural and theological programs generated limited enthusiasm from the Oneidas, he had greater success in construction. Kirkland enlisted numerous Oneidas—especially warriors—in building projects and supplied them with the necessary tools. In June 1773 he noted in his journal that some residents of Kanonwalohale "will probably erect and finish eight or nine dwelling houses this Season." "I have furnished them," he added, "with a number of Carpenters tools, and they have made such proficiency (by the instruction of the carpenter who framed the meeting house) that with a little assistance they are able to finish a house, but perhaps not as elegantly as some in Boston."[42]

By the eve of the Revolution, nearly one-third of Kanonwalohale dwellings were log-framed structures; there was even a steepled church. Indeed, an inventory of war losses attests that at least five of the seven wealthiest residents of Kanonwalohale were warriors, and they all lived in framed houses. The wealthiest was Honyery Doxtator (Tewahangarakhen), the son of a Palatine colonist and an Oneida or Mohawk woman. Second was John Skenandoah, nearly seventy years old, a chief warrior and close confidant of Kirkland's. Captain Bloomfield observed that Skenandoah "lives in a good house built in the Dutch fashion." That Doxtator and Skenandoah had appropriated some of the sachems' power is further suggested by the inventory that records their custody of "national property" in the form of ceremonial wampum—the shell beads that certified the veracity and authority of the speaker's words at a diplomatic event. Similarly, that their houses were listed as the personal property of the warriors shows that they had usurped women's power in that respect.[43]

The ethic of accumulation may have developed in dangerous tension with older norms of redistribution, but it did not supplant them. There was less expectation that the warriors, as non-sachems, would redistribute their wealth automatically. And during the Revolution, when need arose, they voluntarily and generously relieved their kinfolk. We should not be so dazzled by Skenandoah's pewter spoons or his glazed windows that we lose sight of the remaining two-thirds of Kanonwalohale's residents (and probably all who lived at Old Oneida). They lived in houses that, although small, still drew clearly on Iroquois architectural precedents. It was not as though the Iroquois were unfamiliar with any structure besides the classic longhouse. Especially at seasonal migratory settlements, but even in their villages, they had constructed shorter variants as well as bark cabins.[44] Even in the homes of elite warriors, the interiors were still organized in a traditional way, with few European furnishings. It became less common for women to live under the same roof as mothers or sisters, but they were never far from one another. Although traditional norms were being challenged, women's control of the village as a base of female power retained its mythic sanction. As with other elements of Oneida life, continuity prevailed on the whole, parrying the challenges posed by invisible microbes, demanding traders, truculent missionaries, and traditional foes.[45] The Oneidas had yet, however, to experience the full range of trials the outside world had to offer.

Narrowing Paths

Oneida Foreign Relations, 1763–1775

GREATER CHANGE was on the way as Britain's colonies grew more populous and their place in the empire suddenly more tenuous. The Oneida villages may have been localistic, but they were hardly isolated. In addition to their situation near waterways, an extensive and well-maintained system of paths kept Oneida villages in constant communication with one another, the rest of the Iroquois League, and colonial capitals and trading posts. The paths were themselves active sites of communication, where travelers would exchange information with those whom they encountered. Path-side pictographs conveyed messages about war, hunting, or travel. The Iroquois referred to the main east-west road between Albany and Seneca country as the "ambassador road" and Kanonwalohale as the "fallen log" at which travelers were expected to stop, rest, and relate the news. Samuel Kirkland noted that the town was "exposed to crowds of travellers, which has many times reduced a Number of the principle [*sic*] families to a very short allowance, & even to extremity." That the "principle families" were the most generous underscored the continued link between status and redistribution. Like other Native peoples, the Oneidas adhered faithfully to a hospitality ethic that dictated they share their provisions to the last morsel. Although it was two o'clock in the morning when Capt. Joseph Bloomfield arrived at an Oneida settlement in June 1776, he and his two companions, he wrote, were still "Hospitably given . . . a Dish of sour Bread & Milk & a Blanket to lie before the fire which we thankfully accepted."[1] While this practice demanded much of the hosts, it also ensured the "principle families" a greater measure of influence over relations with other villages and nations.

In the 1750s and 1760s, the network of relations between the Iroquois nations and their neighbors had been convulsed by the Seven Years' War, as well as its powerful aftershock, Pontiac's War. In the wake of this upheaval, the Oneidas had to carefully reassess the condition of many of those paths, as well as the destinations to which they led. Since Oneida diplomatic and military responsibilities were generally oriented southward, Oquaga was sometimes even referred to as one of the Longhouse's "southern doors." Many of these southern neighbors were refugee peoples from the south and west who had been displaced by Euro-American expansion. Under Oneida patronage, the Susquehanna Valley became the adopted home of Nanticokes, Conoys, Tutelos, Delawares, Mahicans, and others.[2] Placed in the valleys through which white settlers or hostile southern Indians such as the Catawbas or Cherokees might threaten the Longhouse, the refugees served an important defensive purpose. In 1758, the Moravian missionary Frederick Post described the arrangement: "They settle these New Allies on the Frontiers of the White People and give them this as their Instruction. 'Be Watchful that no body of the White People may come to settle near you. You must appear to them as frightful Men, & if notwithstanding they come too near give them a Push. We will secure and defend you against them.'"[3]

These refugee tribes were integrated into the Longhouse scheme as "props" or "supports." The only refugee group to be accepted into the league itself was the Tuscaroras, who became the sixth league nation and a member of the younger-brother moiety in 1722 or early 1723. In the wake of the Tuscarora War of 1711–13, dozens of Tuscarora families emigrated to Iroquoia and settled in villages along the Susquehanna and between the Oneidas and Onondagas. More Tuscaroras made the journey north during the eighteenth century, and as time passed their population moved deep into Oneida territory, where they were given the right to settle but not sell land. By the 1760s the Tuscarora population in Oneida country was in the range of six hundred to eight hundred, with the largest cluster settled at Canaseraga. They enjoyed full political rights in the councils of the Iroquois Confederacy but were nevertheless expected to defer to their Oneida benefactors.[4]

Exposed Positions

The Oneidas' nearest European neighbors were several hundred Palatine Germans. Those closest were settled at Burnetsfield (now Herkimer), about forty miles east of Kanonwalohale, on lands purchased from the Mohawks.

The Palatines had followed a trajectory remarkably similar to that of the Tuscaroras. Beginning in 1709, these impoverished Germans had emigrated to Iroquoia to distance themselves from war in their homeland. They began to settle at Burnetsfield in 1723. Like that of their Tuscarora counterparts, the Germans' location had been dictated at least in part by the defensive needs of their patron, Great Britain.[5] The Palatine colony represented an early British attempt to use continental Protestants to secure the colonies from attack (and maybe make a little money, too). This strategy, the historian Warren Hofstra has noted, was expanded greatly in subsequent decades, helping to make the entire American backcountry a place of significant ethnic diversity by the era of the Revolution. Indeed, royal officials planning the Palatine migration from its inception hoped it would be even more diverse than it became. They anticipated the Palatines would provide "a good barrier between Her Majesty's Subjects and the French & their Indians in those parts, and in process of time by intermarrying with the neighbouring Indians (as the French do) they may be capable of rendring great Service to Her Majesty's Subjects there; and not only very much promote the Fur Trade but likewise the increase of Naval Stores [i.e., tar and hemp]."[6]

The naval stores enterprise was a dismal failure, however, largely because of a lack of planning and sustained government support. The Palatines proved more successful as farmers and traded foodstuffs, alcohol, and milling and blacksmithing services for land, furs, fish, and food, especially with their close Mohawk neighbors. Evidence that the intermarriages anticipated by the royal officials did take place is attested by the appearance of Oneida families with the surnames Doxtator (Dachstätter) and Summer (Sommer). At the time, the historian Ann Laura Stoler points out, "from the Indies to South Africa, mixed unions . . . were condoned and actively encouraged as part of the strategic tactics of conquest."[7] When the Seven Years' War broke out, these relations had given the Germans a sense of security. Despite their exposed position, the Germans were confident that they were exempt from attack by France's Native allies. The Oneidas remained neutral for most of the war but maintained open diplomatic channels with the French, whose closest Indian allies in the region were the St. Lawrence Valley Iroquois, many of whom were kin of Oneidas. Thus, even when the Oneida sachem Conoghquieson warned the settlers at Burnetsfield of an imminent attack in 1757, he said they "paid not the least regard to what I told them; and laughed at me, slapping their hands on their buttocks, saying they did not value the Enemy." About 100 French-allied warriors did refrain from striking that particular target, but others did not. Forty Germans were killed and 150 carried off as prisoners and the settlement was torched.[8]

The wartime trials of the Germans initiated a sea change in their attitudes toward both their British and their Indian neighbors. Although the Oneidas had done the Germans no disservice, an undercurrent of distrust developed among them. When another Palatine settlement was attacked the following spring, Germans wondered aloud why none of the Oneidas in the vicinity had sounded an alarm. As the historian Philip Otterness has observed, after the war the Germans "no longer relied on good relations with the Indians to ensure the security of their settlements" and became more active participants in British colonial society. In other words, their self-identification as Germans or Palatines diminished as they became increasingly aware of themselves in terms of the newly important category of "white."[9] Many colonial settlements on Iroquoia's southern and western borders had been ravaged by wartime Indian raids. Traumatized by their experiences, Euro-Americans became increasingly inclined to lump Native allies and enemies together in the monolithic category of "Indian." Doing so simplified the task of finding acceptable targets for retributive rage. It also simplified the process of dispossessing the Indians. After all, the lands of friend and foe were coveted equally. Now there was no need to distinguish among them.

The greatest point of friction between the Germans and the Oneidas was at the Oneida Carrying Place. Its strategic importance had led European powers to build fortifications there from an early date; the first of these had been erected by the French in 1689. During peacetime, Oneidas and Onondagas reaped some benefit from commerce at the Carrying Place by working as porters moving goods and boats between Wood Creek and the Mohawk River. They also traded there. In exchange for the Oneidas' toleration of the British forts that succeeded those of the French, Sir William Johnson guaranteed the Oneidas "cheap and plentiful trade." Unfortunately, things did not work out as promised. In December 1758, Conoghquieson complained about high prices: "After all it seems these fair Promises came from your Lips, for we find that goods are sold us dearer than ever."[10] To the Oneidas' further chagrin, neither the fort nor the blockhouse at the lake's eastern end had been dismantled when the Seven Years' War ended. In June 1766, Sir William reported to Thomas Gage: "Several Cayugaes & Oneidaes . . . addressed me concerning the posts lately abandoned, which they said they expected would have been demolished according to promise at ye end of ye War, but they are sorry to find that the Soldiers have been

Succeeded by Settlers, who are equally disagreeable to them & may in time be more so, as they may draw people there to Cultivate Lands, that they dreaded ye consequences."[11] The five or six families who settled at Fort Stanwix by the 1760s were primarily Germans. Among them was the Swabian Johannes Rueff, a trader in furs and provisions as well as an occasional land speculator. He also provisioned the garrison, and he had a reputation for aggression when it came to protecting his business interests. The Oneida sachems, concerned with their waning power over their young men, complained that such white settlements in hunting and fishing areas were nothing but "so many springs of Rum where their Young Men were constantly drunk."[12]

Not surprisingly, the young Oneida men who sought liquor and occasional employment as batteaumen at the Carrying Place also sometimes found trouble. And sometimes they made it. In 1764, British lieutenant Francis Nartloo reported that some Oneidas "drove off a Flock of 25 Sheep . . . 20 of which they Killed and the remaining 5 they absolutely refused delivering when I sent to the Castle without a Ransom of Two Dollars a Head." By targeting sheep, the perpetrators of this act of mischief and resistance had chosen a significant symbol of European culture. Kanonwalohale leaders were unable or unwilling to do anything about it. Some Oneidas claimed that the sheep had strayed (possibly into some Oneida gardens, causing damage) and were killed as recompense only after the British had refused to pay the customary reward for their return. A British officer said that "as he passed the Encampments of some Battoemen . . . he found them Stored with Carcasses of Mutton." Whatever the motivation for the theft of the sheep, the Indians' resentment of the white community at the portage and around the fort was certainly still apparent three years later, when they harassed the colonists and ignited a fire, threatening to burn "the Town" entirely.[13]

Murder at Minisink

After Pontiac's War, reports of grisly murders of Indians by colonists abounded to the south and west. As Conoghquieson put it, "We and our dependants have been for some time like Giddy People not knowing what to do, wherever we turned about we saw our Blood."[14] The events surrounding a 1766 murder provide a window on the deteriorating relations between the Iroquois and their white neighbors to the south. That April, an unidentified Oneida man from Oquaga traveled south to trade at the settlement of Minisink, New Jersey, where a busy path crossed the Delaware River. There he encountered Robert Seymour, "a base Vagabond fellow" who had declared publicly his intention to "destroy any Indian that came in his Way." With the aid of an accomplice, Seymour killed the Oneida. He then broke the dead man's legs and back and buried him, keeping his goods and gun. Two sachems from Oquaga set out the following month to register their outrage with Sir William Johnson. The sachems told Johnson that the deceased "had always been a firm friend to the English, accompanying their Armies every Campaign."[15] Reacting to this incident, and a similar one in Pennsylvania, Johnson commented to a superior, "Both these Murders appear to Spring from the ill timed resentment of ye Country People, who think they do good Service when they Knock an Indn in the Head, and I am well informed they intend to do so with all they meet in small partys." Johnson predicted ominously that until the social climate changed, "many more will share the same fate." Indeed, no sooner had Seymour been apprehended than a mob of two dozen of his Sussex County neighbors liberated him from prison. Governor William Franklin, concerned that frontier rabble-rousers would provoke a war on New Jersey's border, noted with dismay that "the Fellow at length returned to his Dwelling and appeared as publickly about his Business as any other Farmer of the Neighbourhood." Killing an Indian was no great dishonor, so Franklin countered with cash, offering a hundred-dollar reward.[16]

In September, the slain Indian's widow arrived at Minisink with two of her brothers. Sir William furnished them with a letter of introduction addressed to the people of Minisink that read, in part:

> The Bearer hereof is Widow to the Indian who was murdered last Spring in your parts, & now goes with two of her Brothers in search of the Gun &c which belonged to the deceased and which I doubt not you will be good enough to procure for her, and if you were to make her a present of something handsome, it would remove from hers and her Friends remembrance any Malice or resentment, and appear well to that Nation he belonged to, namely the Oneidaes. This I recommend to you as the most necessary Step that can be taken to remove the ill impressions which that unhappy Affair has occasioned.[17]

With these instructions, Johnson sought to bring the Jerseyans' actions into line with Iroquois conceptions of justice. Having married into a prominent Mohawk family, Johnson understood their view. For the Iroquois, the emphasis lay not on punishing the perpetrator but on appeasing the kin of the deceased, who risked mental derangement if not properly condoled. The equanimity of the bereaved could be restored through a gift that symbolically replenished the power of the clan. The satisfaction of female kin in this matter was especially important, for the decision over whether or not to pursue retributive violence lay in their hands.[18]

Sir William had already publicly condoled the Iroquois for their loss with three strings of wampum and a black stroud cloth. The locals of Minisink acquiesced to Johnson's suggestion, motivated no doubt by the knowledge that the Iroquois considered the entire community to which the perpetrator belonged as a legitimate object of retaliation. Fear was present where shame was not. They accordingly "collected Forty four Dollars which together with the Rifle Gun, they had given to the Squaw, who went away seemingly satisfied." But when three warriors returned shortly thereafter and threatened a major assault, the entire community had reason to be fearful.[19] No attack materialized. The warriors were apparently restrained by the woman, who deemed the gifts sufficient to "cover" the dead man, assuaging ritually her grief over his death.

With the assistance of the sheriff of the adjacent county, Seymour was again remanded to jail. His trial was held on December 19, 1766, under military guard. The accomplice pleaded guilty to manslaughter, for which he was branded on the hand and set free. According to the *Pennsylvania Gazette*, Seymour "behaved with great Boldness" throughout the proceedings. He denied the allegations and insisted that he had obtained the deceased Oneida's goods from a sailor. During the trial, the special commissioner, the provincial Supreme Court justice Charles Read, did everything within his power to reinforce the prosecution's case. The newspaper account indicated that he "took much Pains to explain to the Jury, with absolute Clearness, the Nature of this Kind of Evidence, and to shew the absolute Certainty arising from the Facts." The jury returned a guilty verdict, and Read pronounced a sentence of death the following morning. Read's address "paint[ed] the Heinousness of the Crime; the terrible Effect it might have had on the Frontiers, if the Indians had been possessed by the same Spirit of Revenge with the Prisoner; [and] the Ingratitude of it, as it was well known that the Oneida Nation . . . had, during the whole Course of the late War, cooperated with His Majesty's Troops." Seymour was apparently confident that his fellow citizens would rescue him from his fate until near the end, when, "for the first time," according to the report published in the *Gazette*, "he seemed dismayed; for he was encircled by a strong Detachment from the adjacent Companies of Militia." He confessed to the crime at the gallows and was hanged before the assembled crowd.[20]

The pursuit and punishment of Seymour was exceptional. Considering the obstacles the colonists placed in the way, it can be understood only as an outcome of the governor's personal action. Franklin's motivations were complex. His moral outrage appears to have been genuine, resembling the visceral reaction of his father, Benjamin, to the Paxton Boys' murder of twenty Delaware Indians in Pennsylvania two years earlier. William Franklin's indignation was also inseparable from his contempt for the statement of political defiance that Indian killing had become for frontier whites. In taking strong action, the younger Franklin was determined that New Jersey would not witness a repeat of the Paxtonite disorders. In the wake of the Stamp Act controversy, the Indian killings provided Franklin with an opportunity to assure British ministers at Whitehall, the government's administrative nerve center, of his firm control over colonial affairs. Interestingly, Franklin was deeply involved in a pair of land speculation schemes in Indian country.[21] The first was an attempt to secure lands in western Pennsylvania as recompense for the losses suffered by traders in Pontiac's War. The second was considerably more ambitious. Franklin sought to organize a new colony from a massive territory between the Ohio and Illinois Rivers. In this venture he was joined by his father, as well as Sir William Johnson and the Indian department agent George Croghan, among others. For the proposal for the "Illinois colony" to succeed, however, Franklin had to assuage Lord Shelburne's misgivings about the management of relations with Natives by existing colonies. Franklin eagerly pointed out that such depredations were rare in his province and were punished effectively.[22]

Thus, Seymour's trial and execution was performed for an audience that ranged from local settlers in New Jersey to lords in London. It was also performed for the Natives, although they demonstrated some ambivalence about the proceedings. Indeed, New Jersey officials had to go to some pains to find a Native to serve as an official witness to the execution. Little Abraham, a Mohawk, reluctantly agreed to observe the trial and execution and to report what he saw to various Indian communities along the path back to Sir William's Mohawk Valley mansion, Johnson Hall. Little Abraham's reluctance reflected the Natives' wariness of legitimating the colonies' assertion of jurisdiction in matters of criminal punishment. Punishment by hanging did not accord with Iroquois notions of justice. But by the 1760s, Natives had come to understand the meaning of hanging to whites, and they appreciated the gesture, especially in the climate of violence that pervaded the post–Seven Years' War frontier. Perhaps the hanging would deter further anti-Indian violence. At a treaty nearly two years later, Iroquois representatives acknowledged Franklin's actions by bestowing on him the honorific name Sagorighweyoghsta, or "great arbiter of justice."[23] By doing so they did not simply pay tribute to him. Pennsylvania delegates were in attendance, and the Iroquois were implicitly criticizing them for their province's relative impotence.

In general, the Indians' worries over the frequency of reports of anti-Indian violence on the Virginia and Pennsylvania frontiers had only increased. Johnson reported that an Onondaga speaker expressed Iroquois concerns that these events "might end in a troublesome War," adding that they "plainly saw the Clouds gathering around 'em very fast."[24] The Oneidas responded to the situation by bolstering the Native presence in their homeland. In June 1766, Johnson was informed that 220 or 230 Tuscaroras intended to remove to Oneida territory from North Carolina. Johnson's "Journal of Indian Affairs" recorded their arrival on December 18 and the trials they had endured en route: "They with great difficulty were allowed to pass in safety thro' the Frontiers of Pennsylvania, Md., Va. &c notwithstanding they had [Johnson's] Pass, as also that of the Magistrates of the sevl districts—that at Paxton in Penn. in their Return from North Carolina they were plundered of sev[era]l things." It was recorded further that "these with many more Complaints were made known to the Six Nations, altho' [Sir William] endeavoured all he could to keep it private from them, knowing their tempers were already much sowered by such like treatment shewn to sevl of their People this year as they passed thro' them Governments." The arrivals were disappointingly few in number—they had been reduced to 160—and the tales they told only reinforced the Oneidas' conviction that they needed to consolidate Indian strength in the region, especially along their southern frontier.[25]

Drawing the Line

The Natives demanded a revised—and enforced—boundary beyond which whites would not venture for purposes other than trade. The existing boundary, the Proclamation Line of 1763, which prohibited settlement beyond the Appalachian ridge, was vague in the north. Frustrated by what they perceived to be Britain's insufficiently aggressive efforts to secure the lands to which they felt entitled in the wake of military victory, settlers breached the line everywhere. In October 1767, Johnson reported, "[The Indians] complain Grievously of the Want of the Boundary Line of their having met with no redress about their Lands, of their not obtaining Justice on the frontiers, of the Insults & Murders committed by the Inhabitants at the back of the Settlements to the southward, of Intrusions &ca on which heads they have been long assured of redress."[26]

Johnson and other colonial officials were clearly sympathetic to the Indian request but were under no illusions about the government's ability to check white settlers unless Whitehall was willing to commit the additional resources for policing the border. Gen. Thomas Gage, commander-in-chief of the British forces in North America, expressed his opinion that, in the absence of such a commitment, simply drawing imaginary lines to separate Indians and whites left "the Wound . . . only skinned over, and not probed to the Bottom." He added, "If means are not fallen upon to protect the Indians in their Persons and Property's, it matters little where the Boundary's are fixed. The frontier People [who] have now transgressed them, have neither been effectually removed or punished for their Encroachments. . . . I despair not of living long enough to hear that they have transgressed them also."[27] Still, such a line would buy time during which Johnson and his associates could use their privileged access to the Indians to buy land from them. Johnson objected to settlers' forcing their way into Indian territory, but that did not keep him from aggrandizing himself from their presence. By positioning himself as a more benign alternative, he persuaded the Natives to sell land to him. Indeed, the Oneidas and Mohawks had recently sold him a tract of their hunting territory north and west of Oriskany.

Sir William chose Fort Stanwix, abandoned but still standing at the Carrying Place, as the site for the autumn treaty that would determine the new boundary. Iroquois delegates from the west tarried at Kanonwalohale before proceeding. The extended layover was mandated by the death en route of a Seneca chief. It was the Oneidas' obligation as members of the younger-brother moiety to condole his kin. The stop, however, had been planned from the outset. This offered the western tribes an opportunity to consult with the Oneidas, in keeping with the custom of holding meetings at clan, village, tribe, and then supra-tribal levels to establish consensus at each tier before proceeding to further negotiations. Since any treaty line would be drawn through their territory, it was assumed the Oneidas would play a forward role in this negotiation. Indeed, the Oneida chief Tagawaron even complained that "he thought his Nation disagreeably circumstanced the rest having thrown so much of the transaction . . . on their hands."[28]

When the treaty opened officially, more than a month behind schedule, Oneidas comprised nearly five hundred of the more than three thousand Indians in attendance from more than a dozen tribes. Roughly one in two Oneidas was present. Such general attendance bespoke the treaty's great importance, but it was also necessitated by Iroquois politics. Chiefs were representatives only in the most limited sense of the word: they were not vested with any binding decision-making power. Native politics operated strictly on the principle of consensus, and any decision was only as legitimate as the proportion of the whole that consented to it. The chiefs—as mediators, really—discussed terms with Johnson publicly and privately and then returned to consult with their respective delegations.[29]

During the negotiations, Tagawaron acknowledged to Johnson that his people were "much divided in opinion."[30] Since older women wielded more power over the warriors of their matrilineages than did the sachems, the relative absence of women as a result of the corn harvest probably gave the warriors freer rein. The Fort Stanwix negotiations therefore involved a confrontation not only between Indians and whites but also between the most clearly opposed elements of mid-eighteenth-century Oneida society, the warriors and the sachems. The stakes were high for both. The warriors' imperative was to maintain access to the Carrying Place and hunting territory. The sachems were bound to their prescribed role as peacemakers, and in signing a treaty they hoped to secure the goods necessary to retain their flagging influence with the young men, as well as to promote the general well-being of their communities.

The British policy of imperial retrenchment after the Seven Years' War had destabilized the political order in Euro-American and Native communities alike. Faced with large debts arising from its recent victories, Whitehall had tried in vain to relieve itself of at least some of the costs of colonial administration. First it tried reducing those costs by curtailing supplies to its Indian allies. The massive Indian resistance of Pontiac's War forced a partial resumption of those expenditures, but smaller quantities of clothing, food, guns, powder, knives, tomahawks, or even razors, made it harder for pro-English headmen in Iroquois towns to retain their influence among their people. The British attempt to shift the cost to the colonists bore similarly bad fruit. The Stamp Act engendered even greater resistance and made it increasingly difficult for the ultimate English chief, George III, to retain his influence among his own people.

With Iroquois warriors eager to demonstrate their martial prowess and to exact revenge against white frontier folk, the sachems had arrived at the treaty ground anxious to deal for goods that would enhance their faltering control over the young men and shore up their prestige. On this level the sachems and warriors shared an interest in getting the most out of the treaty. The sachems allowed the warriors to dictate the Oneidas' predictable opening move: to propose a line that formally acknowledged the de facto frontier, asserted their suzerainty over tribes to the south and west, and limited further white settlement.[31] The Oneidas hung tough during the negotiations. Johnson complained that "the greatest trouble and difficulty" he "met with was to bring the Oneidaes to allow the line to run any farther West than Oriskane Creek." This effort, he said, "engaged all my Interest & Influence three Days & almost 3 Nights." His goal was nothing short of procurement of the Carrying Place itself, and he pressed the Oneidas relentlessly. The sachems enumerated the difficulties that would arise from any cession beyond Oriskany. A more westerly line would place whites in closer proximity to Indian villages, with all the attendant ill effects. They also noted that some of the lands in question were "the property of a few Familys who did not incline to part with so Valuable a Tract." And when it came to the Carrying Place itself, the Oneidas, according to the official proceedings, "observed that . . . as Game grew daily scarce they purposed to keep Horses & Carriage to carry over Goods &c as formerly to earn some Money for their Familys." Johnson countered with predictions of conflict if the Iroquois revived dormant schemes to expand their activities. To underscore this threat, Johnson cited the Oneidas' familiarity with uncontrollable white frontier folk. He pleaded his inability to rein them in if not given enough "room" so that "the Boundary would be so well known, and secured by Laws before there would be occasion to invade it, that people would act with extreem caution . . . rather . . . than transgress" it.[32]

The new boundary that the Iroquois and Johnson eventually agreed on in 1768 permitted white settlement as far west as Canada Creek and the Unadilla (fig. 3). Two Mohawk towns and the Oneida village of Oriske were to remain enclaves of Indian territory, though they were east of the dividing line. Concessions were made for the benefit of Iroquois warriors. The Carrying Place itself remained under joint Oneida-British control, so the possibility of employment there remained. Furthermore, the Indians did not permit the line to extend north of the portage, allowing the Oneidas for the

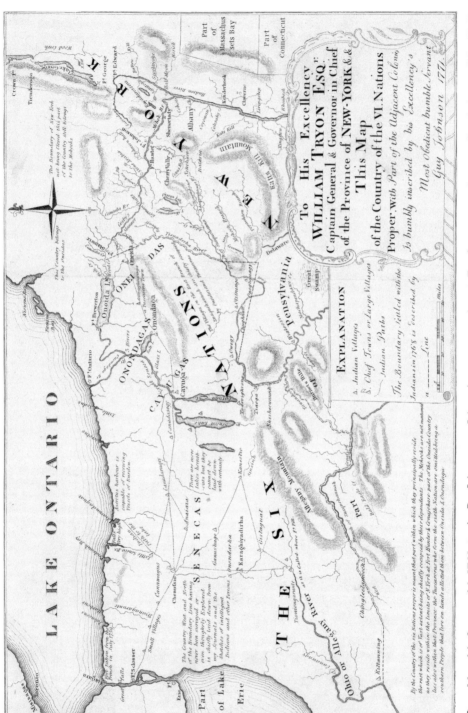

Fig. 3: *Map of the Country of the VI Nations* by Guy Johnson, 1771. Johnson's map portrays the 1768 Fort Stanwix treaty line, as well as the limits of New York's pretensions to Iroquoia. Courtesy of New York State Library, Albany.

present to preserve their northern hunting territories. In addition, in a provision that reflected the Native emphasis on usufruct in reckoning land rights, the sachems laid down the "condition that all our Warriors shall have the liberty of hunting throughout the Country as they have no other means of subsistance and as your people have not the same occasions or inclinations That the White people be restricted from hunting on our side of the Line to prevent contensions between us."[33]

Eleventh-hour entreaties by Sir William for more territory were unsuccessful. In return for their concessions, the Oneidas received their share of the twenty bateaux loads of gifts valued at £10,460 sterling. They were also given a special consideration of $600, and another $1,000 to vacate their claims to the lands previously covered by the Oriskany patent, "over and besides the several Fees which were given in private." One observer described the scene: "The large Present given by Sir William, consisted of the greatest Quantity of Indian Goods & Dollars, I ever saw on such an Occasion and they were most judiciously displayed on the Parade of the Fort, that so all the Indians might see them & in the center of the Parade, circumscribed by the Goods & Dollars on *three sides*." The Indians may have been symbolically occupying the fort, but the Oneidas were well aware that they had given the king "a great and valuable Country." "And we know," they declared during the proceedings, "that what we shall now get for it must be far short of its value." In exchange they demanded explicit assurances that these cessions would be the last, "forever binding & conclusive."[34]

The Treaty of Fort Stanwix was a compromise between the British and the Iroquois, and also between rival factions within the Oneida tribe. In this instance, Oneida factionalism had not weakened them. It enabled them to secure a better bargain because the sachems' negotiating position was strengthened by their ability to match Johnson's threat that he could not control frontier folk with the threat that their control over the young men would break if subjected to further pressure. All Oneidas, like the rest of the Six Nations to the west, also took solace in the fact that part of the price of this bargain was going to be paid by Indians other than themselves. While Oneida territory remained partially intact, the treaty line veered sharply west as soon as it reached their southern border. The Six Nations as a whole had made much of their supposed sovereignty over hundreds of thousands of square miles of Shawnee and Delaware lands. As Johnson explained to his superiors, "The Six Nations insisting on their right to the Lands as far South as the Cherokee River have [ceded] the same to his Majesty and notwithstanding that the Report of the Board of Trade spoke of the Great Kanhawa River as their Southern bounds, I found from what passed at several private Meetings, that I could not deny them the liberty of asserting their pretensions to the Southward without highly disobliging them, and preventing the Settlement of the rest." While ceding the territory of the Shawnees and Delawares increased the sum dispensed to the Six Nations, it had the still more important effect of diverting the stream of white settlement to the south of Iroquoia. This strategy had worked on numerous occasions in the past to keep the Longhouse relatively free of white settlers. It worked again. Croghan commented in 1770, "All this spring and summer the roads have been lined with wagons moving to the Ohio."[35] The relief, however, would be short-lived.

Borderline Indians

Even if the Oneidas had diverted most of the settlers away from themselves, there was little question that the area east of the treaty line would begin filling up quickly now that the line had been formally revised. A large number of new patents were registered in the wake of the Fort Stanwix treaty, and a number of small settlements sprang up to the south and east of Oneida territory in the Delaware and Susquehanna watersheds. A group of speculators from Burlington, New Jersey—including Justice Charles Read and William Franklin—patented lands along the Upper Susquehanna. In 1772, the province of New York created the county of Tryon; it stretched west from Schenectady all the way to the Line of Property, as the 1768 treaty boundary was called. By 1775, the county would already boast a population as high as five thousand. Signifying their partnership, Johnson named the county for the governor but its seat, Johnstown, for himself. That very summer, Tryon defied Whitehall and bargained for land with the Mohawks and Oneidas, promising them the resolution of outstanding land complaints in exchange for nearly one million acres. The Albany grandee Philip Schuyler jealously remarked, "Governor Tryon's fees, alone, will exceed £22,000; a good summer's work, that."[36]

The Indians were hardly naïve about their prospects. When the treaty to establish the line was convened, one Iroquois speaker observed, "Dayly experience teaches us that we cannot have any great dependence on the white People, and that they will soon forget their agreements for the sake of our Lands."[37] Shortly after the creation of Tryon County, the Oneidas moved to buttress the Line of Property by placing more Natives on it. The latest recipients of the Oneidas' self-interested largesse were Christian Algonquians primarily from southern New England and eastern Long Island. They would create a community that would become known as Brothertown. The idea of a Christian Algonquian settlement in Iroquoia was probably formulated by the Montauk schoolteacher David Fowler and the Mohegan preacher Samson Occom, who had visited the Oneidas in 1761. During the 1760s, Rev. Eleazar Wheelock, the head of Moor's Indian Charity School in New Hampshire, had deployed Fowler and the Mohegan Joseph Johnson as teachers at Kanonwalohale, as well as the Delaware Joseph Woolley at Oquaga. Fowler preceded Kirkland at Oneida by a year, and Fowler and Johnson had stayed on to assist Kirkland when he arrived in 1766. Eight Oneida children had attended Wheelock's school, but none remained by 1769. In 1855, the Brothertown Indian Thomas Commuck said that the Oneidas had initially invited Fowler to settle among them because of his "'book learning,' and other useful knowledge of the 'pale faces.'" Bringing in the Algonquians would enable the Oneidas to gain further understanding of colonial culture while adhering to their stated desire that "no white p[eo]pl[e] shall ever live among us, or near us, except ye minister and schoolmaster."[38]

The Oneidas' need for Indian emigrants to reinforce the boundary with the colony was matched by many Algonquians' need to find a new home. In the 1760s and 1770s, the Indians of southern New England and Long Island found their situation "much streightened." They had shared a common experience in the century since the catastrophe of King Philip's War. Euro-American settlers increased in numbers and encroached on Indians' already diminished lands with impunity. Some whites had purchased lands from venal sachems such as the Ninigrets among the Narragansetts, who sold off tribal territory to support an opulent lifestyle. Others had purchased lands from Indians seeking to pay off debts incurred for food, medical care, and alcohol. Still other whites occupied Indian land by no right at all.[39]

The coastal Algonquians had made significant adaptations to life in the midst of white settlement. While village horticulture continued to be the mainstay of Algonquian subsistence, they compensated for the loss of game resources by raising livestock and adopting sheep and cow husbandry. Men's roles were by tradition located away from the village, prompting Algonquian men to seek opportunities in the whaling industry and the colonial army. Moreover, many Algonquians had converted to New Light Christianity during the religious fervor that swept British North America in the

1730s and 1740s. The First Great Awakening had briefly increased whites' interest in converting the Natives and produced a brand of Christianity that, in its emphasis on the individual's personal relationship with the supernatural, the zeal of the preacher, and its downplaying of formal doctrine and dogma, had a greater chance of appealing to Indian religious sensibilities.[40]

The New England Algonquians attempted to emigrate to Oneida territory in 1775. Their timing could not have been worse. New Englanders were alarmed by the prospect of their Indian neighbors' taking refuge among the hated and feared Iroquois just as a war with Britain threatened to erupt. Connecticut governor Jonathan Trumbull used the fact that "the whole Country is full of Suspicion" and that "these are dangerous times indeed" to deny the emigrants a passport. As Joseph Johnson related it, the emigrants' neighbors "said that . . . it wou'd be best to knock all the Indians in the head rather than that they Shoud go to the Mohawk Country." Threats were made that, as he put it, "my head shou'd soon be Seperated from my body." White New Englanders also applied financial pressure. "Many of our People who used to labour hard for the Inhabitants," Johnson complained, "were refused payment unless they wou'd stay." This practice probably had the desired effect, for those who set forth for Oneida country did so only under "the ignominious burthen of real Poverty." When the first group of emigrants (now probably fewer than a dozen) arrived at Johnson Hall they had to beg for provisions, because, they later reported, "we had but just enough to bring us up thus far." Johnson reflected on the irony of the situation: "I told them . . . it seemed to Me [a] matter of great Surprize, that as the People of New England had got almost all our Lands from Us, and thereby oblig'd us to go elsewhere, shou'd want to Stop us now, when a Year ago, they wanted to get rid of us."[41] New Englanders were willing to threaten murder on Christian Algonquians because they suspected that their joining the Iroquois would unlock the murderous savage many believed lurked within every Native. They believed the Indians' conversion and adoption of Euro-American habits were but a façade concealing an essential, unchangeable, violent Indian-ness. But if Johnson thought he had encountered the ultimate irony—or overcome the ultimate obstacle—in the New Englanders' unwillingness to let the Algonquians leave, he was in for another "matter of great Surprize."

Many Natives had also come to believe that Indian identity was fixed and distinct from that of Europeans. According to some Oneidas, those who failed to uphold the "old customs & . . . traditions, & live like true

Indians" perpetrated a grave offense against the Great Spirit. This "nativist" ideology, to use the historian Gregory Dowd's term, emerged as a response to the acute problems of declining power and material dependency that followed the departure of the French during the Seven Years' War. It found votaries among a wide array of Eastern Woodland tribes, especially in western Iroquoia and the Ohio Valley, and had inspired Pontiac's War. Nativists believed that adoption of European traits hastened the day when Indians would be subjugated alongside another nonwhite people in Euro-American society: Africans. One Seneca predicted, "The spirit of the brave warrior & the good hunter will no more be discovered among us. We shall be sunk so low as to hoe corn & squashes in the field, chop wood, stoop down & milk cows like *negroes* among the dutch people." Warning Indians off from a Moravian mission, nativists also claimed that they would be made "slaves, where they would be harnessed to the plough, and whipped to work."[42]

As if to offer visual proof of the nativist argument, many of the Christian Algonquians were of at least partial African descent. The common social and economic marginalization of Indians and blacks in New England society, combined with the lack of men in Indian communities and the lack of women in African American communities, had resulted in significant intermarriage. Thus, despite Native Americans' historic indifference to race as a criterion of community membership, the Oneidas' grant to the New England Indians specified that the land "shall not be possessed by any persons, deemed of the said Tribes, who are descended from, or have intermixed with Negroes, or Mulattoes." This ban, which contributed further to the small size of the emigrant party, reflected the concerns of Iroquois nativists, as well as some Algonquians, including Occom himself. Their experience taught them that Africanization compounded the already intractable problems in their relations with Europeans. The Iroquois and the Algonquians suspected that the colonists might enslave them, and Wheelock's students had witnessed the degradation of slavery first-hand.[43] As a result, many of those who were not personally disqualified from the emigrant group were probably unwilling to leave behind spouses and other relatives who were.

As soon as the New England Indians "had got Cornfields planted and gardens made" in Oneida territory, they began to fear that "the distant Indian Nations . . . [might] fall on, and take up the Hatchet against the new settled Indians." Joseph Johnson reported that "therefore the New England Indians with the consent and advice of the Oneidas, thought best for their Safety and the Peace of the Country to return for the Present from whence they came, until the present Troubles shall be ended." Apparently Connecticut was not the only "Country full of Suspicion" in which "dangerous times" prevailed. No violence seems to have erupted, but the Oneidas' relations with their western brethren—not to mention Oneida pride—was a casualty of the failed Algonquian settlement. The Oneidas had previously assured the Brothertowns, "We shall be ever ready to defend you, and help you, or ever be ready to protect you according to our Abilities." As one Oneida confided to Kirkland about their relations with the Iroquois to their west: "We are despised by our brethren, on account of our christian profession. Time was when we were esteemed as honorable & important in the confederacy: but now we are looked upon as small things; or rather nothing at all."[44]

The Oneidas' failed attempt to settle Christian Algonquians on their eastern flank shows how times had changed since the initial Tuscarora migration. The middle decades of the eighteenth century had seen the advent of European colonial settlement in Iroquoia. The significance of that development had initially been muted by the imperial rivalry between Britain and France. But France's military defeat allowed English- and German-speaking colonists to begin pushing west in earnest. Coupled with residual bitterness from the war, the settlers' attitudes and behavior toward their Indian neighbors changed, as did their understanding of themselves. As friction grew, the peoples of and around Iroquoia increasingly thought of themselves in racial terms that were simple and exclusive. This development did not bode well for groups like the Christian Algonquians who blurred racial categories. Nor was it promising for the Oneidas, situated as they were on the very frontier of Euro-American settlement. A border war was brewing, and it would come in the form of the American Revolution.

3

The Dilemmas of Alliance

The Oneidas' American Revolution, 1775–1784

THE AMERICAN REVOLUTION has helped to define the distinct national identity of the Oneida people more than any other episode in modern history. In that war, the Oneidas broke with mainstream confederacy opinion and aligned themselves with the colonists. As with the abortive Algonquian settlement, this policy did little to enhance their standing among their fellow Iroquois. However, the Oneidas determined it was the only way to protect their homeland. Their judgment was vindicated at least in part by the Patriot victory. Thus, when Oneidas tell the story of their participation in that war, they emphasize the special relationship it established with the United States—even if that relationship has been honored only fitfully by their partner. In recounting the war, the Oneidas often dwell on the experience of one Oneida woman. Her English name was Polly Cooper. According to oral tradition, Cooper accompanied a contingent of Oneidas to Valley Forge. They carried large quantities of corn to feed the Continental Army in its hour of greatest distress. Cooper taught the grateful Americans how to prepare the corn but refused payment for her labor. As a gesture of thanks, George Washington's wife, Martha, took Cooper to Philadelphia and bought her a shawl, hat, and bonnet.[1] This presentation of gifts epitomized the Native ethic of reciprocity and symbolized the vitality of the U.S.-Oneida relationship.

The documentary record bears out some of the story's details but is silent in regard to others. Nevertheless, the Cooper tradition conveys larger truths that are beyond question. As the story suggests, the Oneidas' wartime efforts were recognized by American officers including Washington himself.[2]

By virtue of its sacredness, the gift of corn signifies that the Oneidas' contribution to the Patriot cause was of the highest magnitude. Through combat, spying, and scouting, the Oneidas were indispensable to the survival of Patriot communities on the New York and Pennsylvania frontiers. The Oneidas were the United States' most important Native allies. Their sacrifice was great as well. After their villages and fields were burned by Britain's Native allies as retribution for siding with the Americans, hundreds of refugee Oneidas suffered through privations and exposure to smallpox. Disease, displacement, and other war-related traumas reduced the number of Oneidas living in their homeland to fewer than 650.[3]

Because the American Revolution had divided the Six Nations, Iroquois warriors were faced with the disconcerting prospect of harming one another in the course of fighting someone else's war. Although enough hostile acts took place that some historians refer to the Revolution as an "Iroquois civil war," most Iroquois balked at taking the lives of their fellows. Indeed, on many occasions, they attempted to mitigate the impact of the war on other Indians by negotiating prisoner exchanges and urging their white allies to exercise restraint toward Native foes. Like other Native Americans, the Oneidas experienced the American Revolution as a prolonged trial in which they constantly tried to balance contradictory imperatives. They had to protect the independence of their communities by assisting their respective allies without killing kin or otherwise diminishing the Native power on which their long-term interests depended. In other words, they behaved toward the United States as allies rather than subordinates. This alliance strategy was adopted by many Indian communities seeking to navigate the treacherous shoals of a conflict not of their own making.[4]

Neutralism

When New England rebels issued an appeal for Iroquois support in the spring of 1775, the Oneidas replied with a declaration of neutrality that reflected the Iroquois Confederacy's initial official position. The New Englanders prudently declared themselves satisfied.[5] The Oneidas were content to buy time, as were most of the rest of the Iroquois. Neutrality had benefits recognized by all. The Six Nations had historically taken advantage of divisions among Europeans to protect their own autonomy. Because of their military prowess, diplomatic skill, and strategically crucial location, the Iroquois had effectively held the balance of power between the British and French until the end of the Seven Years' War. Iroquois political culture admitted scant central authority, however, and so factions favorable to one side or the other constantly threatened the equilibrium. Europeans faced a chronically volatile situation that required their attention and sometimes felt more than a little like extortion. During a conference at Albany in 1775, a Six Nations spokesman put the Patriots' good will to the test by requesting substantial trade and the return of two parcels of land that he claimed had been taken from them without compensation. On hearing their demands, the secretary to the Patriot treaty commissioners observed privately, "It is plain to me that the Indians understand their game, which is to play into both hands."[6]

The Iroquois' game, however, was more one of canny diplomacy than cynical ploy. The Iroquois were making the best of a bad situation. Beneath the assertion of neutrality, the confederacy's constituent members were truly at odds over how to proceed. Samuel Kirkland reported after a March 1776 council involving the Oneidas and Cayugas, "Many of the Indians have observed to me that they never knew Debates so warm and Contentions so fierce to have happened between these two Brothers . . . since the Commencement of their Union."[7] Both could sustain a belief that their alliance best served the long-term interest of the Iroquois, and they fought sincerely and effectively for their chosen side for the duration of the conflict. Indeed, although the pendulum of fortune swung back and forth during the war, there was relatively little switching of sides by those who early on committed themselves freely to either the crown or the colonists.

To the extent that the English concept of liberty made sense within the Natives' noncoercive political context, the Iroquois already enjoyed more of it than any British subject or American citizen ever would. The question was how to protect it. The Iroquois recognized that they had a stake in the war's outcome, even if this was primarily a war among whites. But Iroquoia was large, and it offered many different vantage points on what that outcome and its implication for Natives would be. The westernmost nations had witnessed some of the most violent manifestations of white aggression during Dunmore's War. This war, triggered in 1774 by competition over Ohio Valley lands, had pitted Virginians against Delawares, Shawnees, and Mingos, some of whom had Seneca and Cayuga relatives in Iroquoia. Many Senecas and Cayugas had been deeply frustrated by the Six Nations' collective decision to remain aloof from Dunmore's War. When the Revolution broke out, their lack of sympathy for the rebels was predictable, and calls for retribution became harder to resist. Besides, the presence of Fort Niagara made the crown's strength—and patronage—more palpable than the rebels' in western Iroquoia. Fort Niagara's personnel included an experienced cadre of Indian agents, many of whom spoke Native languages.[8] There was little reason for the Indians there to question British officers' confident counsel that the crown would prevail.

Pro-British sentiment among the Mohawks sprang from somewhat different sources. The Revolution presented the Mohawks with their last hope of slowing, arresting, or perhaps even reversing the white settlement around them. More than a century of contact with sharp-dealing white neighbors and speculators had left the Mohawks with little land and considerable hostility toward expansionist white settlers. Mohawk allegiance to the crown had been cultivated and sustained by the Mohawk family of Sir William Johnson, who died in 1774. Joseph Brant, the brother of Johnson's Mohawk widow, traveled to Britain in 1776, where he was further impressed by the power and grandeur of the empire. Brant's influence extended to Oquaga, whose population included more than a hundred Mohawks who had emigrated there in the middle decades of the century as Europeans took over the Mohawk Valley. Many Oquaga Oneidas followed the Mohawks into the British camp.[9] The Oquaga experience demonstrates that although personal conscience was always the final arbiter of behavior, allegiance was generally decided at the village, rather than the national, level. No nation was homogenous in its support of crown or colonists. Among the Mohawks, many of those from Fort Hunter remained neutral throughout, and a peace party led by Great Tree existed among the Senecas. Then there were the Iroquois among the "Seven Nations" of the lower St. Lawrence Valley. Although no longer represented at confederacy councils, most of the Seven Nations Iroquois were Mohawks (but with a substantial number of Oneidas) who resided at Akwesasne and Kahnawake. They maintained their autonomy from the Iroquois Confederacy and had exhibited a consistent disinclination to take up arms in the wars of others. The American Revolution was no exception. Although they were officially allied with the British, their assistance was generally apathetic, and some actively aided the Patriots.[10]

Winning Oneida Hearts and Minds

Why did the majority of Oneidas defy their fellow Iroquois and take up arms against the British? Historians have generally assumed that, as Washington put it, the Reverend Kirkland enjoyed "uncommon ascendancy" over them.

As we have seen, however, the Oneidas did not blindly follow Kirkland in matters of politics, diplomacy, and war any more than they did in matters of religion. Nevertheless, his presence took on a new importance as the imperial crisis deepened. In the years immediately preceding Sir William Johnson's death, the stakes in Kirkland's initially asymmetrical relationship with the superintendent had risen dramatically. A New Light Presbyterian dissenter from New England, Kirkland was deeply sympathetic to the emerging colonial resistance. As among the Oneidas, political divisions in the colonies corresponded roughly with religious ones. The gifts Kirkland distributed came to symbolize, in addition to his good will, that of the like-minded rebel colonists who supported him. Kirkland boasted that between his harangues and his stores, he had pre-empted many Natives' visits to Johnson: "My house has been crowded with visitors from remote parts great part of the winter & some have returned from Oneida without going down the country which I suppose has given great uneasiness to a certain Sachem [i.e., Sir William]."[11]

Furthermore, whenever Kirkland returned to Kanonwalohale from his regular trips to Massachusetts to visit his family and sponsors, he disseminated the latest news of unrest from a New England perspective. Accused by Conoghquieson in January 1775 of causing "much trouble" by "always collecting news and telling us strange matters of the white people," Kirkland denied propagandizing the Oneidas, admitting only that he "occasionally explained the prints." Kirkland was less coy in a June letter to the Albany Committee of Correspondence. He acknowledged his clerical obligation to remain neutral and insisted the Oneidas had demanded information of him. But he was willing to take credit for the result. In his estimation, "my Interpreting the doings of the Congress to a number of their Sachems has done more real service to the Cause of the Country, or the Cause of Truth & Justice than five hundred Pounds in presents would have effected."[12]

Kirkland's statement says something about his relationship with the Oneidas. He surely helped frame the Oneidas' perception of the conflict. But the point Kirkland was really making had to do with the mutual need he shared with leaders of the rebellion. Without the patronage of New England dissenters, his mission would not survive; as an ambassador for the Patriot cause, however, he was invaluable to them. If we can judge the diplomatic aplomb of New England Patriot leaders by the appeal they drafted and sent to the Indians, they needed all the help available. Their message solicited Native sympathy by reciting that the colonists had "purchased . . . land with their own money, and . . . have built our houses, and cut down the trees, and cleared and improved the land" only to find that "Our Fathers in *Great Britain* tell us our Lands, and Houses, and Cattle, and Money, are not our own." Although they raised the specter of shortages of powder and guns for colonists and Indians alike, their argument was hardly likely to convince the Indians to "whet [their] Hatchet, and be prepared with us to defend our liberties and lives." It seems that Kirkland dared recite it to the Oneidas only, and probably with considerable redaction at that.[13]

A second Patriot representative at Oneida by 1776 was James Dean of Connecticut, who had moved to Oquaga in the late 1750s, at roughly the age of ten. He had been sent there by his missionary step-uncle, Benjamin Ashley, to gain linguistic competence, as well as to serve as a token of good will to ensure the acceptable treatment of Native children at Wheelock's missionary boarding school in New Hampshire.[14] Dean seems to have succeeded in his new life. He was adopted by an Oneida family and given the name Cologhquadeal ("the sun's halo"). Adoption in Iroquois culture represented a serious commitment, and he was looked after by his mother or other senior women in the community long beyond his childhood. In 1761, the missionary Gideon Hawley remarked that young James had become "a perfect Indian boy in language, manners, and dress." Later, Hawley and his fellow missionary Amos Tappan "advise[d] [Dean's] Father to bring him off," suggesting that Dean was a bit too successful for some. "We think it proper," they said, "[that] he should be placed where he may be further instructed in his Mother Tongue, and the principles of the Christian Religion." Dean apparently lived alternately at Oquaga and Spencertown, New York, for the remainder of the 1760s.[15] He attended Dartmouth College (as Wheelock had renamed his school) in the early 1770s. In 1775, Dean was dispatched by Wheelock to Kahnawake, the Mohawk reserve outside Montreal. Dean was to serve a dual purpose there: his duty was, in his words, as much "to conciliate and confirm their friendship to the common Cause of America, as to instruct them in the Principles of our holy Religion." Since the causes of the conflict appeared opaque to many Natives, Dean reported, "[they] took the opportunity of my being among them to inquire into the Origins & Reasons of the [conflict]. I gladly improved all such Opportunities to inform them of the Grounds of the present Controversy."[16] The Kahnawake Mohawks became at best tepid allies of the British during the war, a fact that is probably partially attributable to Dean's influence.

By 1776, the Continental Congress employed Dean to continue his important work at Kanonwalohale. Kirkland acknowledged Dean's influence in a letter to the Northern Department commander, Maj. Gen. Philip Schuyler, stating, "The Oneida put great Confidence in Mr. Dean as your Honor's Deputy and admit him into their Cabinet Councils. Had he not been on the Spot at this Juncture to strengthen and encourage the Oneidas, and remove objections the Cayugas would probably have carried the Day & had they brought back the Ax 'tis thought our Frontiers would have felt it before many months."[17] But the greatest testament to Dean's influence came in the form of threats to his life from pro-British Iroquois. Specifically, he was warned away from an early spring conference at Onondaga in 1776. Having stopped en route at Canaseraga, the "female Governesses of the town, and those who were present from [Kanonwalohale]" urged him not to go on—a clear testament to the concern his adoptive family felt for his welfare. They told him, he wrote, "Our hearts have trembled and our eyes have not known sleep . . . while we consider the danger that appears to . . . threaten you at Onondaga." Dean thanked them but felt duty-bound to proceed to the council. He did so with an Oneida, Tuscarora, and Kahnawake escort.[18]

As the Revolution approached, Kirkland and Dean had explained the complex and quickly evolving situation to the Oneidas in terms favorable to the rebels. Kirkland and Dean enabled the Oneidas to see beyond the already demoralized Tryon County militia and understand the Patriots' true strength. That Dean and Kirkland were biased was obvious, but the Oneidas could and did regularly compare notes with their pro-British peers. Perhaps most important to the forging and maintenance of an alliance, Kirkland and Dean conveyed to Congress the Oneidas' needs and dispositions toward the United States. And by satisfying the needs of the Oneida people, Congress hoped it could improve their dispositions.[19]

"Constrained to a Compliance"

The Oneidas' wartime policy was fundamentally shaped by the fact that they occupied the front line of Indian country as defined by the 1768 Treaty of Fort Stanwix. In early 1775, one of Kirkland's converts and closest assistants, known as Deacon Thomas, had told royal officials that the Oneidas were "greatly alarmed at the endeavours of people to cross [the boundary] lately, and requested that they might be immediately prevented."[20] But the limits of Britain's ability to rein in frontier settlement were already obvious, and if the Oneidas alienated their white neighbors, they could expect to be dispossessed. New York Patriots regarded the Carrying Place as "the Key of the Western Frontier." It would be closely watched. As prospects of armed conflict grew, the Oneidas realized that they would have to come to terms with neighboring Patriot communities. In a statement to a British officer explaining his nation's alliance with the Americans, the Oneida sachem White Skin noted, according to the reported proceedings, that "their People lived so near to the Rebels that they were constrained to a compliance." The statement may have been made under duress, but as a description of extant power relations it was only a modest exaggeration. The Oneida chief Good Peter (fig. 4)

Fig. 4. *Good Peter, Chief of the Oneida Indians* by John Trumbull, 1792 (detail). Courtesy of Yale University Art Gallery, Trumbull Collection.

later put forth the same argument more positively when he recalled that "the love of peace, and the love of our land which gave us birth, supported our resolution" to back the United States. At Oriske, the Oneida village near the portage adjacent to colonial settlement, warriors mustered with the local militia in 1775 and reassured them that no Indian hostilities were imminent.[21]

When it came to consolidating Oneida allegiances, a little patronage did not hurt. The Patriot commissioners of Indian Affairs noted ruefully, "The Enemy have a very capital advantage over us in their intercourse with the Indians as they have it in their power to afford them such ample supplies, and those in their interest are continually drawing Comparisons." To nurture Native support, Congress loosened its purse strings and promised to keep its Indian allies supplied with gunpowder, provisions, and clothing. Diplomacy carried a hefty price tag, too. Convening a treaty with the Six Nations in August 1776, General Philip Schuyler noted, "The Consumption of provision and Rum is incredible. It equals that of an army of three thousand Men; altho' the Indians here are not above twelve hundred, including Men, Women, and Children."[22] Entertaining small touring Indian delegations proved a more cost-effective form of persuasion. Kirkland escorted a small contingent of Oneida warriors to New England and New Jersey in March 1777. The missionary had informed Schuyler that six or seven Oneidas wished to travel to the coast for an "occular Demonstration" of "French gentlemen or French vessels," if available. Kirkland understood that the promise of an alliance with France gave the rebels crucial credibility in the eyes of many Oneidas. Oneida francophilia dated to the seventeenth century, but its present incarnation was largely born of nostalgia for the era of imperial competition. It was strong enough that British agents or their Iroquois supporters felt it necessary to stridently deny the existence of any Patriot-French alliance.[23]

According to the pastor (and soon-to-be Yale College president) Ezra Stiles, who met the touring Oneidas in Rhode Island, the Native delegates came "to inspect and report the Preparations & Strength of these States." At Boston they "were shewn the Fortresses & went on board . . . one of the American Men o' War. They desired to see the Canon discharged, & asked Capt Manly to fire one with Ball for Congress, two without Ball for G. Washington, & six without Ball for the Six Nations of Indians." Stiles reported that the Rhode Island Assembly "made an Entertainmt for them &c to amount of Expence 300 Dollars—among the rest a Gun or Musquet made in N. Engld exceedingly decorated worth 20 Dollars, tho' they gave 40 & presented it to the Chief Warrior." On March 29, Washington informed the president of Congress that the six Oneidas had visited him at his headquarters, where, he said, "I shewed them every civility in my power and everything I thought material to excite in them an Idea of our strength and independence."[24]

These diplomatic efforts bred a certain degree of camaraderie between the Oneidas, the diverse array of colonists gathered under the Patriot banner, and, later, their French allies as well. Captain Bloomfield noted in his diary that Oneida warriors tutored Continental Army officers in lacrosse. Exhibitions of song and dance also brought Natives and whites together as they shared in a recreational activity that surmounted the language barrier. At a dance during a November 1777 council, an Army surgeon reported, "One of the chiefs . . . took the commissioners, one at a time, by the hand, and danced them around the circle, then rubbing his hand about the grease and blacking of the pot, he blackened the face, first of General Schuyler, and then the other gentlemen, which excited much laughter." Claude Blanchard, the French commissary general, recalled the visit of an Oneida-Kahnawake delegation to Rochambeau's fleet in Newport in 1780. He found their table manners satisfactory and commented that their dancing reminded him of French peasants pressing grapes in a vat.[25] Such socializing promoted cohesiveness that was helpful during the trials of war.

Soldiers, Scouts, and Spies

Those trials had begun in earnest in 1777, when Britain launched two expeditions south from Canada to rendezvous near Albany with forces based in New York City. If successful, New England would be cut off from the other colonies. British major general John Burgoyne headed south from Montreal along the Champlain–Hudson corridor while brevet Brig. Gen. Barry St. Leger marched straight into Iroquoia and laid siege to Fort Stanwix in early August. Oneidas alerted nearby towns to the siege and participated in the fort's defense. According to Henry Powless, son of one of the fort's Oneida defenders, "The British . . . began to dig to undermine the fort, to blow it up; & Oneidas used to say, if they had not been there to aid in its defence, the fort might not have been saved."[26]

Seven hundred Tryon County militiamen under Brig. Gen. Nicholas Herkimer set out to relieve the fort, and roughly sixty Oneidas were with them. His courage having been recently called into question, Herkimer now led them to the fort rather incautiously. Mohawk, Seneca, and British soldiers were lying in wait and ambushed the relief column by Oriskany Creek. The fighting that ensued was intense and carried on at close quarters throughout the day. Recalling the carnage many decades later, Blacksnake, a Seneca, said that he had not seen so many dead bodies then or since. There had been so many, in fact, that "the Blood Shed a Stream Running Down on the Decending ground." An unknown number of Oneidas, perhaps thirty, were among the four hundred Patriots who died. Their losses were considerably greater than those of the British and their Iroquois allies. However, the battle, combined with a Patriot looting raid on their camp, sapped the willingness of British-allied Iroquois to persist in St. Leger's siege. The departure of his Iroquois allies contributed to St. Leger's decision to return to Canada, rather than rendezvous with Burgoyne. Thus, the resistance offered by the Tryon County militia and its Oneida allies contributed to Burgoyne's subsequent surrender at Saratoga, in which they would also play a more direct role.[27]

Historians have cited the Battle of Oriskany as the eruption of a civil war among the Iroquois.[28] But though Oriskany was the first violent exchange among the Iroquois during the Revolution, it was also the last. Nothing like it happened again until the Battle of Chippawa in the War of 1812. Indeed, some of Britain's Iroquois allies, particularly Senecas, had been reluctant to engage the Patriots at Oriskany and had perhaps been brought there under false pretenses. The captive-turned-Seneca Mary Jemison observed that the British had sent for Seneca men merely "to come and see them whip the rebels . . . to . . . just sit down, smoke their pipes, and look on." When violence appeared imminent, the Senecas proposed a parley with the Oneidas and militiamen, only to be shamed by Joseph Brant into joining the march. And although the Indian participants in the battle were not particularly repentant about the death of fellow Iroquois, when they exacted retribution for this battle, they did so by destroying Oneida property, not lives. By contrast, the Senecas made up for the loss of thirty-six warriors—a heavy blow to a tribe of only about a thousand—by clubbing to death some of their Patriot prisoners. Oneidas and Mohawks sacked one another's villages at Oriske and Canajoharie, but they were already evacuated and their inhabitants were not pursued.[29]

For the remainder of the war, Indians on opposite sides of the conflict generally avoided hostile encounters with one another. In September, almost immediately after accepting a war belt from the Americans, the Oneidas, Tuscaroras, and Onondagas dispatched at least 150 warriors to join Patriot

General Horatio Gates to meet Burgoyne. The Patriot-allied Indians took prisoners and intercepted communications between British officers. Of the Oneidas and the other Patriot-allied Indians, a Euro-American veteran of the Battle of Saratoga said, "They where Brave men and fought Like Bull dogs till Burgoine surrendert." Gates praised the Indians' "great service." To the likely relief of all the Iroquois, however, the Battle of Saratoga itself did not pit them against one another. As one British soldier noted, the British-allied Indians "ran off through the wood" before any engagement.[30] Although angered with one another and divided in their allegiances, the Iroquois were still primarily committed to fighting Europeans or Euro-Americans rather than one another. They continued to try to limit the terms of their entrapment in the war, even as it grew more intense.

The Oneidas' willingness to serve was also limited by some of the same factors that limited the Patriot militia's. Although the average Oneida warrior possessed greater martial skill than his colonial counterpart, neither was a professional fighter. For each, defending home communities was the overriding priority. They would not travel far to serve if their families faced imminent danger at home. Although the Marquis de Lafayette boasted in March 1778, "The love of the french blood mix'd with the love of some french *louis d'or* [i.e., money] have engag'd those indians to promise they would come with me," the Oneidas did not go anywhere until the French and Americans agreed to build a fort to protect their village. As the U.S. Indian commissioners observed, "It is not reasonable to suppose that they will march to the southward and leave their families defenceless."[31]

The approximately fifty Oneida warriors who finally left for Pennsylvania late that April proved themselves particularly useful adjuncts to the Continental Army during their service there. Drillmaster Friedrich von Steuben, imported from Prussia by way of France to train the Continentals, valued Native warriors for their ability to "keep the Enemy Compact, prevent Desertion in our Troops, [and] make us Masters of Intelligence." Drawing a European analogy, he noted, "The Austrians always use the Croats (a kind of white Indians) for such Purposes and to so good Effect that the King of Prussia imitated them by enrolling a Body of Irregulars to Cover in like Manner his Army." On May 30, the *Pennsylvania Gazette* accordingly reported that forty Oneidas had arrived in Trenton, New Jersey, "to scout near the lines, to check the unlawful commerce, too much carried on at present, between the country and the city."[32] But the Oneidas had come to fight as well. A week earlier, after the Battle of Barren Hill, the Oneidas' French commander had occasion to praise "their hability in firing." About four of them fell in battle. The Oneidas' service ultimately yielded them ten officers' commissions at the ranks of captain and lieutenant. Among those honored with a lieutenant's commission was Hanyost Thaoswagat, who had distinguished himself in the British campaign against Montreal in the Seven Years' War. One Kahnawake Mohawk who served with the Oneidas, Louis Atiatoharongwen, was made lieutenant colonel and a Tuscarora, Nicholas Cusick, lieutenant. These commissions represented important marks of respect for the Six Nations allies.[33]

The Patriots had anticipated a major British offensive to the south at the time they had called up the Oneida warriors. After it became clear that no such confrontation would materialize, Washington suggested that the Oneidas be sent home, with the request that they remain "in readiness to cooperate with us on any future occasion, that may present itself in advancing our mutual interest." In fact, the future occasion had already arrived. In a letter from Kanonwalohale dated three days earlier, James Dean related that "the Indians have been constantly ranging the Woods in quest of [a] party who fired upon their people." By the month of June it had become apparent to Congress that they faced "the commencement of an Indian war; which threatens with extensive devastation the frontiers of these United States."[34]

In mid-summer, Oneidas brought Schuyler first news of an assault on the frontier settlement of Wyoming. In early November, the Oneidas passed along a crucial warning regarding a Tory-Indian raid that had yet to take place. An Onondaga had informed them that a large number of Indians and Tories had resolved to attack Cherry Valley. The warning went unheeded, and thirty-three persons were killed in the ensuing assault. The source of the Oneidas' Cherry Valley intelligence—the oral report of an Onondaga— indicates that the Oneidas' effectiveness as intelligence-gatherers lay in their relationships and contacts as much as in their scouting skills.[35] Kinship ties enabled Oneida scouts to venture into hostile settlements. In one of the war's more daring feats of espionage, Deacon Thomas had concealed himself in the rafters of the council house at the Akwesasne Mohawk village while a British officer unfurled General Burgoyne's 1777 strategy. Deacon Thomas had promptly relayed this intelligence to the Patriots. He continued to operate there and in other villages in the region with the consent and protection of friends and relatives until his assassination at Kahnawake by the British in 1779. The controversy sparked by his killing only underscored the fact that the St. Lawrence Iroquois tolerated his activities.[36]

A "Civil" War

Most of the Iroquois recognized that volatile situations were more effectively managed when lines of communication with the opposing side were maintained. By lobbying the Patriots for the better treatment or outright release of British-allied Iroquois prisoners, the Oneidas expected a modicum of protection for their own captured warriors. When a party of Seneca warriors arrived at Washington's headquarters to fulfill the terms of a prisoner exchange in June 1778, Washington reported that they were "attended by a few of our Oneida and Tuscarora friends, who were thought necessary to proceed with the truce." The Oneidas also assured the Cayugas that they had used "their Influence to relieve from close confinement some of their People." These good offices were reciprocated in September, when a British-Indian raiding party captured five Oneidas. While the Tories planned to keep them under close watch, the Natives let them escape. In November 1778, the Oneidas pleaded successfully for the release of a Kahnawake warrior who had been captured by the Patriots.[37]

The Oneidas also used their influence to pre-empt Patriot retaliation on Iroquois communities after the frontier raids of 1778. In the wake of the Wyoming raid, Oneidas and Onondagas insisted that Iroquois diplomatic protocol demanded the formal return of some wampum belts that had been languishing unanswered before any action was taken. They implied that any retaliation prior to a formal response to the wampum would jeopardize whatever support the Patriots enjoyed among the Iroquois. Dean decried this as a ploy "only invented to gain Time and keep the Commissioners in suspence & to retard the operation of any plan that might be formed to do ourselves Justice upon them."[38] The first months of 1779 saw a similar flurry of diplomatic activity to this end. In January, the Oneidas claimed to have won the support of a significant number of Onondagas, some of whom traveled to Oneida in April to surrender "a number of large Silver medals which had been given them by the agents of the King of Britain" as tokens of their support. Two parties of Oneidas were dispatched to "the hostile tribes of the Six Nations." On their return, one Oneida with "a relation at Quiyoga [Cayuga] informed him the Quiyogas were determined to hold a conference with the Oneidas very soon." Taking note of such proceedings, Lieut. Gen. and Governor of Quebec Frederick Haldimand, Britain's supreme commander in North America, railed that "the perfidy of the Rebel Oneida Nation is come to that pitch that they even presume to debauch & invite the five nations to be of their sentiments & come over to them."[39] Wartime Six Nations diplomacy frustrated British and Patriot officers alike, but it mitigated the war's effects on the Iroquois.

Washington nevertheless remained committed to striking those Iroquois nations responsible for the devastating 1778 raids on Wyoming and Cherry Valley. He acknowledged that the only way the Patriots could take Fort Niagara would involve the Oneidas convincing fellow Iroquois to betray it, but he regarded that as unlikely. It was unclear that the Patriots could even find their way to Niagara through Iroquoia. In February 1779, when Washington sought to better understand Longhouse geography, he wrote, "I have thought of no way more likely to gain this information, than from Mr. Deane or Mr Kirkland to endeavour to get it from the Friendly Oneidas." He added that it should be obtained "in such a manner as not to give them any suspicions of the real design." Also, in a meeting with Oneidas shortly before carrying out his orders to destroy the Onondagas' village in April, Colonel Goose Van Schaik disingenuously professed ignorance of any planned attack. This prompted the Oneidas afterward to ask him sarcastically whether "all this was done by design or mistake."[40] The situation was exacerbated by the fact that "all this" involved more than the killing of a dozen warriors and the capture of thirty-three prisoners that Van Schaik reported. An Onondaga chief later claimed that "some of the Young Women . . . [were] carried away for the use of their Soldiers & were afterwards put to death in a more shameful manner." While the accusation is not evidence, New York governor George Clinton had warned, "Although I have very little apprehension that any of the soldiers will so far forget their character as to attempt such a crime on the Indian women who may fall into their hands, yet it will be well to take measures to prevent such a stain upon our army." After Van Schaik's raid, most of the 800 Onondagas fled to Niagara, where they received arms and encouragement to repay the favor. About 130 others sought refuge among the Oneidas, many among kin relations.[41]

Washington and Van Schaik recognized the unwillingness of the Iroquois to wage war on their fellows, a fact that was nowhere more strikingly confirmed than by an encounter between a party of Oneidas and St. Lawrence Valley Indians under the leadership of a British officer, Claude-Nicolas-Guillaume de Lorimier. When De Lorimier's men encountered several Oneidas, the Indians united and chased away the officer and a métis, or Franco-Algonquian, member of the party. De Lorimier's Indian confidants later disclosed that the Oneidas appealed for cooperation on the grounds that they shared the "same blood." According to De Lorimier, the Oneidas claimed to have allowed pro-British Indian scouts to operate undetected and unmolested. They asked that "shoud any of the Canada Indians discover their scent, not to tell of them until they were gone back & not to be prevailed upon to fire upon them or to accompany the King's scouts." In order that the Natives on both sides would be able to maximize their freedom, he added, the Oneidas also "particularly requested they [the Canadian Indians] woud never come to that quarter accompanyd with whites & told them they must give up any white people which would accompany them & they woud scalp them to prevent their discovering how they shoud be given up." The Oneidas had, in fact, asked Continental officers for permission to reconnoitre alone before but were denied. To make the best strategic decisions for themselves, Natives on opposing sides sought opportunities to communicate with one other and gather information independently of their Euro-American allies. Before the parley ended, the Oneidas even asked that the Canadian Indians surrender one of the white members of their party, "that they might not return empty handed to the fort." This request was refused, but the Canadian Indians apparently agreed to fire some random shots to give the impression that an engagement had taken place.[42]

De Lorimier's superior, Alexander Fraser, believed there was "reason to think that something worse has been transacted between them than they think proper to divulge." This "something worse" was an agreement to trade scalps. Given the basis of the Oneidas' appeal—kinship—and their allusion to having cooperated with another party of British-allied Natives, the British captain Walter Butler's concern that "the Six Nations would aid one another" seems reasonable. Indeed, one pessimistic British officer saw little prospect of curtailing Oneida spying, and noted, "I doe not think that Indians will doe any thing to hunt those of their own Colour, Especially those that are Related . . . unless there shal happen to be a sufficient number of white people present."[43]

Although the Oneidas raided Tory bases in 1779, their alliance with the Patriots slackened when Natives were targeted. After the Onondaga fiasco, the Oneidas provided scant support to the much larger expedition against southern and western Iroquoia under Gen. John Sullivan later that summer. Sullivan complained in September that only four Oneidas had assisted him "and they [were] totally unacquainted with every part of the country through which I have yet passed." Replying to Sullivan's complaint, an Oneida delegation told him they had intended to send a hundred warriors but received word en route "that they were too late." The speaker then tweaked the Americans' frequent boasts regarding their strength with the nonchalant statement that they thought "that you had men enough." The chief warrior present antagonized Sullivan further by requesting clemency for the Cayugas. The Oneida warriors claimed to "know there is a party of the Cayuga tribe who have ever wished to be at peace with their American brethren" under the leadership of Tegatleronwane, who was related to an Oneida sachem. They held out hope for negotiation, adding, "[We] therefore request that you would not for the present destroy their cornfields."[44]

Unmoved, Sullivan proceeded to destroy forty Indian villages, 160,000 bushels of corn, and "a vast quantity of vegetables of every kind." Of the western end of the Longhouse, he reported, "we have not left a single settlement or a field of corn in the country." But Sullivan might have done well to exercise the restraint the Oneidas had advised. Although Sullivan had executed his orders competently, nothing he accomplished directly impaired the ability of hostile Iroquois to strike again. His actions only left them bitter toward the Patriots and more dependent on the British than ever. The following year, a British officer noted with satisfaction, "We would not have had one third of the Six Nations in our interests at this time" if the Patriots had exercised "more prudence & less severity."[45]

The circumstances surrounding the death of one of the Oneidas accompanying Sullivan—Lieutenant Thaoswagat—sheds light on Iroquois attitudes toward each other. He had been part of a small party that was captured. According to a Seneca account, he was executed by a Seneca, and his corpse "cut almost all to pieces." Although killed by a fellow Iroquois, his mutilation had been mercifully posthumous. His fate stood in sharp contrast to that of two white soldiers, both of whom were ritually tortured before being allowed to die. The Seneca account noted that a Stockbridge Indian captive was allowed to escape, because Little Beard, a Seneca, reminded his party that "they were at war with the whites only, and not with the Indians."[46] Likewise, in September 1780, on being informed by their Mohawk leader that the Oneidas were their target, a Mississauga (Ojibwe) party from the north shore of Lake Ontario "declared to a Man they would not act against the Oneidas" and all but three deserted. The remaining men attacked a rebel party, killing four and wounding five. When they caught an Oneida, however, they let him go, "declaring they knew him to be a neutral Indian." On repeated occasions that autumn, joint British-Indian scouting parties came across Patriot scouts accompanied by Oneidas. They took the whites prisoner and released the Oneidas, to the exasperation of British of-ficials.[47] Clearly, Natives' qualms about taking the lives of other Natives in this conflict transcended tribal or confederacy identities.

Despite the rising anti-Patriot sentiment among the Iroquois following Sullivan's campaign, the Oneidas and a small band of neutralist Mohawks believed that their relations with the Six Nations were not beyond repair. In the winter of 1779–80, two pro-Patriot chiefs (Oneidas Good Peter and John Skenandoah) and two neutralist chiefs (Mohawks Little Abraham and Johannes Crine) went to Fort Niagara with hopes of effecting "a perfect and permanent reconciliation" with their counterparts. Brant encountered the four some distance from the fort and immediately warned the com-manding officer, Guy Johnson, of their approach. Brant suspected that they might be greeted with some sympathy even among his own warriors, so he took steps to ensure that they would not stop at any Indian villages along the way. He also asked Johnson (nephew to the late Sir William) to "pretend to be friendly with them at first before those Indians who are going with me to war."[48] At Niagara, the Seneca Sayengeraghta questioned Skenandoah point-edly about Oneida assistance to Sullivan. Skenandoah downplayed it, but the other Iroquois expressed their contempt by refusing his wampum. The fort's commander then proceeded to incarcerate the delegates in the fort's "black hole"—an unlit, unheated dungeon. Despite their contempt for the embassy, Sayengeraghta and others protested this treatment on more than one occasion. Johnson put them off by disingenuously promising the prison-ers' release as soon as the "next" raiding party left Niagara. Only after the last party departed did he let three go—and then only on the condition that Skenandoah aid the British. The fourth prisoner, Little Abraham—the witness to Seymour's execution—had died.[49]

In June, the Oneidas at Kanonwalohale received a warning from a pro-British Onondaga chief warrior who had recently been at Niagara. The British regarded the destruction of Kanonwalohale as a strategic necessity, although Guy Johnson reported a certain reluctance on the part of the Na-tives. The Oneida chiefs informed the commanding officer at Fort Stanwix of their expectation of "a general Invasion." The Oneida women, who had authority over determining village locations, decided that the nation would "move down into the Country and seek a place of safety among the Inhabit-ants of the United States." Their wishes were accommodated since the Amer-icans feared that the Oneidas would join most of the rest of the Six Nations at Niagara if protection were not forthcoming.[50]

The raiders arrived in force and parleyed with Oneida representatives for two days. Although about thirty Oneidas defected to the British, four hundred took shelter in Fort Stanwix. Before the raiders and the Oneida and Tuscarora defectors left, Kanonwalohale was reduced to ashes, the crops destroyed, and the cattle driven away. The Oneidas fled to Schenectady, only sixteen miles west of Albany. The majority of the population of the Mohawk Valley went there as well. Governor George Clinton conceded gloomily, "Schenectady may now be said to become the limits of our western Frontier."[51]

Fear and Loathing in Schenectady

Schenectady during wartime presented a bleak prospect. Everything except misery and fear were in short supply, and neither Patriot nor Oneida interests were well served by locals who took Oneida weapons in exchange for liquor. Proximity to the white population also facilitated the transmission of disease, including smallpox. Schuyler made repeated appeals to the Continental Congress on the Oneidas' behalf. He assured his superiors that "As to Cloathing . . . if [the Oneidas'] whole Stock was collected, it would but tolerably cover an eight part of their number, and to add to their calamity, the small pox prevails with, and has already been fatal, to some of them, in this complication of distress, which beggars all description, I am overwhelmed with their lamentations."[52] Schuyler also noted that, if "the dictates of humanity and a regard for the interest and honor of the United States" were not enough of a motivation for Congress, self-interest was: "I fear their virtue will at last yield to a continuation of distress, which no human beings can endure, and that they will renounce an alliance which has exposed them to such variety of calamity, to form one with those who can amply supply every of their wants." Gen. Pierre Van Cortlandt offered a similar assessment, and he did not trust feelings of humanity or gratitude to carry the argument, either. He observed, "The Oneida's naked and precariously subsisted and threatning to go over the Enemy; the Effects of which will be severaly [severely] felt by the frontier Inhabitants." The entreaties of the two generals bore meager fruit, and only very slowly at that. Most Oneidas repaired to a spot north of the town and toward Saratoga "in hopes to gain some subsistence by hunting" and where they might "more easily and plentifully be accommodated with fuel, which in their naked condition is an object of importance." They maintained what the Marquis de Chastellux described as "an assemblage of miserable huts in the woods."[53]

The reasons for the Oneidas' flight to the outskirts of town, however, had to do with more than mere subsistence. Initially they had been quartered in the town barracks, and the soldiers sent to live among the townspeople. This distance between the soldiers and Indians was insufficient. In March 1781 Schuyler reported, "Disagreeable Controversys have frequently arisen between the soldiery and the Indians . . . and one of the latter having lately been barbarously murdered and others Assaulted and dangerously wounded it became necessary to remove them to the neighboring woods."[54] What had gone wrong since the amicable lacrosse lessons and dances? Part of the answer lies in the fact that officers—not common soldiers—had been more regularly involved in those events. On Sullivan's expedition, the plebeian attitude toward Natives was manifested in the offering of toasts such as, "Civilization or death to all American savages" and the skinning of a dead Indian to make boot legs. Moreover, although Schuyler and other officers now lamented the friction between Natives and soldiers, they were also partially responsible for it. Horatio Gates had exploited the anti-Indian frenzy that followed the 1777 murder of Jane McCrea, supposedly by Canadian Indians, to gain new recruits throughout the upper Hudson Valley. And by employing Natives to track and capture deserters—in short, as enforcers of military discipline—officers widened the breach between Indians and soldiers. When about thirty Continentals deserted Fort Stanwix in June 1780, a party of Oneida warriors was sent in pursuit. When sixteen of the deserters were overtaken, they opened fire on their pursuers, who returned it, killing thirteen. Similar incidents had occurred earlier. Whether or not fellow soldiers approved of the deserters' desperate measures, they could testify that the grievances that spurred them were very real. Washington noted, "The want of pay and the necessary Cloathing, particularly Shirts, is assigned as the primary cause" of the 1780 escape.[55] From the common soldier's perspective, the Natives who made them more secure also enforced their submission to harsh conditions.

Patriot soldiers valued their Oneida allies for their ability to keep them safe from surprise attack through the scouting and intelligence-gathering activities that only Natives could perform. However, they also feared and distrusted them for precisely the same reason. Dependency on Indian allies generated anxiety and, in turn, anger. When Oneidas withdrew from a scouting party under the command of Lt. Thomas McClellan in 1779, he wrote his superior, "my Pen must fail to Describe to you the situation we wair in to See the Infernil Villins Deserting us in the Wide Wilderness, to

See the Gloom that Set on the Braws of Each of our Brave Men."[56] Because the Oneidas were the Patriots' principal source of information on the enemy's movements, they instantly came under suspicion whenever Patriot soldiers or settlements were attacked. In 1778, when a soldier who had left Fort Stanwix to catch a horse was scalped and killed, soldiers at the fort openly accused the Natives of having countenanced the attack. It was the second such fatality in that many years. In response, as many as a hundred Oneida and Tuscarora warriors appeared at the fort to reaffirm their allegiance to the Americans. The soldiers' concerns, however, were not entirely without foundation. There was a price to be paid for the intelligence they needed, and the Oneidas maintained their end of the quid pro quo by allowing Native opponents a modicum of freedom to act in the territory they controlled. In 1779, Butler even asserted that "the Caghnawago [Kahnawake] Indians who lately took the Prisoners at Fort Stanwix were not only with some Oneydas a little time before but were even directed by them where to make their Blow."[57]

Despite these conflicts, the Oneidas successfully kept the balance in the Patriots' favor. In the summer of 1780, Senecas complained that Oneida scouts were altogether "too officious, & making Report to the Americans of every Tract [track] they discover." In October, the depredations of a British-Indian raiding party were limited because of their interception by an Oneida scouting party. Haldimand complained to Lord George Germain that the Oneidas were "troublesome and treacherous to the last degree."[58] Displaying his usual animus toward the Oneidas, Brant "fixed in his Mind to take Revenge on [them] . . . for sundry insults that he as well as his Sister received from them." (He kept his planning highly secretive, presumably because he was idiosyncratic in his determination to harm them, and he was concerned that Iroquois warriors might leak word.) Another testament to the Oneidas' effectiveness came from Schuyler in January 1781. Noting that "the enemy in small parties have already reappeared in Tryon County," he expressed his fear that "if the Oneidas should be driven to desperation by the hardships they endure, and join the enemy all beyond [Albany] will be one dreadful scene of desolation and slaughter." Schuyler's concern about the Oneidas, however, was ill-founded, since they continued to serve the Patriots effectively through that year. Haldimand groused that they "much impede our Scouts and Recruiting Parties, & are in many Respects very useful to the Rebels."[59]

Schuyler's sense of the Oneidas' crucial place in the defense of the frontier had been magnified by the fact that the Patriot population of the Mohawk Valley was unwilling to unite in its own defense. Col. Abraham Wemple voiced a suspicion that "the Inhabitants along the Mohawk Rivers being all farmers, and a great many . . . not faithful to us[,] may immediately go and inform the Enemy of our weakness." And even if they did not do that, he believed they could not be rallied effectively because they would instead "protect their own families in the little forts they have built and are building." For Col. Marinus Willett, those small fortifications inspired both admiration and despair. Willett acknowledged that "they have discovered sufficient skill to justify the saying that necessity is the mother of invention" but mused that "to draw the men from there places to which they have fled for refuge for themselves and their families is a difficulty I fear I shall not be able to get over."[60] Mirroring the Oneidas' dilemma before departing for Pennsylvania in 1778, the security of the local community figured prominently in the complex calculus that determined wartime activity for nonprofessional combatants.

Only in 1782 did Dean's ability to mobilize Oneida scouting parties seemed to flag. On February 20, he wrote an apologetic letter to Schuyler after a party he had engaged "declined the service & are gone to the Woods to hunt." It took multiple negotiations to convene another scouting party, only to have them turn back prematurely, ostensibly for want of acceptable snowshoes. Persistent tension between the Oneidas and the white inhabitants of Tryon County did not help the alliance. On May 1, 1782, Schuyler had to publicly appeal for calm amid rumors that an Oneida or Tuscarora warrior had killed some whites. Schuyler was assured by deputy quartermaster general Henry Glen "that he had full evidence that the Indian supposed to be concerned was not guilty of the fact." But the guilt or innocence of any particular Indian was beside the point to the would-be vigilantes. According to Schuyler, "the Inhabitants had threatened to put to death any of those Oneidas and Tuscaroras they might meet with." Exasperated, he reminded the public, "It would be extreamly Imprudent & unjust to retaliate for any offence committed by an individual on others not Guilty, for the consequences would prove extreamly distressing as all those Indians might thereby be tempted to join the Enemy Increase their force, and thus still more distress the frontiers . . . casting an odious imputation on our national faith. I have therefore most earnestly to Intreat you to prevent any injury to them in their persons or property."[61] Such conflict heralded trouble for the Oneidas at war's end, when the threat of Oneida defection would no longer be a check on abuse.

Friction only increased as the approach of peace revived competition for land. On September 9, 1782, a group of Oneidas and allied Indians complained to the commissioners of the subterfuges of "people who want to take away our Lands by Piece Meals."[62] The problem the Oneidas faced is exemplified in a February 1783 letter from a Continental officer, Pliny Moor, to his father in Massachusetts. Moor began with a description of the Patriots' arduous march to British-held Fort Oswego on the southern shore of Lake Ontario. The Oswego expedition had been an aggressive move to assert Patriot control over both the lake and central and eastern Iroquoia. It ended in failure after the Oneida guide, Capt. John Otaawighton, led them astray in the final hours of the nighttime approach. Moor seethed "that by the perfidy or Ignorance of one Savage guide (the former of which is more probable) the Continent is at more than a Thousand pounds Expence besides the loss of several good men a number of Toes frozen & a quantity of good health." The remainder of Moor's letter indicates precisely why the Oneidas might have considered early Patriot control of the fort to be detrimental to their interests. During his service, Moor had been systematically reconnoitering Indian land, identifying particular spots conducive for farms, mills, and trade. His letter indicates that he was already making arrangements to stake a claim.[63] It was clear that early U.S. dominance of the northern frontier would only hasten white settlement in Iroquoia. Thus, the expedition's failure did not necessarily harm the Oneidas, who were anxious to return to their burned-out villages even before the peace was made official, lest someone else lay claim to them.

Peace

Still, as the Revolutionary War neared its conclusion, some Oneidas saw cause for optimism. After all, they had chosen the winning side. Some even taunted their pro-British fellows about their far less certain fate. Speaking to an audience of British-allied Iroquois, one Oneida mischievously mocked the king as having said, "What can I do, nothing, you have conquered me, therefore do with them [the Indians] what you please." This imaginary statement nicely captured Native consternation at Britain's generous concessions to the United States. At the Treaty of Paris, signed in September 1783, Britain bequeathed to the United States their claims to the entire area east of the Mississippi, south of Canada, and north of Florida. This area included the territories it had controlled, conquered, or purchased and those of its Native allies as well. The Oneida went on to suggest the pro-British Iroquois move to the British Isles, since "these parts still belong to the King."[64]

The state of New York, however, was anxious to seize control of Iroquoia as quickly and decisively as possible. Reflecting on the character of the war, Congressman James Duane counseled a unilateral approach toward the Six Nations: "If we adopt the disgraceful system of pensioning, courting, and flattering them as great and mighty nations . . . this Revolution, in my Eyes, will have lost more than half its Value."[65] New York had to make up with swagger what it lacked in fact because, as Guy Johnson's 1771 *Map of the Country of the VI Nations* suggests, the state's claim to the Longhouse was not self-evident, even to other Euro-Americans. Massachusetts was another key rival. Massachusetts had a larger population, and the boundaries described in the Bay Colony's charter, which predated (and was therefore legally superior to) New York's, could be construed to resume west of the Hudson Valley. The dispute between the states would take several years to resolve, but New York was taking no chances. The state had already lost its northeastern fringe when part of Albany County broke away to form the Vermont Republic, so now it moved quickly to claim the area west of the 1768 treaty line.

Seizing the land of British-allied Iroquois seemed the first order of business, but the Oneidas' swath of territory stood in the way. As early as March 1783, the state legislature instructed its Indian commissioners "to accomplish an Exchange of the District claimed by the Oneida's and Tuscarora's for a District of vacant and unappropriated Lands within this State," presumably in Seneca country. The plan was shelved because this risked renewing the war with the Natives. When New York called the Oneidas to meet at a treaty at Fort Stanwix in September 1784, the Oneidas were wary. They attended only on the condition that no land cession be demanded of them, and they reminded the governor that "General Washington assured them during the late Troubles, that they should possess and keep their lands," including the square-mile enclave at Oriske which, although east of the Line of Property, was retained by them under the 1768 treaty. Governor Clinton prudently ignored Duane's advice and replied with generally soothing statements about the state's respect for their territorial integrity, though he indicated his belief that the Oneidas had sold the land at Oriske.[66]

If nothing else, the treaty had set a precedent for the state's formal dealings with the Indians. Holding the treaty at all challenged the Articles of Confederation, which reserved to Congress the "sole and exclusive right and power of . . . managing all affairs with the Indians, not members of any of the states." New York looked to that final phrase to legitimize its dealings, though few at the time thought the Oneidas qualified as "members" of New York State. The Oneidas certainly saw nothing in their recent history that diminished their status with regard to New York. Apparently neither did James Madison, who wrote James Monroe that the New York negotiations usurped the powers of Congress and were a clear violation of both "duty & decorum."[67] However, "duty & decorum" were far from Governor Clinton's mind. Even if nothing else could be accomplished, Clinton had called the treaty simply to assert the state's jurisdiction over Iroquoia at the expense of other states or the federal government. To that end, Clinton instructed Peter Ryckman and Peter Schuyler to stay at the treaty ground and disrupt the proceedings of the federal commissioners who were to hold their own treaty at the fort soon after. Clinton told them, "where You find they have in View any thing that may eventually prove detrimental to the State, You are to use your best Endeavours to counteract and frustrate it." Their "best Endeavours" involved dispensing substantial quantities of liquor, which caused irate federal commissioners to eject both men and the liquor peddlers who assisted them. When a U.S. Army officer confiscated the liquor, the peddlers retaliated by filing a complaint with the local sheriff and attempting to have the officer arrested.[68]

The Marquis de Lafayette was another interloper at the federal treaty. His presence was less obnoxious but nevertheless discomfiting to commissioners clearly struggling to establish their nation's authority even within its own bounds. Lafayette formally addressed the Oneidas and laid the groundwork for an ongoing relationship with France. He promised, "The manufactures of France . . . will be to you a token of the alliance."[69] Lafayette's words played on the aboriginal association of trade and diplomatic alliance: alliances were solemnized with goods, and the health of diplomatic relationships was reflected by ongoing exchange. The Oneidas were not displeased.

When federal negotiators at Fort Stanwix finally got their proceedings under way, they offered the Oneidas further reassurance. The commissioners remarked, "It does not become the United States to forget those nations who preserved their faith to them, and adhered to their cause, those, therefore, must be secured in the full and free enjoyment of their possessions." The final treaty document, signed by Oneida chiefs Dagaheari and Otyadonenghti, enshrined that guarantee.[70] Dagaheari's and Otyadonenghti's satisfaction with the United States and France was doubtless marred, however, by the commissioners' contemptuous treatment of the other Iroquois nations. Griffith Evans, secretary to the Pennsylvania delegation, noted that the commissioner's speech to them was "delivered . . . in a language by no means accommodating or flattering." They interrupted Iroquois speakers, pointed fingers at them, and demanded hostages. Because of the tremendous importance the Iroquois attached to council etiquette, this was a serious affront and did not bode well for peace and reconciliation. This untoward behavior, Evans noted, "made the Indians stare."[71] Some simply left. Others yielded grudgingly to the commissioners' bullying and ceded Six Nations' claims to Ohio. They gave up most of the land they had claimed in Pennsylvania in a separate agreement with representatives from that state.

If the Oneidas had planned any appeal on behalf of the other nations, it was stifled by the federal commissioners' hostility. The harsh terms of the 1784 Treaty of Fort Stanwix fed a postwar alienation of the Iroquois from one another. The western Iroquois were powerless to do anything except curse Washington (to whom they now gave the name "Town Destroyer") and the Indians whom they accused of abetting his crime. Although the Oneidas would become occasional mediators between the Six Nations and Euro-Americans, they were not able to win them any better treatment, because the threat posed by the Iroquois Confederacy was so much diminished. The humiliating peace amplified resentments among the Iroquois that had been muted during the conflict itself. It ultimately obfuscated the cooperation and cohesion the Iroquois had exhibited throughout the war, even to themselves. A chill set in among the various nations of the Iroquois League that would never thaw completely. All the Oneidas could do was to try to keep their territory by reminding the Americans of the contributions they had made to the Patriot cause and downplaying the rest.[72]

4

Misplaced Faith

A Decade of Dispossession, 1785–1794

I expected when I returned to my Country to have sat down in Peace and enjoyed pleasant Days. I was even encouraged to hope this, Brother, from you,
from your own Declarations. You welcomed me home on my Return. The
United States there planted the Tree of Peace with four Roots, spreading
Branches and beautiful Leaves, whose Top reached the Heavens.

—GOOD PETER, 1788

FOUR YEARS AFTER the end of the Revolution, the chief warrior and
spokesman Good Peter contrasted the postwar expectations of many
Oneidas with their reality. Within that brief period, white settlement surrounded the Oneidas, who lost nearly all their lands and suffered tremendous internal strife. Things were not supposed to have worked out that way.
For the Oneidas, the gratitude of the United States and New York proved
to be thin reeds on which to rely. In the Oneidas' difficult circumstances
New York found an irresistible opportunity to begin replenishing its war-
depleted coffers and making good on claims to lands beyond the Hudson
and Mohawk.[1]

Decimated and impoverished by war, the Oneidas could not physically
resist the arrival of thousands of Euro-Americans who flocked to Iroquoia
in the Revolution's wake. The Oneidas did their best to parry this challenge.
They engaged with the cultural and economic notions of the Euro-American
settlers. Many Oneidas adopted elements of Christianity to augment their
spiritual resources and help them cope with the wrenching changes to their
lives. In this context, the advice and insights of their missionary, Samuel
Kirkland, took on an enhanced importance. As before, however, they accepted his religious advice as they did his political advice, selectively.

Real estate was a different matter. When pressed to cede land, the Oneidas sought an intermediary to manage transactions with whites. Since they
were at a disadvantage in dealing with English-language legal documents,
English measures, and the Arabic numeration system, the Oneidas required
an agent in whom they could repose absolute trust—"one Great Man," as

they put it. Kirkland, who had pledged never to acquire land west of the Hudson, seemed a suitable candidate.[2] Surrendering their land outright was repugnant, but thwarting the aspirations of Euro-American farmers became impossible. Leasing part of their lands seemed like a workable compromise. The Oneidas came to grief, however, as their plans were refused or subverted. Kirkland was but one of numerous intermediaries who took advantage of the Oneidas by misrepresenting or otherwise failing to explicate fully the terms of proposed agreements.

The Oneidas' poor living conditions increased their vulnerability. The war had left them destitute. Their houses had been burned, their fields had become overgrown, and their caches of corn and grain had been emptied. Capt. John Otaawighton said of his village, "We found it consumed to ashes and all our improvements destroyed." A survey undertaken by the federal government counted seventy-three houses destroyed in Kanonwalohale alone. On an abbreviated visit to the Oneidas in 1784, Kirkland said, he subsisted "intirely on strawberries, with now & then a little fish." In 1785 he reported, "The most of my people are degenerated as much as our paper currency depreciated in time of war."[3]

As the Oneidas returned, they rebuilt Kanonwalohale, but in an even less concentrated settlement pattern than before the war, and also established many smaller settlements. "The number of small Villages since the resettling [of] the Country," Kirkland complained in late 1785, "has increased my travelling to near thirty miles when I make a general visit." This dispersed pattern helped the Oneidas make the most of available resources, but it also reflected family rivalries, the broad political competition between sachems and warriors, and disputes over religion, temperance, and wartime allegiance. Oriske was dominated by members of the sachem faction and Kanonwalohale by the warriors. François Barbé-Marbois, a French nobleman who was present at the peace treaty, witnessed a brawl between Oneida brothers that he explained thus: "One of the two brothers had followed the English army, and the other had joined the American."[4] Indeed, over 150 Oneidas took refuge along the Grand River in Canada, alongside nearly 2,000 pro-British Iroquois settled under Brant's leadership. Some, but not all, would trickle back over the next ten years. Questions also lingered over John Skenandoah's service to the British. Most excused him, recalling his time in Niagara's "black hole" and accepting his explanation that whatever services he had rendered the British had been performed under duress. Jacob Doxtator of Oriske and others, however, were skeptical. Nearly a century later, the Oneida John Cornelius said, "Some of the Oneidas bitterly re-proached [Skenandoah], & one even knocked him over the head, felling him, with his tomahawk, & came near killing him."[5] The attack may or may not be true in its particulars; after all, Cornelius was not yet born at the time. But his very understanding of what had happened is evidence that tensions related to the war dissipated exceedingly slowly. These and other family, clan, and factional resentments were inflamed by alcohol—a problem that grew worse with the increasing presence of white peddlers in the region. In such an atmosphere, many Oneidas chose where to live with the under-standing that the potential for friction was cooled only by distance.

Landlords

In November 1784, Col. John Harper, an Oneida-speaking officer under whom some Oneidas had served, obtained a cession of approximately 100,000 acres of land along the Susquehanna River. Most of the seven Oneida signatories were prominent men—they included the sachems Peter Oney-anha and Cornelius Otatshete and prominent warriors such as Lodwick Gahsaweda, as well as Jacob Reed, a warrior who had learned to speak and write English at Eleazar Wheelock's school. How Harper obtained their consent became a matter of dispute when the Oneidas challenged the deed: Harper claimed that they had offered him the land, but the Oneidas said he had misrepresented himself as an agent of the state and plied them with li-quor. Whatever promises he may have received from individual Oneidas during the war, he apparently never obtained the general consent of the na-tion. The state legislature deemed the transaction null and void. The state's objection, however, was not to the sale itself but simply that it had been ex-ecuted by private interests. The 1777 state constitution granted the state a "pre-emption right," or a monopoly on the purchase of Indian land. This provision was ostensibly to protect Indian land rights, though whether it actu-ally did is dubious. Thus, the legislature moved to arrange its own treaty with the Oneidas at Fort Herkimer the following June. The treaty commission-ers were especially hopeful because, they said, "from [the Oneidas'] peculiar Situation as to Provisions and other Necessaries . . . the Treaty is well timed for the Advantage of the State."[6]

The Oneidas who showed up said they had been led to believe that the purpose of the meeting was not to sell more of their lands but simply to find ways to avoid such embarrassments in the future. Significantly, the state did not inform the Oneidas that Harper's deed had been quashed but rather allowed them to believe it would be enforced. As Good Peter put it, "The Message which was sent by Mr. Ryckman was well delivered, except one Word which We did not comprehend, which was, that You wanted to *purchase* Lands" (emphasis added). Perhaps the Oneidas were merely posturing; perhaps they had been deliberately misled about the purpose of the meeting. Or, perhaps, the interpreter, Peter Ryckman had, in fact, erred; Governor George Clinton had earlier complained that the Dutchman's command of English was not good enough "to give a perfect Translation."[7]

Under pressure, the Oneidas offered up a tract, but the state deemed it too small and mountainous to be worth purchasing. Before revealing their next offer, the Oneidas aired their grievances about lands taken but never paid for by "the German Flatts People" and others. They also hoped to secure the state's "assistance," they said, "to prevent your People for coming among Us" to buy land. Finally, Good Peter offered to "lease one Tier of Farms in the Manner they are done by the White People, along the Boundary Line throughout the Extent of our Country, and that People of Influence might be settled on these Farms to prevent Encroachments, and that a Person might be appointed to collect our Rents annually." Explaining this proposal, Good Peter said, "We cannot sell any more of our Lands and this Leasing may be an Income to our Children."[8]

The Oneidas' willingness to become landlords was a creative solution to the territorial conflict that constituted a middle ground between aboriginal and European ideas about land tenure. Several aspects of Good Peter's statement merit closer examination. His expression of concern for future generations was in keeping with the traditional Iroquois view that the current generation were stewards of the land for their descendants. The idea of preserving the nation's territory by creating a buffer zone of trustworthy clients also reflected a traditional Iroquois strategy. This idea was rooted in the long-standing practice of settling dependent allies on vulnerable frontiers. To shore up their position on the front line of Indian country, the Oneidas encouraged the immigration of other Indians to their lands. Although most of the Tuscaroras resettled near Niagara after the Revolution, some fifty returned, bringing the local Iroquois population to approximately eight hundred. The New England Algonquians were invited back and created a durable community known as Brothertown. The Stockbridges, among whom some Oneidas had found refuge during the latter phases of the war, and whose lands in the Hudson Valley, Vermont, and Massachusetts had been overrun by white settlement, also accepted an Oneida invitation.[9]

The Oneidas' proposal also contained significant innovation. When Good Peter alluded to leases "in the Manner they are done by the White People," he meant for money. The Oneidas did not expect any material compensation from Native tenants, but they certainly did from whites—and they were well aware of the economic potential of leasing. During the colonial and Revolutionary War periods, the Oneidas' closest official liaisons had been with Sir William Johnson and Maj. Gen. Philip Schuyler. Johnson had settled hundreds of tenants on his Mohawk Valley lands. Schuyler was a Hudson Valley manor lord. Numerous Oneidas had visited one or the other man's estate and had come to understand, at least in general terms, the reasons for the material disparity between the homes of landlords and tenants.

Good Peter, however, also openly acknowledged the limits of that understanding. As the historian Patricia Cline Cohen has observed, even among late-eighteenth-century Euro-Americans, most economic transactions, even simple ones, relied on trust. Devising leases that would satisfy tenants and protect the landlord required technical skills of literacy and numeracy that no Oneida possessed.[10] In fact, the state of mathematical knowledge was rudimentary among the general public, as well as college graduates, because numeracy was still regarded as the province of men of commerce. Native Americans were in an especially problematic position. Transactions involving land were complex, and each one involved translation into a different language and a different numeration system and involved arbitrary and amorphous units of measurement, such as acres. Land was paid for in currency whose denominations had yet to be standardized or even decimalized. Interest was also an alien concept. Furthermore, the Oneidas needed someone who could evaluate the credentials of men like Harper who sought to do business with them and also command their respect for the purposes of negotiation. Thus, Good Peter freely admitted that the Oneidas needed assistance in administering a leasing program, and sought "People of Influence" to settle nearby. Good Peter also implied that they needed someone of skill, status, and familiarity with the law, when he asked for "a Person . . . to collect our Rent." Ultimately, Oneida reliance on Euro-Americans to craft and enforce leases undid the Oneidas' plans.[11]

Clinton told the Oneidas that he considered their leasing proposal to be "highly disagreeable" and that it merited the "disdain" of the legislature. He pointed out that "if accepted, [it] would make the Government of the State tributary to You." Clinton insinuated that the Oneidas had acted in bad faith by offering such a meager sale and a lease. The governor was likely trying to extort the land from the Oneidas when he fretted that "Disorder and Mischief . . . may be difficult to prevent" in areas "remote from our old Settlements and where We have too little Lands to form new ones, large enough to give Force and Energy to our Government." The governor realized that buying and reselling Oneida land offered the state more revenue than leasing it. Nevertheless, his response was surprising in its vehemence. Landlordship was an elite prerogative, and its practice by Natives was an unthinkable inversion of the racial hierarchy, even for an anti-elitist "people's man" like George Clinton. As Good Peter recalled in a 1792 interview with the federal commissioner Timothy Pickering, Clinton called it "a dishonourable proposal: that he and his Com[missione]rs were not in the condition of tenants; and that they should be ashamed to return home with such an account of the negociation." Ideology dictated that New York would not become the Oneidas' rent collector.[12]

According to Good Peter, Clinton "produced a heap of money, & told some of our nation to take up a handful; but they would not consent to do this; it was too heavy. He then himself grasped a few handfuls, and gave to one and another." At least initially, these tactics did not work, but treaty proceedings record obliquely that "the Evening [was] spent in private Conference with several Chiefs and Warriors" and then allude to "the favourable Turn the business took." Alcohol often played a role in such situations. A young Oneida chief of the sachem party, Captain John, later told a sympathetic federal representative that Oneida leaders were "often overreached by white men of not half their natural understanding" who "bring a bottle with them, and pour out a glass." "We drink and we drink again," he explained. "By and by, our hearts grow light, and we do not well know what we say."[13] The historian Alan Taylor speculates, however, that the women of the nation shifted their position, placing the immediate procurement of needed goods and food over warriors' future use of the territory for hunting. Indeed, when the negotiators reconvened the following morning, the sachem Peter the Quartermaster (Beech Tree) replaced Good Peter as speaker. Beech Tree declared that the nation had reached a consensus concerning selling lands to the south, which they offered "more out of Friendship" than for the money. Clinton immediately taxed that friendship a little further, demanding that the sale be enlarged. The cession amounted to more than 300,000 acres. In return, the Oneidas would receive $11,500, or roughly $.04 an acre, payable half in cash and half in goods and provisions. Most Oneidas acquiesced, believing they would lose more and receive less if the state sat by idly while illegitimate, unsanctioned private dealings like Harper's took place. Grasshopper, a sachem, underscored the Oneidas' expectation that this agreement would be "the last application for Lands."[14]

Reasoning that the most effective barrier against white settler encroachment was other whites, the Oneidas made a strategic cession of the lands on which they had earlier hoped to settle loyal tenants. This five-thousand-acre buffer lay along their eastern border directly athwart the path of settlement. On this strip they granted land to a cadre of cultural mediators whom they hoped would prove trustworthy and useful. These included James Dean, Samuel Kirkland, and the blacksmith Abraham Wemple. The Wemple family had a long history as Iroquois traders, though one observer said of Abraham that "from his familiar knowledge of the Indian tongue and manners, and his own disposition, [he] can promote all their vices." The Oneidas hoped that placing these men on their eastern frontier they would promote peaceful trade and diplomacy while screening them from frontier folk who had less respect for Indians. But George Washington's words would prove prophetic: "Scarcely any thing short of a Chinese Wall, or a line of Troops will restrain Land Jobbers, and the Incroachment of Settlers, upon the Indian Territory."[15]

Although the state refused any kind of leasing arrangement in 1785, the Oneidas did not abandon their aspirations to landlordship. In the years that followed, they found private individuals who were interested in leases, largely because of the state constitution's ban on the purchase of Indian land by private parties. For example, Archibald Armstrong, a tavern keeper, received a lease of one mile square for thirty years. Jedediah Phelps, a silversmith, received six miles square for the annual rent of five hundred skipples of corn. Isaac Carpenter, a blacksmith, paid the Oneidas ten pounds a year for a hundred acres. Although another man pressed the Oneidas for a purchase of lands (in the hope that the legislature would grant him an exception), the Oneidas "utterly declined an absolute sale." William Colbrath, an officer at Fort Stanwix during the war and one of the traders expelled from the federal treaty in 1784, leased a tract south of the Stockbridge settlement. (Ironically but fittingly, he would soon become sheriff.) The Oneidas also leased a Kanonwalohale tract to Ebenezer Caulkins, a schoolteacher, for twenty-one years.[16] These leases brought the Oneidas very modest monetary benefits, but the lessees often possessed skills or access to goods—including alcohol—the Oneidas desired, and the land would revert to the nation after a fixed term.

Postwar Oneida Christianity

The Oneidas sought to reconcile their ways to those of the settlers in other realms as well. Christianity was a potential means for the Oneidas to make sense of and cope with dispossession, along with related difficulties such as famine and alcoholism. Examining Oneidas' various beliefs during this period makes the dichotomy of "Christian" and "pagan"—which has been used to describe religious divisions among almost every tribe—appear less rigid. These labels only roughly approximate the Oneidas' engagement with Christianity after the war and hide the complexity of their religious beliefs. The Oneidas neither abandoned traditional beliefs nor unthinkingly resisted the colonizers' faith. Instead, eclecticism and syncretism prevailed.[17]

Those Oneidas most deeply committed to Christianity sought to appease a new deity in order to revitalize their community, but they did not simply substitute a set of new beliefs for their traditional ones. Instead, they took selected aspects of Christianity and reinterpreted them to render them congruent with preexisting beliefs and practices. For their part, many traditionalists (identified in the documentary record as "pagans") engaged with Christianity to oppose it, but they did not leave the engagement unchanged. The majority of Oneidas appear to have lived by flexible, even idiosyncratic, syntheses of traditional belief and Christian doctrine. At times of heightened factional tension, more Oneidas gravitated to the "pagan" or "Christian" extremes of the religious spectrum, but for the most part kept their spiritual options open. They were baptized but not active communicants; they attended the missionary's sermons, but they sought out traditional healers when they believed themselves afflicted by witchcraft.

The Oneidas drew on their traditional religious ideology to understand the missionary's message. When Kirkland preached from Proverbs 27:19, "as in water face answereth to face," he evoked in the minds of his audience the day the prophet Deganawidah arrived on the roof of Hiawatha's cabin and looked down into the smoke hole to see Hiawatha preparing a cannibal stew. Hiawatha was transformed when he saw Deganawidah's face reflected in the water rather than his own. Good Peter echoed this episode during an exhortation the following spring: "O! Sinners, look on the word of Jesus that is a glass in which you may see what you are." As the historians George Hamell and Christopher Miller have demonstrated, for all Eastern Woodlands Indians the reflective qualities of glass and still water were semantically associated with mind, soul, and greatest being.[18]

Even if Kirkland was not describing personal visions or dreams (which for the Iroquois constituted the normal mode of transmission of information and power from the spirit world), the Oneidas understood that the Bible was the equivalent medium of revelation for whites. For the Oneidas, Kirkland was a channel to the contents of the whites' holy book and its power. Testifying to the iconic status of the Bible among Natives, Kirkland observed that Oneida Christians looked to "*holy Book* evidence (as they phrase it)" to indicate the fate of their souls. The legitimizing authority of the book was so great that when the Quaker Joseph Sansom saw Good Peter preaching in 1791, he noted that "he preached with a Bible in his hand, though he could not read."[19]

Except during hunting or fishing seasons, Kirkland's sermons frequently drew one hundred to two hundred Oneidas, even in poor weather. His audiences were numerous and diverse, including professing Christians and non-Christians. A common explanation for Indian submission to sermonizing—that they were exhibiting customary politeness—simply cannot account for the size, diversity, or consistency of the turnout. Nor can the numbers be attributed to Kirkland's oratorical prowess, because he had little. He was a newcomer to the Oneida tongue. (By contrast, Good Peter's eloquence was well-known and contributed to his attaining the position of chief. He occasionally preached with Kirkland, who described him on one occasion as speaking "like an apollus & with the energy of a son [of] Thunder.") A more likely explanation is that the Oneidas attended Kirkland's sermons to better understand the spiritual power of the Euro-Americans who had begun swarming to the region. Although tribal factionalism had provided the missionary with a foothold, Oneidas also experimented with Christianity as a way to come to grips with the spiraling problems they faced and to understand why the Great Spirit allowed the white people to prosper.[20]

As Kirkland's audience expanded, however, so did opposition to Christian influence. The contest for souls was not always a zero-sum game. Soon after Kirkland reported signs of proselytizing success, "some instances of violent opposition" arose. "Encouraging appearances on the one hand" were met by "discouragement on the other." On New Year's Day 1787, members of the pagan party fired shots into the air during Kirkland's service. Invoking nativist rhetoric, they demanded that his listeners adhere to "the true religion of Indians" lest they should "come to ruin." They held a feast and dance and then forced Kirkland to flee the town temporarily after threatening his life.[21] The exercise was a gesture intended to noisily and emphatically reassert the boundaries between Indians and whites. It appears to have been limited in its disruption of the mission; Kirkland continued to report increasing numbers of visitors in the spring. But an ebb tide was coming.

Witches and Healers

A crop failure reduced the Oneidas to dire want yet again in the summer of 1787, and Kirkland noted, "A number of families have had no corn for several weeks, but the scanty portion, which I have dealt out to them from my own stores." To explain the crop failure, the Indians were inclined to scrutinize actions of their compatriots that may have displeased the spirits or otherwise interfered with their access to sacred power. Such explanations projected conflicts within the community on to a higher plane of significance. In September, Kirkland reported, "Their ancient superstition respecting the power of witchcraft had revived among them and prevailed to a great degree notwithstanding their instruction & professions of belief in the Christian religion."[22]

Attention focused, he said, on a "poor old Squaw lately returned from the Senekas country . . . where she had been very famous in the magic art" and who, it was rumored, "had been instrumental in the death of several persons in that quarter." Exemplifying the pitch of the enmities that threatened to tear Oneida society apart, Kirkland noted, "Her arrival was welcome to many families among the Oneidas; they expected all old grudges would be revenged." Before long, he continued, "This creature was very soon seen by several persons flying thro' the town in the shape of an overgrown owl;—& at another time, running with incredible swiftness in the appearance of a fox" (see fig. 5).[23] In addition to seeing apparitions, those who believed themselves bewitched exhibited what appear to be psychosomatic symptoms. Bemoaning "the strong propensity there is in Indians to superstition," Kirkland wrote:

Fig. 5. *A Man Bewitched within the House by a Woman Without,* anonymous copy of a painting by George Wilson (Cattaraugus Seneca), ca. 1845. This mid-nineteenth-century Seneca image reflects elements of Oneida witchcraft beliefs in the 1780s. The caption notes that in preparation "for a journey to a distant land or tribe, [the witch] put on the dress best adapted for her object. When upon a tour of revenge, . . . she dressed with fox's skin, flames of fire coming from her mouth." She transmitted "a fatal disorder" to the victim with the point of her forefinger. A second witch appears "in the tree in a spying expedition." (Four-poster beds, however, were not in use among the Oneidas in the 1780s.) Courtesy of the National Anthropological Archives, Smithsonian Institution (neg. 45516A).

> The Sachem then told me (as a profound secret) that the two Indians then sick (whom I knew) were poisoned by the incantation of . . . the Supposed witch. The two persons alluded to, had been suddenly seized with the most excruciating pains & continued so for several days. I was sent for at the time to visit them, & prescribe, if I knew of any remedy. I told them the disease appeared to me to be nothing more than the rheumatism, so called, among the English people. They appeared to pity my ignorance or incredulity. They applied to some Doctresses, who pretended skill in the same art, for an antidote.[24]

The illness and then the recuperation of the afflicted under the care of the "Doctresses" validated traditional witchcraft and counter-witchcraft practices, which involved herbalism and ritual activity ranging from prayers and offerings to dances and feasts. From the Oneidas' perspective, the missionary's knowledge, power, and skill had been surpassed by those of the witch and the "doctresses." Embarrassed as a minister—and perhaps also as a man—Kirkland recorded his chagrin that the outbreak of witch fear confirmed to the Natives that "what they feel & see must be truth without any deception." The crisis and its resolution provided the Indians with apparent empirical verification of the efficacy of traditional methods of ritual healing and reinforced personal commitments to traditional cultural practices. This episode highlighted a sense of difference between Natives and Euro-Americans. Kirkland's medico-spiritual ministrations had been found wanting when applied to Indians.[25]

Before year's end it was clear that the earlier Christian fervor had been eclipsed. Good Peter voiced his regret that "so many of the Oneidas have turned back to their old ways," and Kirkland noted that "the profligate & pagan party have gained great strength by the conduct of some, who apparently began in the Spirit, but ended in the flesh."[26] In the following year, 1788, many Oneidas would come to feel this description was true of Kirkland himself. For the time being, however, Kirkland's dismay over the witchcraft outbreak and the backsliding of converts contributed to his questioning the possibility of Christianizing the Indians as long as traditional subsistence patterns remained intact. He was not the first Protestant missionary to conclude that the two traditions were incompatible.

"One Great Man"

In January 1788 the Genesee Company of Adventurers, led by John Livingston, sought to lease the entire Oneida domain for 999 years. This agreement mirrored similar leases that the company had already signed with other Iroquois nations. The company's none-too-subtle purpose in proposing this strange deal was to circumvent the state proscription against private land sales. Kirkland came out in favor of the proposal. The state Indian commissioner, John Tayler, reported, "In one of his Sermons . . . previous to the Long Lease . . . [Kirkland] observed that his Thoughts were too extensive, their Country so large that he could not collect himself, and urged the Propriety of selling a Part and then his Ideas would be more confined and he would preach better." Kirkland was echoing a longstanding English judgment that Native societies and mentalities were anarchic, a quality that was exemplified and exacerbated by the Natives' tendency to spread their subsistence activities over a wide range.[27]

Livingston's proposals, according to Good Peter, gave the Oneidas "much anxiety and great pain." Why, then, did they accede to them? There are several reasons, but they all speak to fundamental disadvantages under which the Oneidas labored in negotiations over land. One is what the historian J. David Lehman has described as "white factionalism." Natives were lobbied for their lands by a welter of individuals competing for the same prize. They represented private companies, the governments of various states, the United States, and foreign nations. Some represented only themselves. With the nation's legal institutions still nascent, the respective rights and powers of all these parties were still hotly contested. Indeed, even distinguishing who was who, or represented what, was not always possible. According to the Oneidas, Harper had presented himself as acting with state authorization, and Col. Louis Atiatoharongwen testified that John Livingston did likewise. Good Peter recalled, "By [Livingston's] appearance and company, we supposed they came from the Great Council of that State, and would not deceive us." Livingston was a sitting assemblyman, and three of the men flanking him—Peter Schuyler, Abraham Cuyler, and Matthew Visscher—had met with the Oneidas on previous occasions as state treaty commissioners. And they spoke quite literally with the voice of state authority, too: their interpreter was none other than Peter Ryckman, New York's interpreter in 1784.[28]

Ironically, the Oneidas reasoned that the Genesee Company lease offered them a way to reduce the risk of being misled. Good Peter said they decided, "It would not be for our advantage to lease a small piece to one and a small piece to another, or to listen to every one that should say to us, Cut me off a slice from your loaf. It may be better for us that one Great Man should undertake to manage the whole."[29] The Oneidas believed Livingston was that "one Great Man" who could assess the credentials of their various suitors, as well as the merits of the offers. The Oneidas were correct about their needs. As Good Peter's son put it in a 1793 speech to New York land agents, "Your people are very wise, we are not half so wise."[30] In this particular transaction, the Oneidas did not seem to understand that the compensation they were to receive was limited—one thousand dollars a year (rising to fifteen hundred dollars after fifteen years) for nearly six million acres. Good Peter said he "thought [it] was a great sum." His credulous assessment was seconded by another Oneida, who described it as "a generous Rent."[31] The Oneidas signed. There is nothing to suggest that any of the individuals who knew better and had the Oneidas' trust stepped forward to disabuse them of these misconceptions. Although direct evidence of Kirkland's compensation is lacking, Colonel Louis, Jacob Reed, and James Dean had already been compensated with cash or company shares.

The "anxiety and great pain" the Oneidas experienced during the negotiations dissipated in its immediate aftermath, only to be replaced by a greater anguish when the true nature of the transaction was revealed to them. Good Peter recalled, "The voice of the birds from every quarter, cried out you have lost your country!"[32] The birds on that occasion were Natives who had heard about the lease from British agents at Niagara and Peter Penet, a French trader who had taken up residence locally and now perceived an opportunity to augment his influence. For his role in promoting the lease, Kirkland became the object of great resentment (or at least greater resentment than usual). According to Tayler in May 1788, "they have discovered his Views and despise him." In the face of Oneida "abuse," Kirkland set off to assist in other Indian land deals, most notably the extensive Phelps-Gorham purchase from the Senecas.[33]

The 1788 Treaty of Fort Stanwix

The Livingston Lease provided Governor Clinton with an opportunity to repeat the tactics that had proven so successful in forcing the Oneidas into a cession in 1785, but on a grander scale. Once again, the state commissioners also sought to take advantage of the Oneidas' hunger due to lack of provisions. Tayler recommended that the meeting take place late in the summer because, when the Oneidas' supplies would be "exausted," he pointed out, "they will be more anxious to meet the Governor." In fact, it was only late June when the state received an Oneida request for "two Batteaux loads of Corn" lest "when you come up you will find some of us dead of Hunger." On July 22, Kirkland noted in his diary that the Oneidas were "exceedingly straiten'd for provisions" and "all on their way to their fishing quarters."[34]

Just as it had in 1785, the state sought to take advantage of the Oneidas' uncertainty over the previous transaction. When Clinton met with the Oneidas at Fort Stanwix at the end of August, he concealed the fact that the "Long Lease" had been quashed by the legislature in February. The lease made a mockery of the state's self-proclaimed preemption right, and furthermore, the Genesee Company shareholders were primarily members of the legislature's Federalist minority. But the governor shared none of this information with the Oneidas and insisted that they had lost their homeland. Clinton coyly asked the Oneidas not to suppose "that it was our Intention to kindle a Council Fire at this Time in Order to Purchase Land from You for our People." He asserted it was the Oneidas' own imprudence in dealing with actors other than the state that necessitated this meeting. With regard to their lost lands, Clinton predicted, "I think I can raise it from its present drowned condition" but admonished the Oneidas that if they did not grant most of their lands to New York, he would "do nothing but let it go." Following Clinton's directives, the Oneidas reserved a quarter-million-acre tract for "themselves and their Posterity forever for their own Use and Cultivation, but not to be sold, leased, or in any other Manner alienated or disposed of to others." Leasing was to be permitted in a four-mile strip along the southern border, provided the leases were for no longer than twenty-one years. Half-mile squares along the north shore of Oneida Lake were to remain open to them as well.[35]

The rest of the Oneidas' territory, nearly six million acres, was granted to the state, though the Oneidas claimed, "We returned home possessed with an Idea that we had leased our Country to the People of the State." Good Peter recalled that at the end of the proceedings, "[Clinton] sais to us You have now leased to me all your territory, exclusive of the reservation, as long as the grass shall grow & the rivers run. He did not say, 'I buy your country,' Nor did we say 'We sell it to you.'"[36] Unfortunately for the Oneidas, an outright sale is precisely what the treaty document recorded. The Oneidas traded almost all their lands for five thousand dollars and an annuity of six hundred dollars. Negotiating a lease had certainly been the Oneidas' goal; according to Good Peter, Colonel Louis had been placed at the forefront of the negotiations because "he was acquainted with the method . . . of leasing land . . . & receiving rent." Good Peter later asserted that, unbeknownst to him, Colonel Louis had been bribed. The proceedings make some references to an arrangement that the Oneidas might have interpreted as a lease. For example, the state agreed "annually forever to furnish you with some Provisions and Clothing, or to make an annual Payment in Money instead."[37]

The Oneidas made a formal complaint composed in the national council in January and bearing the names of nine eminent Oneidas, including John Skenandoah, Good Peter, Peter Oneyanha, and Lodwick Gahsaweda.

Since we had time to consult the Writings and have them properly explained, and have seen the Proceedings of your Surveyors, we find our Hopes and Expectations blasted and disappointed in every particular. Instead of leasing our Country to you for a respectable Rent, we find that we have ceded and granted it forever for the . . . inconsiderable sum of Six hundred Dollars per Year. We find our Reserve much smaller than we expected, as your Surveyors by beginning at the wrong Place, different from what was agreed on, have run the East and West line almost by our Doors.[38]

The interpreters at the 1788 Treaty of Fort Stanwix, John Bleecker and Samuel Kirkland, were rewarded by the state with one and two square miles, respectively. Kirkland undoubtedly had reasons for betraying his earlier oath never to acquire land west of the Hudson: his family was growing, his financial need was acute, and the Oneidas' landholding now appeared to him as an obstacle to their salvation. Cessions to other whites (most of whom had rendered the Oneidas far less service than he) had become a regular occurrence. Nevertheless, Kirkland's credibility suffered permanent damage. He did not hang around long after the treaty was signed but instead headed deeper into Iroquoia to explore the possibility of establishing a mission elsewhere.[39]

The French Connection

When Kirkland returned briefly in November, Good Peter informed him of myriad "artifices made use of by the French traders to increase their influence & introduce an easier religion & broader path than the presbyterian doctrines would admit of." Kirkland left, this time to promote his plans for an Indian school among prospective sponsors in New England. His departure allowed Frenchmen in Penet's party to boast to the Vatican that they had ousted the Presbyterian and spread their influence across the Six Nations. They bragged, "Our Title of French has contributed much to our gaining the friendship of these Nations, by their agreeable recollection of the honesty and the generosity of the French towards them" and appealed to the Pope for "spiritual and temporal help."[40] The Oneidas were, in fact, rather nostalgic for the French, or at least for the days when the French provided a counterweight to Anglo dominance, and so Penet remained in their good graces.

At the 1788 Fort Stanwix treaty, the Oneidas had rewarded Penet for exposing Livingston. They granted him a square tract, measuring ten miles on each side, in the northern reaches of their territory. Penet promised "ten thousand French settlers" on the lands he had acquired. Although a private trader, Penet misrepresented himself to the Oneidas as an agent of the French king. The Oneidas understood him to be the representative to which Lafayette had alluded at Fort Stanwix in 1784. At the 1788 treaty, Penet bolstered his false credentials by appearing in the company of the French minister plenipotentiary to the United States, Count Élénore-François-Élie de Moustier. Moustier played along with Penet's misrepresentations even so far as to refer to Penet publicly as his representative.[41] Once again, the Oneidas were presented with the impossible challenge of assessing the credentials of their negotiating partner.

New York State officials were galled by the French ambassador's crashing their treaty, but they did not challenge Penet's false claims at the time because so many millions of acres had been riding on the successful completion of the negotiations. Why did Moustier participate in the ruse? It was his job to promote France's commercial interests and influence, and Penet's plans promised to do both. France recognized the fragility of the new nation and was interested in maintaining power bases within the American domain. Personal issues also played a role in Moustier's actions. Moustier was accompanied to Fort Stanwix by his sister-in-law, the Marquise de Bréhan, whom Gouverneur Morris, a businessman and one of the framers of the Constitution, described as "a singular, whimsical, hysterical old woman whose delight [was] in playing with a negro child and caressing a monkey."[42] But the real problem was that she also caressed her brother-in-law. The couple's choice not to conceal their relationship had resulted in their ostracism from polite New York society and ultimately to Moustier's recall. Although Moustier and Bréhan were shunned by Governor John Hancock on a visit to Boston, the Oneidas welcomed them warmly. In this light, the Iroquois' conventional diplomatic rhetoric of kinship was doubly gratifying to their "father" Moustier. The marquise was hailed as the "mother" of the nation, and Moustier repeatedly referred to her as such in his correspondence with them.[43]

Moustier was genuinely sympathetic when the Oneidas complained to him of the Americans' twin crimes of liquor peddling and land frauds. They told him, "All these troubles remind us of the time when we lived with our French brothers. Never did they bring us such liquor; and we were happy." Though utterly false, for the time being, this rose-colored history flattered France and pressured its ambassador to set things right. It made the most of the old French legitimizing myth of the *génie colonial*—the notion that France had a particular way with Native peoples and was therefore more entitled to guide them than, say, the more culturally obtuse English. It also reflected the Oneidas' nostalgia for France, which Lafayette had activated at Fort Stanwix. After returning to New York, Moustier continued to correspond with the Oneidas and went so far as to share his wisdom in a form most appropriate to an enlightened nobleman of the 1780s: in consultation with Penet, he drafted a constitution for them. As he explained to the French foreign minister, "The assertion that the . . . Indians are not susceptible to civilization is an injustice with which they are generally treated by the whites. . . . The chiefs and elders of the Oneida nation addressed themselves to me to learn how they might remain in possession of [their] lands. . . . After numerous conversations . . . *they asked me to give them laws by which they could govern themselves.*"[44]

Thus, in October 1788 twenty-seven prominent Oneidas, including four women, spanning all three clans and both political factions, signed the Oneida constitution. Among the signers were senior leaders as well as up-and-comers, sachems and warriors, including Peter Bread (Kanadarok), a leader of the Christian party. The constitution differed in many ways from traditional Iroquois values and precedents. Most notably, it provided for severalty, or dividing the collectively held reservation lands and distributing them to Oneida families and individuals. The constitution also proposed to centralize power in the hands of two "men of principle and interest" who would be the nation's official intermediaries with the outside world. The first men so designated were Colonel Louis and Peter Otsequette, the latter of whom spent about two years being educated in France at Lafayette's expense. The constitution also designated "one man . . . to have strict lookout that no strong liquors . . . are sold." These officers were answerable to the Grand Council, which was made up of two hereditary chiefs and one head warrior from each of the Oneida nation's three clans—certainly a win for the sachem-leaning pagan party, who were Penet's more reliable backers. But the content of the constitution was too radical and its provenance too alien to be implemented at the time. The Oneidas may not even have understood them as translated. There are two likely reasons why the plan received wide Oneida approbation anyway: acquiescence to the French minister's plan bolstered relations with France, and, since New York had recently ratified the U.S. Constitution, the Oneidas' constitution was a pointed assertion of their own sovereignty. The Cherokees would make a similar gesture, with greater substance, decades later.[45]

The state of New York finally moved to limit these French machinations. New York had already lost Vermont, and the proximity of Penet's grant to the Canadian border made it prone to British and even French subversion. Thus, John Tayler told the Oneidas that two letters purported to have been sent to the Oneidas by Moustier were fakes, and that "the Indians in the future should not believe anything from a foreign country, be it France, Spain or Germany—none but the Governor of the State."[46] Indignant, pro-French Oneidas noted in a letter to Moustier that Tayler must have forgotten the Revolutionary War, for "who would he be without the French?" This quip aside, they were disturbed enough to ask Moustier to verify his authorship of the letters. He did so and even sent them a suit of clothes he designed for them and had made in Paris as a sign of friendship. Reassured, the Oneidas appealed to him in late 1789 for his "protection against the usurpation which has been done us by the surveyors of the state of New York." Moustier accordingly sailed upriver to meet with four Oneida chiefs in Albany. He gave them some interesting and sound advice, gleaned no doubt from his proximity to Congress and his close study of the U.S. Constitution. He had noted earlier that the governor was not the final arbiter in Indian relations— the federal government was. The Oneidas were apparently pleased with this information, stating that in the future they would go to George Washington and Congress with their problems, convinced that justice would be done them at the federal level. As they put it, "We wish no longer to find ourselves in the grasp of the state commissioners . . . who are of the belief that they can do nothing better than destroy the Indians."[47] Thus, the substance of Moustier's meeting with the Oneidas highlighted the very heated contest between the states and Congress for jurisdiction over Indian affairs. This contest compelled Congress to pass the Trade and Intercourse Act the very next year to affirm federal supremacy over the states in dealing with Natives.

By the time the act was passed, Moustier had been recalled. His departure precipitated the collapse of French influence. Penet also ran into financial difficulties and Oneida resistance to granting him any more land. His 1790 attempt to lease lands at Canaseraga met the opposition of Oriske Oneidas led by Col. Honyery Doxtator, a hero of the Oriskany battle, who claimed it in the name of the wolf clan. Penet left for St-Domingue (now Haiti), where he sold fellow Frenchmen deeds to his extensive square. He apparently drowned there. Peter Otsequette also died far away from Oneida territory. He was serving as a member of a high-profile Six Nations diplomatic mission to the federal government in Philadelphia in 1792 when he took ill. He was buried there amid much fanfare, courtesy of the government and the citizens of the capital. Colonel Louis beat a partial retreat, dividing his time between Oneida and Akwesasne. Yankees, not Frenchmen, lay in the Oneidas' future.[48]

A Plague of Yankees

By 1790, a massive influx of white settlers into the Oneida country was well under way. In New England, population growth and land depletion were twin spurs to emigration. The first white settlers of the nearby towns of Lee, Bridgewater, Clinton, Paris, New Hartford, and Westmoreland all arrived between 1786 and 1790. The canal promoter and merchant Elkanah Watson noted of Whitestown in 1788, "Settlers are continually pouring in from the Connecticut hive, which throws off its annual swarms of intelligent, industrious, and enterprising settlers. . . . They already estimate three hundred brother Yankees on their muster list." The onrush did not abate. Three years later Watson reported that the numbers of settlers were still "swarming into this fertile region, in shoals, like the ancient Israelites, seeking the land of promise."[49] Speculators and settlers were further encouraged to emigrate by increasing land values resulting from rising European demand for wheat. The development of transportation infrastructure also promoted the growth of white settlement. In 1793 the Western Inland Lock Navigation Company began clearing Wood Creek to improve navigation between the Mohawk River and Oneida Lake.[50] Roads through the Oneida Reservation were being built and improved to connect the Hudson Valley to the growing Euro-American settlements deeper in Iroquoia, particularly the town of Canandaigua, about a hundred miles to the west. Whitestown landowners included the Democratic-Republican George Clinton and the Federalist George Washington, who jointly held more than six thousand acres along the Mohawk. According to the 1790 federal census, the population of Whitestown had reached 1,891. Of the neighboring town of Westmoreland, Kirkland marveled that "this place, which six years ago, was in a state of nature, a mere wilderness, should so suddenly appear like the garden of Eden, the fields around us whitening for harvest, or clad with verdure." Having failed to find greener fields elsewhere, the missionary was back to stay.[51]

According to Kirkland's estimates in December 1790, there were 588 Oneidas living in five villages. He also counted 287 Tuscaroras, Stockbridges, and

Brothertowns.[52] Despite declining game, the Oneidas continued to practice their traditional economic pattern of hunting, fishing, and horticulture as best they could. Shortly after a measles outbreak and in the grip of yet another famine in 1789, Christian and pagan Oneidas alike expressed their anguish that "while blessings of every kind flowed down like a river upon the white people, as though God begrudged them nothing; Calamity, wretchedness and poverty were the lot of the Indians." Kirkland wrote in his journal that he was asked "whether this displeasure of Heaven or curse of God was not inflicted on them for some great sins against God, committed by their forefathers?" And if not, "What did the Great God mean by what is said in the second Commandment; that he would visit the iniquities of the Fathers upon the Children unto the third and fourth generations?" In debates with their Christian peers, Oneidas who opposed the mission had been cannily deploying Christian doctrine to argue against conversion on the grounds that doing so would change nothing until the curse expired some time hence. Those Oneidas who sought to discredit Kirkland's doctrines often found that the most effective way to do so was to engage it on its own terms. Kirkland had to acknowledge that among the mission's foes were "some Indians of very considerable abilities; (who have become most acquainted with divine revelation)." Kirkland denied vehemently that the Indians were cursed for sins that were not their own and explained that the threat "to visit the sins of the Fathers upon the Children" referred to temporal matters exclusively. For example, he said, to the extent the Indians continued to suffer as a result of prior land sales, they were feeling the effects of their forefathers' sinful love of liquor. Kirkland admonished, however, that their souls were in jeopardy as long as they imitated the immoral ways of their ancestors—drinking and "persisting in wicked doctrines and practices they received by tradition from their fathers."[53]

Although Kirkland's remarks won a chorus of "*togeske, togeske, very true, very true,*" one chief spoke out to criticize God's judgment and, by extension, white society. Challenging Kirkland's explanation, the chief questioned why the whites who had acted sinfully by debauching and defrauding the Indians' forefathers seemed to elude similar divine retribution. The chief said, according to Kirkland's account, that "he understood it had become a proverb among the white people to say, '*as dirty as an Indian.*' '*as lazy as an Indian,*' '*As drunk as an Indian,*' '*lie like Indians.*' And we Indians can only say '*Cheat like white man.*' And poor Indians must bear it." The chief used his understanding of Christian definitions of morality to throw light on the hypocrisy of its votaries and the asymmetrical justice of their God. The rhetoric of Christian morality, which whites could neither ignore nor dismiss easily, became a powerful anti-Christian argument whose use only expanded as the balance of power in Iroquoia tilted against Indians. "Argue with them upon the internal evidence of the excellency of the Christian system & the tendency of its doctrines," Kirkland noted of his conversations with a visiting Onondaga, "& they will urge against it the wicked practices of its professors." The Natives suggested that whites were reaping the rewards not of right action but simply of sharp dealing. For many Oneidas, this observation enhanced their sense that when they recouped their own spiritual power the whites would pay for their misdeeds. By engaging in the debate on Christian terms, however, they also imbibed and accepted a new relationship between religion and personal morality.[54]

The difficulty Indian converts faced in reconciling temporal expressions of God's judgment with the observable behavior of whites militated against their uncritical acceptance of Christianity, as well as any desire to erase the cultural and geographic boundaries that separated them. As an Oneida told two Quakers in 1790, "They looked at the flourishing state of the white people & were ready to apprehend the Great Spirit loved the white people more, because they were better, yet they saw the white People did not do right." On another occasion, Oneidas complained to the governor than "when the white people saw [a group of young warriors] they kill their neighbor's hogs, and told their neighbors that the Indians did it, and so our people were put to trouble for it."[55]

If Kirkland's gospel preaching resonated in this context, it owed more to elements of the Oneidas' culture than to whites'. Even if Euro-Americans did not "do right" toward Indians, the Christian concept of fellowship remained attractive to Natives, since it could be the basis for renewal of indigenous norms of comity that had broken down. It was obvious too that, although whites also drank heavily, their communities did not suffer the same disruptions. Some Oneidas therefore perceived Christianity as a powerful resource to combat the very great danger that intemperance and violence posed to their communities—and to these more limited, pragmatic ends many remained adherents to Kirkland's church. One chief noted that "some Indians did love God and Jesus Christ so much that they get drunk no more, and walk in strait path." This description would have applied to both of Kirkland's staunchest supporters, Good Peter and Skenandoah. As a corollary to their search for an effective temperance strategy, Oneida Christians also looked to Jesus as a resource to combat the often fatal violence that had become endemic to the reservation community. Beech Tree, a sachem who was sympathetic to the mission, delivered an impassioned oration in 1788, saying, Kirkland recorded, that "he was afraid there was something in the hearts of the Indians that w[oul]d [have] killed Jesus were he now in the world, if Jesus himself did not hold it down or restrain it," and he hoped Jesus would restrain the Indians in their festering hatreds toward one another.[56]

Oneida interest in Christianity was still concerned with reforming traditional practices and beliefs rather than discarding them. Aspects of Christianity that could not be made congruent with the indigenous belief system were generally rejected. In 1790, Kirkland admitted in a private note to himself, "Some subjects, upon which I may have bestowed much labour & study, seem to have no kind of effect upon the minds of Indians, as tho' it did not concern them or was altogether unintelligible: & another discourse where much less labour has been bestowed, will by some means or other, at once gain their ear, wake up their attention & seem to get fast hold of the mind, as they themselves have expressed it." For example, Kirkland observed that when he "Discoursed upon Psalms 99, 1, 2, 3: 'The Lord reigneth, let the people tremble,'" the subject seemed to him "beyond the reach" of his audience, "except a few persons"—possibly because it disrupted the equation of Puritanism's wrathful God with the benevolent twin, Sapling, of Iroquois myth. By contrast, Kirkland found his audience "more than usually attentive" when he preached from Thessalonians, "Pray without ceasing." Good Peter's remarks indicating his satisfaction "for this warrant granted to guilty sinners" suggest that he and his peers assimilated prayer into the indigenous category of thanksgiving rituals that were quite literally regarded as gifts from the spirit beings above. Nothing could be of greater import to a people whose religion was essentially, as Seneca ethnologist Arthur C. Parker described it, "a continuous doxology," or song of praise.[57]

The Oneidas' continued interest in hymn singing is the most striking example of how the Oneidas modified Christianity to better accord with their traditional style of worship. Few Europeans or Euro-Americans who visited the Oneidas, even for a short time, failed to hear and comment on the Oneidas' hymnody. In 1791 Rev. Nathan Ker said that their singing exceeded "*all description.*" In 1794, the Quaker James Emlen wrote, "Their singing exceeded anything of the kind that I remember to have heard, the voices of the squaws were truly melodious." Singing provided a point of convergence for Native and Christian religious practices. Hymnody appealed to Indians on their own terms because they considered singing, like baptism, to be inherently spiritually efficacious. The marked popularity of hymnody among the Oneidas, and other Native groups, suggests that it was relatively easily incorporated into indigenous frameworks of religious meaning and practice. Although unaccompanied by drum or dance, singers' activity nevertheless represented concerted effort and heartfelt sentiment, and was appreciated as such. Those who participated enhanced their own status, as indicated by Kirkland's comment, "Their proficiency in Psalmody is become so great as invites the notice of the whole village, except a few of the pagan party."[58]

But it also entailed considerable risks from the missionary's perspective, since Christian concepts could be compromised in the process of accommodating them to the indigenous vocabulary. The linguist Thomas McElwain's analysis of nineteenth-century Seneca hymns demonstrates that much of their specifically Christian content was lost in translation, that "non-Iroquoian feelings and expressions are largely omitted" and that, in the effort to find theological common denominators, "totally different sentiments have replaced eighteenth-century Anglican expression."[59]

War in the West, Tension at Home

Tensions among the Oneidas were exacerbated by the ongoing hostilities between the United States and the so-called western confederacy of Indians. Although the Euro-American settlement of Iroquoia was proceeding quickly in the early 1790s, expansion in the Ohio Valley had slowed in the face of coordinated military resistance by Miamis, Shawnees, Wyandots, Delawares, and others. The western confederacy handed the U.S. Army humiliating defeats in the Ohio country, inflicting nearly a thousand casualties in two encounters in 1790 and 1791. To some Natives, these events suggested that they might recoup their spiritual power and mount an effective resistance after all. While the Oneidas displayed little of the *rage militaire* present among the warriors of some other Woodland tribes, Kirkland acknowledged in September 1793 that "be the war ever so unjust on the part of the Indians, still they have a feeling for them as Indians."[60] Indeed, the pagans were galvanized, and the rhetoric of nativism—and its concomitant repudiation of all things European—was amplified. There is little evidence to suggest that this repudiation was a result of outside influence, even though contacts between tribes continued, especially among kin. Instead, it represented a spontaneous expression of sympathy and solidarity. Late in the summer of 1791, an Oneida claimed a vision that demanded the revival of the White Dog sacrifice and a host of other "ancient feasts, religious dances & ball-plays . . . or no good should come to the Six nations." The dream—which foreshadowed more Iroquois prophecy later in the decade—does not seem to have been fulfilled in its particulars, but Kirkland reported in 1791 that some Oneidas grew "very violent in their opposition to all means for promoting civilization & Christianity."[61]

The nativists' patience with Kirkland grew strained, especially with regard to his interference in family relations. Kirkland had long insisted on that "obligation which lay on heads of familys to maintain the worship of God in their respective families"—a coercive model that created tensions wherever members of a household did not hold the same beliefs. In 1790 when a Christian chief, Lieut. Joseph Kanaghsatirhon, "forbid his daughter to company with" a young pagan suitor, the young man "took a large potion of the muskrat root & soon after . . . was so convulsed as to be speechless in a few moments & expired in about two hours." In the wake of this fatal protest, Kirkland reported, "The fury of revenge, the warmth of natural affections, the dictates of conscience, and the fear of God, discordant passions seem to be all alive in town."[62]

Kirkland observed that "when Indians are at variance with *Indians* & a deep rooted mutual prejudice has taken place, their dispositions are inexorable, & their spirit of resentment towards each other, much more keen than when offended with a white person."[63] Although they met frequently in council to overcome their differences, unity at the national level consistently proved elusive. Kirkland provided details of one of the numerous plans for national reconciliation and reorganization that was debated in 1793. This plan, which Kirkland no doubt favored—and very possibly had a role in formulating—called for the Oneidas to create "two grand settlements, instead of six or seven insignificant ones" and to divide their territory into private familial allotments that could be exchanged with other tribal members but not sold to whites. Canaseraga would be home to "all those who did not like to promote agriculture and civilization, and such as could not bear the restraints of the Christian religion, nor love its doctrines." Kanonwalo-hale would have "none but such as were desirous of promoting husbandry, and will study for peace, and endeavour to advance the true religion" and

"No ardent spirits ever to be brought into the town, unless in case of sickness." When the plan could muster the support of only a "bare majority," Skenandoah spoke of beginning a settlement for those who were "resolutely determined to live like white people" anyway. Others, however, "opposed the plan, merely for its being too much like white people, and [because], in the course of a few years, there would be no trait in the town of the genuine Indian." Although the plan laid out the apparent choices facing the Oneidas in their starkest form, Kirkland reported that, "their various reasonings upon the subject, and the objections which were raised, would fill a small volume, if all were to be written, and serve as a portrait of their different dispositions, improvements, and prejudices."[64] Though the culture of the colonizers defined the terms of the debate, the response of most Oneidas defied a simple espousal or rejection of Euro-American ways.

By 1793, Skenandoah lamented the Oneidas' "apparent declension in regard to [the Christian] religion."[65] Native military victories in the Ohio country, Kirkland's absences, his role in their dispossession, his frequent illness, and his preoccupation with building an Indian academy all contributed to the waning of his flock. In 1796, when the New England divines Jeremy Belknap and Jedediah Morse came to audit the mission, they found church membership (which was a formal status) to be still only approximately thirty. This figure, however, did not reflect the Oneidas' ongoing engagement with Christianity. Standards for membership were high, and many might attend worship regularly without seeking the distinction of membership. Church membership lacked an Iroquois analogue, except medicine societies, and these, like Kirkland's church, were small and exclusive. Belknap and Morse observed, "When the present missionaries decline to baptize any of their children, [the Indians] carry them . . . down the Mohawk River, where, on payment of the usual fee of half a dollar, they find no difficulty in obtaining baptism, and are perfectly easy about the salvation of their children. As far, therefore, as this kind of baptism may denominate them Christians, the whole nation, except the few Pagans above mentioned, may be said to be so."[66] Belknap and Morse's disdain aside, the simple fact that so many Oneidas went to the trouble of traveling to obtain baptism demonstrated a definite desire for the sacrament. If Kirkland's baptismal standards were not to their liking, Oneidas went elsewhere to obtain it—but they did obtain it. In short, even when it came to Christianity, the Oneidas remained the arbiters of their spiritual needs.

Kirkland's conversation with a very ill Oneida named Cornelius Hanwaleao in 1800 suggests the continued relevance of Christianity for many non-communicants. Hanwaleao had received instruction in the precepts of Christianity early in life but had ceased attending worship at least fifteen years earlier. Nevertheless, Kirkland found that Hanwaleao "would not intirely renounce christianity" even though "he rather inclined to rest upon the tradition of the Fathers." Hanwaleao furthermore acknowledged, in his words, "two great crimes of which I have been guilty, & for which I must be punished: (Viz) the Sin of *Adultery* . . . & drunkenness." Strangely, though, he did not see fit to enlist the minister's aid as he lay dying. Instead, Hanwaleao observed: "Having no more deadly sins, my punishment will be of short duration. I shall have to pass thro' two fires only. I have had a glimps of the peaceful country which lies beyond these tremendous fires. I have seen the man (such as one by name in english *Big Bear*) who had three fires to pass thro', but he has survived it & has safely arrived." Hanwaleao had accepted certain Christian norms—although he had violated them—and he incorporated the Protestant hell in such a way as to maintain the traditional Iroquois afterworld ("the peaceful country") intact, along with the two-way connection with this world. Presumably he believed his baptism would limit or at least help him survive the coming ordeal. "It frequently happens," Kirkland observed drily, "that some doctrine of revealed religion will be intermingled with their ancient superstition," and Hanwaleao's testimony suggests how Christian beliefs had been appropriated and indigenized by Oneidas who considered themselves traditionalists. New beliefs were consciously considered, and those aspects that were accepted were authenticated by their incorporation into dreams and visions, the content of which circulated widely by word of mouth.[67]

Timothy Pickering and the Treaties of 1794

With nativism on the rise, federal policy makers—and Secretary of War Henry Knox in particular—recognized that a more conciliatory policy toward the Indians was needed to avert a wider war that the United States could ill afford, in either money or men. The Washington administration placed a high priority on keeping the Six Nations out of the fray, launching a goodwill campaign to keep them at peace. The 1790 Trade and Intercourse Act was a central element of this policy. It provided that traders must be licensed, that crimes by whites against Indians would be punished, and that no purchase of land was valid unless it was made in a public treaty with the federal government. As Washington told a delegation of visiting Senecas, "You will perceive, by the law of Congress for regulating trade and intercourse with the Indian tribes, the fatherly care the United States intend to take of the Indians."[68] The president signed the bill into law on July 22. Although New York's state government cohabited with the federal government in lower Manhattan, New York ignored the act. The state soon authorized funds for continuing its own independent Indian diplomacy and pursued a strategy that ran directly counter to the federal one. Governor Clinton wished to promote divisions among the Six Nations, on the grounds that Iroquois "disunion produces impotency and secures inaction." Meanwhile, the Washington administration thought the more efficient and effective way of neutralizing the Six Nations was to deal with them as a whole and to reassure them through respectful treatment. An exasperated Washington complained to Alexander Hamilton, "The interferences of the States, and the speculations of Individuals will be the bane of all our public measures."[69]

Washington dispatched former quartermaster general Timothy Pickering to Iroquoia to achieve his aims. Pickering began his diplomatic enterprise in Iroquoia in October 1790 by affirming peace and friendship with the Senecas in a conference at Tioga Point.[70] It might be said that Pickering was the point man for a federal "charm offensive," although most of Pickering's acquaintances found him somewhat lacking in that quality. The self-conscious rectitude that irked Pickering's peers was certainly in evidence in his conduct of Indian affairs. When the federal government named Gen. Israel Chapin agent to the Six Nations in 1792, Pickering wrote him that the president "manifested much concern to have a good man selected, who would act uprightly, & especially one *who was no speculator in Indian lands, and who had too much honesty ever to be made the instrument of deception, or silently to suffer deception & imposition from others, in any negociations with the Indians, particularly in bargains for their lands.* . . . For he has seen that in most of those bargains heretofore made, the Indians have been shamelessly imposed on."[71] Indeed, Pickering probably had the state treaties with the Oneidas in mind when he wrote this letter, because he raised the Oneidas' predicament in a letter to Knox three days later. In that letter, he made the wry observation that "the 'consequences' of their attachment to us [in the Revolutionary War] . . . have not been 'good' unless it is good for them to lose almost all their lands for a trifle." Pickering had interviewed Good

Peter at length about the Oneidas' treaties, and he had taken down twenty-five pages of detailed testimony.[72]

Good Peter died in 1793, so he did not participate in the culmination of Pickering's diplomatic efforts with the Six Nations, the November 1794 Treaty of Canandaigua. As the parties gathered at the treaty grounds in October, they were still absorbing the news that the western confederacy had suffered a decisive defeat at the Battle of Fallen Timbers, near modern-day Toledo. The Oneidas were the first to arrive, and they spent some time with Pickering discussing their particular problems. Captain John told Pickering: "Our minds are divided on account of our lands. Not that we are to blame: —'Tis you, Brothers of a white Skin, who cause our uneasiness. You keep coming to our seats, one after another. You advise us to sell our lands. You say it will be to our advantage. This, Brother, is the voice we receive from you." After recapitulating the Oneidas' dealings with the state since the Revolution, Captain John requested Pickering's opinion of a recent agreement signed with Peter Smith. Smith was a local fur trader, and the agreement allowed him to rent out the lands in the leasing zone authorized in the 1788 Fort Stanwix treaty in exchange for $200 a year ($250 after three years). In addition, Smith had promised to open a large store with low prices and bring "peaceable quiet" settlers. Smith's Oneida supporters were mostly among the pagans, and this agreement had been lubricated by a secret reward he promised Jacob Reed.[73] In May, Honyery Doxtator and his sons, Cornelius and Jacob, confronted Smith's surveyors, breaking their chain and threatening their lives. Pickering opined that Smith's lease, as well another recent one to Abraham Van Eps, were null and void because they violated the Trade and Intercourse Act. They were also bad deals. Pickering described the leasing zone in terms of the number of farms it could support, and the annual compensation received by the Oneidas for each farm under Smith's terms as the monetary equivalent of a quart of rum. Pickering alluded to the Oneidas' inability "to calculate the quantity & value" of their lands. "Perhaps sometimes," he noted, "the interpreters purposely deceive you: but at other times the interpretations are not exact because you have no words in your language by which the meaning of the English words can be expressed." Furthermore, he added, referring to legal jargon, "few even of the white people understand all these words: and they are not necessary to be introduced into papers which convey your lands." Hoping to help the Oneidas fend off future trouble, Pickering armed them with a copy of the Trade and Intercourse Act.[74]

The Oneidas comprised 264 of the 1,600 Natives present at the general treaty, which was signed on November 11. Its principal effect was to clarify the western boundary between the United States and the Six Nations in Seneca territory. The Six Nations relinquished their claim to lands in Pennsylvania and Ohio, and the United States dropped its claim to a million acres of land farther east. The Six Nations received ten thousand dollars in goods and their annuity was increased to forty-five hundred dollars, payable in "clothing, domestic animals, implements of husbandry, and other utensils suited to their circumstances, and in compensating useful artificers, who shall reside with or near them, and be employed for their benefit." Thus began the practice that continues to this day of sending cloth to each of the Six Nations every year. Most important, the treaty also recognized the Six Nations' reservations as their respective domains until they might decide to sell them to the United States.[75]

After completing the Canandaigua treaty, Pickering and his interpreter, Jasper Parrish, traveled to Oneida to determine appropriate compensation for the Oneidas' Revolutionary War losses. Pickering was making good on his earlier sentiment: "Something more must be done that has yet been done for the Oneidas; and tho' their concerns have been delayed, I will not forget them. Their affairs are not on a footing satisfactory to me; and I fear that neither theirs nor those of any other Indians ever will be." With the assistance of Dean, Parrish, Kirkland, and Reed, Pickering tabulated the Oneidas' individual claims. He concluded: "The aggragate of their losses as given in by them, severally, amounted to near 8000 dollars. After considering characters & merit a proper liquidation was made & the precise sum was determined for each individual, by the Superintendant. The liquidated amt. 5000 dolls. to be a full compensation for the losses the whole nation had sustained by the late war & in consequence of their adhearance [sic] to the United States."[76] At the Oneidas' request, compensation was determined per capita to avoid internal disputes over the distribution of the money. In Kirkland's opinion it was likewise desirable that the sums be paid in money rather than goods. On December 2, Pickering held a treaty with the Oneidas, Tuscaroras, and Stockbridges, about which he stated, "The United States in the time of their distress, acknowledged their obligations to these faithful friends, and promised to reward them." The treaty provided the Oneidas five thousand dollars "as compensation for their individual losses and services during the late war." It also provided for the construction of one or two grist and saw mills (along with one or two millers for three years), and one thousand dollars for the construction of a church.[77]

By the end of 1794, having defeated the western confederacy on the battlefield and settled outstanding boundary disputes with the Six Nations, the federal government dialed back its Indian diplomacy. Pickering returned his full attention to the other duties that had been conferred on him, most notably as the government's postmaster general. It was not long before Washington elevated him to secretary of war and soon after that, secretary of state. The Oneida veterans' treaty marked the end of the Pickering era in Iroquois diplomacy. It was brief, but it would be remembered fondly. As the Oneidas struggled to adapt themselves to their newly restricted domain, the state of New York increased its pressure on them once again. The Oneidas may have already given up the great majority of their acreage, but the acreage that they retained was, from the state's perspective, the wrong acreage. The Oneidas had reserved to themselves the heartland of their territory, but that area, not coincidentally, sat astride a key transportation corridor. While the Oneidas' relations with the relatively distant federal government went into deep eclipse, the state's motivation to press the Oneidas to relinquish more territory would only increase.

5

In a Drowned Land

State Treaties and Tribal Division, 1795–1814

THE ARRIVAL OF "shoals" of settlers in the Oneidas' vicinity promoted an atmosphere conducive to land sales. By 1814 the reservation would be landlocked and surrounded by nearly seventy-five thousand whites. As settlers' cattle invaded their gardens and settlers' seines blocked their streams, the Oneidas found it harder to conduct their customary economic activities. Taverns and trade houses proliferated. The mixture of drink and debt was particularly effective to precipitate land sales. By accepting rewards for signing treaties, leases, or letters granting permission to cut timber, individual Oneidas reaped personal benefit from collective Oneida property. Especially among mixed-blood families, Euro-American notions of private property and values of possessive individualism became more prevalent. In addition, some Oneida individuals adopted land-intensive Euro-American agricultural practices. As they did so, they came to fear the prospect of their fellow Oneidas' selling the tracts on which they had labored. The state was able to use this fear as leverage.

The treaty of 1795, signed in Albany, marked the state's ongoing defiance of federal authority over Indian affairs as established by the Constitution and restated by the Trade and Intercourse Act and the Treaty of Canandaigua. It also marked two significant developments in New York's approach to treaty making with the Oneidas. First, the site of negotiations was moved from the Oneida reservation to the banks of the Hudson, more than one hundred miles from the territory itself. Second, although the state's negotiators later took large swaths of reservation land, they came seeking specific parcels. On these tracts they envisioned strategic "improvements"—canals, roads,

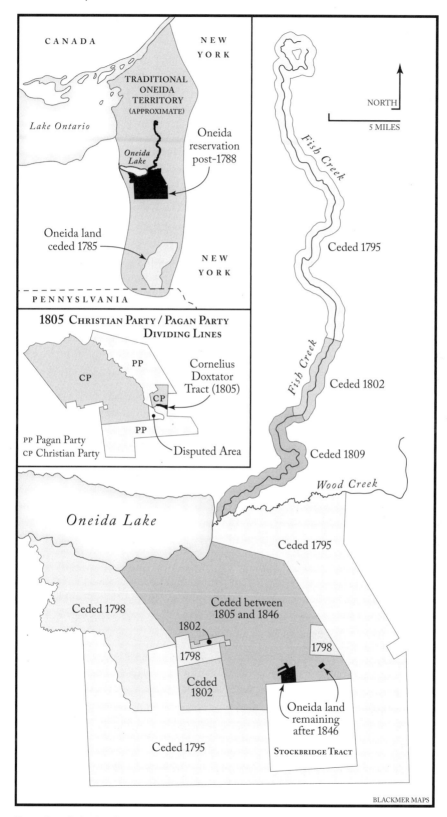

Fig. 6. Oneida land and land cessions, 1785–1846. Map by Kate Blackmer.

taverns, towns—that would link the Oneidas' homeland to the longer-colonized regions of the state. Smaller tracts were also secured for the benefit of local white men such as James Dean, Abraham Van Eps, and a new Frenchman on the scene, Angel de Ferrière. These men had strong connections with the Oneidas and were willing to use them to induce the Indians to sell, provided the state would sanction a reward. As a result, between the signing of the Treaty of Canandaigua and the end of the War of 1812, the Oneidas entered into a flurry of treaties with the state, numbering eight in all. In 1806, the Oneidas complained that land continued to be the "source of our troubles" because of "the folly of a few of our people & the desire of gain in some of the white people, who conspire to filtch [it] away from us."[1]

The Oneidas' position had grown markedly more tenuous within six months of Timothy Pickering's December treaty compensating the United States' wartime allies. In the chain Pickering hoped would protect the Oneidas, the first link to be compromised was, ironically, the Oneidas themselves. In February 1795, nineteen Oneidas, led by John Skenandoah, petitioned the state to appoint Dean and Philip Schuyler as commissioners to help them lease their lands "for a valuable consideration." They needed help, they said, "[because] we do not know how to transact land matters to advantage."[2] That the Oneidas would approach the state is surprising, but they did not view this action as precluding federal involvement. Indeed, the Oneidas probably still associated Dean and Schuyler with the national government, in whose service both men had been most active. More clouds gathered in March, when the federal agent to the Six Nations, Gen. Israel Chapin, died. He was promptly replaced in office by his son and namesake, who bore a captain's title. Although he presented himself to Secretary of War Pickering as a compliant subordinate who shared his father's concern for the Six Nations' well-being, Captain Chapin performed more consistently as a friend to white settlers.[3] In April 1795, the state legislature passed the "Act for the Better Support of the Oneida, Onondaga, and Cayuga Indians, and for Other Purposes Therein Mentioned." "Other purposes" apparently got the better of the "support of the Oneida": the act directed state commissioners to proceed to Iroquoia to negotiate land treaties. They were to pay the Natives no more than four shillings an acre. At the same time, the act stipulated that the land should then be sold by the state for no less than sixteen.[4]

These troubling developments for the Oneidas might have been counteracted by the Federalist John Jay's succeeding George Clinton as governor in July. Pickering raised with Jay the issue of Clinton's failure to comply with the Trade and Intercourse Acts. And though Jay agreed to secure a federal commissioner for all treaties initiated under his administration, he declined to suspend the pending negotiations or review his predecessor's actions. Pickering ordered Chapin to "tell the Indians that [a state treaty] will be improper & unsafe," and that "such a treaty . . . will be void." Chapin conveyed Pickering's message to the Oneidas at the treaty at the Oneida reservation in August. But he was contradicted by the state's lead commissioner— none other than Philip Schuyler. With Dean as his interpreter, Schuyler offered the Oneidas a circuitous and misleading explanation why there were no federal commissioners present. Colonel Pickering, he asserted, "has been misinformed, and has misapprehend[ed] the Business. . . . And therefore the Communication made you by Capt. Chapin ought not to impede the Business of this treaty and the accomplishment of so good an object to you as that we are sent upon, especially as we act *perfectly agreeable to law*."[5] Dean and Schuyler were not the friends the Oneidas thought them to be. According to one of Kirkland's sons, Dean's attitude toward the Indians was one of "disgust." Schuyler had also expressed disdain for Natives and had avoided further contact with the Oneidas after the war. Now, however, he headed the Western Inland Lock Navigation Company, which had been incorporated in 1792 to open a water route between the Hudson River and Lake Ontario. The Oneidas' land along Wood Creek became crucial to accomplishing Schuyler's plans. In 1793, the state surveyor general, Simeon DeWitt, observed that Schuyler "drives it on with all his might," and the French diplomat Charles de Talleyrand noted, "General Schuyler seems to attach a great deal of importance to opening this navigation." As a result, even despite having injured his ribs in a carriage accident in early June, by mid-month he was en route to the Oneida reservation.[6]

Captain John was the spokesman for the Oneidas at the treaty negotiations. Although he greeted Schuyler in a warm and familiar manner, he said, "We hoped, Brothers, when you came, that you had with you an agent from the United States." This ambivalent beginning prefaced a tense negotiation. Captain John observed that the commissioners' initial proposal "marked out too large a piece of land, we will part with a small piece and hope you will give us the value of it." This "small piece" still amounted to a full township of land, thirty-six square miles along the eastern edge of the reservation. Captain John also expressed concern about fishing by whites in Fish Creek. Fishing was of growing economic importance to the Oneidas. One settler described how the Oneidas brought salmon from Fish Creek to the market at Rome, the town rising around the Carrying Place. The Oneidas conveyed them, he said, "in baskets or on their backs, and when extra plenty, the Indian ponies were used as pack-horses, on which the fish were somewhat fantastically, and quite ingeniously, bound with bark, the back and sides of the beast having been previously covered with branches of the large-leafed basswood sapling."[7]

Captain John was offering another buffer cession, but Schuyler did not simply seek acreage. He knew which parts of the reservation he wanted, and these were not in the area proposed by Captain John. In addition to the area he wanted for his canal, Schuyler sought the leasing zone where Smith had already planted tenants. Schuyler argued to the Oneidas that the Wood Creek lands were of poor quality and would be primarily a boat landing and the Smith tract was already lost to white settlers. When his demands were not met, he and his delegation left.[8]

This departure did not, however, mark the end of the negotiations. Although the commissioners had left, the locals Dean and Van Eps were seeking personal grants and thus had strong incentive to maintain pressure on the Oneidas. Less than a week after the commissioners' departure, Dean reported to Schuyler that he had been invited to meet "the Sachems, War[r]iors & Women in Council assembled." He reported that the women asserted their primacy in land matters, upbraided the men for not consulting them during the negotiations with the state, and instructed them to accede to the commissioners' final proposal "with some small variations." Dean urged Schuyler to seize the opportunity and included a letter signed by thirty-two Oneidas of both parties indicating their willingness to accede to an adjusted version of the final proposals. Dean had no doubt traded on the matrons' regard for their adopted son, the "perfect Indian boy" whom they had sought to protect during the war.[9]

A delegation of at least twenty Oneidas arrived in Albany in mid-September to complete the negotiations and sign the treaty. The commissioners offered no additional money but only reassurance regarding the Oneidas' continued possession of Canaseraga, which had been the subject of some debate as a result of ambiguous place-names in the 1788 boundary description. The commissioners also promised a favorable word to the legislature about the fishery. The usual difficulties, such as the language barrier, were compounded by the negotiators' relying now more heavily than ever on rough maps, potentially conflicting recollections, and different place-names. Even in the final treaty document, some of the geographical reference points were vague, such as "a certain creek falling into . . . Fish Creek." The bounds were defined with reference to points that had no relation to natural features, but only distances measured in abstract, culturally specific units. For example, part of the treaty boundary was defined as beginning from "the Chittilingo Branch of Canassaderaga Creek thence Southerly along the said Branch so far as to be One mile distant from the Northern Boundary of the Tract of Land leased by the said Tribe or Nation to Peter Smith, thence East by a Line parallel to the said Northern Boundary so far as to a point four miles distant from the Eastern boundary of the Tract so appropriated as aforesaid thence Northerly by strait lines parallel to the Eastern boundary lines of the Lands so appropriated and Keeping four miles distant therefrom."[10]

Similarly complex was the compensation scheme. The Oneidas ceded three tracts on the western, eastern, and southern sides of the reservation. For one, they were to receive $2,952 as well as an annuity in that amount. A second tract entitled them to $3 per 100 acres, as well as an annuity in that amount; for a third tract they would receive an annuity of $3 per 100 acres. After the survey was complete, the state calculated the overall acreage to be 20,500 and the additional annuity required as $617. Schuyler had achieved his goals at a very modest price, less than a fifth the land's market value.[11]

With the treaty signed, the time now arrived for the intermediaries to claim their rewards from the ceded territory. Dean and Myndert Wemple received one square mile each; Van Eps received two. The treaty commissioners' report explaining the source of these men's influence among the Oneidas helps explain the Natives' consent to the land grants: "Mr. Van Eps has resided some years at Oneida, and to his influence we are in a great measure indebted for the final adjustment, and we have reason to believe that the Indians are indebted to him in a Considerable sum of Money, for supplies from time to time afforded them. Mr. Dean has on all occasions been their friend and interpreter, and Colo. Wemple afforded them very considerable pecuniary aid, during the last War when they were driven from their Teritory and sought refuge at Schenectady." Dean noted that Van Eps had been "very active on the present occasion," which had something to do with an extant receipt titled "Money to Van Eps and who received it." The receipt records payments to more than a half-dozen influential Oneidas. At least five of them signed the request to resume negotiations, as well as the treaty itself. The sums were quite large: one hundred dollars each to John Skenandoah, Martinus Rotshin, eighty-three dollars each to Peter Bread and Tall

William, fifty dollars each to Jacob Reed and an Oneida identified only as
Powless, and ten dollars to an Oneida identified as Hanyost.[12]

On learning of the sale, John Sergeant, the missionary to the nearby
Stockbridges, wrote Pickering, asking his opinion "respecting the unlawful
purchase (as I call it) of the Indians land in this vicinity lately made by the
Government of this State." Pickering's reply has not survived, but his actions hint at his thinking. He had consulted the president over New York's
evasion of the Trade and Intercourse Act. Washington was dismayed but
was willing to live with New York's faits accompli. Correctly anticipating
future compliance under Jay, Pickering beat a partial retreat. He told Chapin,
"You may content yourself with giving the Oneidas the information . . . &
there to leave the matter." Chapin had done exactly that.[13] A temporary accommodation addressing the relationship between the federal and state governments had been reached, but it was not one that worked in the Oneidas'
favor.

"Death and Darkness"

The Oneidas' travails probably only confirmed Pickering's belief that their
sole salvation lay in their immediate adoption of European-style plough
agriculture. To that end, Pickering had invited Quakers to attend the Treaty
of Canandaigua. Pickering placed considerable trust in the Quakers' ability
to promote the Natives' "civilization" without alienating them with speculation of the theological or real estate varieties. As Pickering expressed it to
the Northwest Territory governor Arthur St. Clair, "Most attempts at civi-
lizing the Indians which I have heard of have been preposterous: We have
aimed at teaching *religion*, and the *sciences* before we taught them the simple
and essential labours of civil Life." The Quaker strategy accordingly emphasized training Natives in plough agriculture and the English language rather
than preaching the Gospel and seeking converts. Pickering's endorsement
of the Quakers also amounted to a repudiation of Kirkland's proselytizing
and the Indian academy he proposed.[14] (True to Pickering's predictions, this
academy proved of little use to the Natives but of considerable value to the
settlers, eventually dropping its original name, Hamilton-Oneida Academy,
to become Hamilton College.)

The Quakers offered their services to the Six Nations generally, but the
western Iroquois balked. According to Chapin, "they wished to see the advantages that would arise to the Oneidas."[15] The sachem party, however,

increasingly known as the pagan party, welcomed the Quakers, whom they sought to use as intermediaries with Euro-Americans, thereby reducing their dependence on Kirkland. To the Quakers, the prospect of a mission to the Oneidas seemed a satisfactory beginning, though less than they had hoped for. A Quaker delegation arrived at Kanonwalohale in the late spring of 1796 and spent the entire month of June making arrangements for the three missionaries who were to remain at Oneida: Jacob Taylor, Enoch Walker, and Henry Simmons Jr. "We have . . . found it tedious, to a trying Degree," the delegates reported, "in doing Business with these people." Most of the delays they faced were unrelated to their mission but were symptomatic of the trials the Oneidas were enduring. They were distracted, for example, by the surveying of the lands ceded in the 1795 treaty. Just as the Quakers were setting out for Oneida from a nearby town, a runner had arrived to inform them of a further delay, because the Oneidas whom they were to meet "were gone to Fort Stanwix, to complain of the Surveyors for overrunning the boundaries of the last Sale."[16] The Oneidas perceived a discrepancy between the verbal description of their territory and the final lines run by the surveyors.

Alcohol abuse was another problem that seemed to rise as the reservation contracted. On at least one occasion, the interpreter (probably Jacob Reed) "was disordered with strong drink." So, too, were many of those with whom the Quakers had hoped to communicate. Shaken by the scene, the Quaker Joshua Evans wrote that "a portion of death and darkness was felt rather than a pleasant sensation, in these visits."[17] Death and darkness had, in fact, enveloped the Oneida reservation. Three murders took place there between November 1795 and June 1796. The first involved two Tuscaroras embroiled in a personal dispute; the second involved two Oneidas. The third was of a white man and had been perpetrated by an Oneida named Saucy Nick in the tavern operated by Wemple. All involved liquor.[18]

Adding to the Natives' consternation was the county authorities' efforts to unilaterally apply the settlers' laws to the Natives in these cases. As Gov. Daniel D. Tompkins would later observe, the Indians felt "horror at becoming objects of punishment by laws which they cannot interpret or comprehend."[19] The Oneidas had seen the result when their lands were subjected to New York's legal regime; they were unwilling to subject their persons to it as well. Although they had ceded most of their lands to the state, they had nowhere ceded their sovereignty over themselves and what remained to them. Only months earlier, the Treaty of Canandaigua implicitly recognized that they retained sovereignty by stipulating that if a crime involved both Indians and whites, it should be referred to the federal government and the Six Nations for mediation. Nevertheless, in two of the cases, the accused Indians were jailed and tried by the county. Dean understood how committed the Oneidas remained to their norms of traditional justice. He wrote to Pickering requesting information about the Oneidas' treaty rights. With a phrase well calculated to pique Pickering's patrician sentiments, Dean alluded to "the disagreeable sensation excited by popular prejudice on the present occasion." Pickering's response does not survive but, fortunately for the two Oneidas, "popular prejudice" did not run so deep as to convict them in the absence of sufficient evidence. Five years later, Dean again intervened to limit state meddling in a murder case involving two Oneidas. Kirkland reported that Dean felt that traditional justice must take its course, and that in the absence of the banishment or killing of the accused, "there would never be peace in the Town."[20]

Needs and Desires

The Quakers explained to Kirkland, according to his journal, that "their two leading maxims in order to civilise & reform the Indians, and by which they expect gradually to effect it, are *necessity* & *kindness*. First, to make them see & feel their *need*, & then to shew them *kindness*." Thus, the Quakers aimed to instill needs most Oneidas did not feel so that they might relieve them. The Quakers believed a model farm would reveal to the Oneidas the material comforts provided by plough agriculture and spark a revolution in manners, including the adoption of private property. The Quakers explained to the Oneidas, "our Friends [i.e., the missionaries] are to live plentifully, as their own people do at home." Although the Oneidas placed a high value on redistribution, the Quakers specified that only "the eighth part of the Remainder is to be reserved for the relief of your old and infirm people; and the rest is to be divided amongst the young Indian Apprentices; that they may enjoy the fruit of their Labour; and have something to begin with for themselves." Although some Oneidas began to subscribe to Euro-American values of possessive individualism, most Oneidas still would have perceived a breach of proper behavior if Kirkland's accusation is true. He stated, "The greatest objects of charity, many widdows and orphans among the Oneidas were never once visited, seen or known by the Quakers during their three years residence here."[21]

Federal agent Chapin perceived that the Quakers were only dimly aware of the ambitiousness of the cultural transformation they proposed, and he mocked them. In the fall of 1796, he declared himself "fully convinced *it is much easier to make a well-bread* [sic] *American an Indian, than an Indian a white man, much less a Quaker.*" But not all Quakers in Iroquoia were oblivious to Natives' alternate cultural logic. James Emlen perceived that the Natives valued social and political pursuits highly enough to divert time from strictly economic ones. "They & we estimate time with very diff[eren]t judgm[en]ts," he observed, and of the Six Nations he concluded, "Perhaps no people are greater masters of their time." He also noted, "We are very apt to condemn any natural practices which differ from our own, but it requires a greater conquest over prejudices & more penetration than I am Master of clearly to decide that we are the happier people."[22] Indeed, as the historian Daniel Richter points out, the early republic's Quakers were an especially anxious lot, trapped between competing ideals of simplicity and success, separatism and benevolence. Although his fellow Quakers were disproportionately prosperous and urban, Joseph Clark stated, "My mind was considerably humbled in seeing the manner in which the Indians lived and how free they were of those cares and wants that luxury and pride hath introduced, consequently less afflicted with those disorders which are so prevalent among the rich or those of a higher class of life." The Oneidas presented the Quakers with the surprising fact that, in the words of the anthropologist Marshall Sahlins, "wants may be 'easily satisfied' either by producing much or desiring little."[23]

The Oneidas continued to stick with the latter strategy, and Chapin informed Pickering at the end of 1796 that the Quakers "do not make the progress that could be wished." The letters from the missionaries cited progress but muted their expectations. By the end of 1796 the Quakers could report that they had opened an English school. They also supported a minor building boom. As with Kirkland's mission, architecture was one of the most popular elements of the Quaker one.[24] In addition to construction, the Oneidas looked to the Quakers to help them with their blacksmith work, a persistent concern for the pagans because Wemple, the federal smith, was a Kirkland ally. Unfortunately for all Oneidas, however, Wemple had proven more interested in running his tavern than in fixing their guns and implements, and he was threatening to leave. The Quakers were hard-pressed to replace him with one of their own because of the duty the smith would have of repairing firearms, to which they had conscientious objections. They eventually obtained an elderly Quaker smith, William Gregory, who they claimed had been able to train two young Oneida men in the trade, despite his infirmity.[25]

Progress toward the fundamental transformation the missionaries sought was, in their words, "slow." By October 1797, platitudes crept into their reports: "Altho the progress of improvement amongst the nations may not advance acording to the expectation of man, yet we have no reason to doubt that our labours will be lost or time spent in vain, as we abide under the direction of *him* who is altogether suficient for his work." Unfortunately for the Quakers, the Oneida farm recruits found it difficult to adjust to the rhythm of European-style agricultural labor. The missionaries reported that "some days, near thirty would come to work, and other days scarcely one was to be had." In April, they reported, they could "board none that labour with us except the two boys," probably because of seasonal hunting demands.[26] The lack of sufficient support from Oneida men meant the missionaries had to look elsewhere for ways to keep the model farm going. Clark recommended that "some well-quallified woman . . . cook and mend for them, and leave them at liberty for more important service among the Natives." While she did so, she might also "instruct the Indian women and girls in house-wifery without which an imperfect and slow progress will be made." Thus, the Quakers' involvement with Native women was at its inception an attempt to maximize the usefulness of the male missionaries. Two women, Hannah Jackson and Susanna Gregory, arrived later that year. Although spinning and knitting were soon being taught to about fifteen girls on the reservation, even in March 1799 the women's instructor could only sigh resignedly, "The Women in this Reservation have need of considerable improvement, and as knowledge must precede improvement, so must instruction knowledge."[27]

The Quakers' insistence on realigning Oneida gender roles posed the single greatest obstacle to the achievement of their goals. Oneidas who followed the Quakers' lead transgressed gender norms that had mythic sanction. There is no evidence that the Oneida apprentices ever achieved proficiency. The smith's task of tending hot coals indoors, for example, probably too closely resembled that of a woman tending the kettle of soup. And as the Quaker John Pierce noted of the Tuscaroras among the Oneidas, if a man was seen "ho[e]ing a Hill of Corn, he would appear as much ashamed, as if he had been caught in a dishonourable or wicked Action." There was some flexibility in these roles, since men did routinely help women in the

fields. But pressure to reverse roles outright was checked by traditional attitudes, which for some were actually reinvigorated by their proximity to
whites and more acculturated Indians, such as Stockbridges and Brothertowns. In 1796, Belknap and Morse noted, "The Oneidas affect to despise
their neighbors of Stockbridge and Brotherton for their attention to agriculture, [even though] they are obliged to buy their corn and meat of them."
Furthermore, they added, "They have an idea that to labor in cultivating
the earth is degrading to the character of man, who (they say) was made for
war and hunting and holding 'councils,' and that squaws and hedgehogs are
made to scratch on the ground." It was no wonder that the Quakers could
find only boys to perform what the Natives defined as women's work. For
their part, women were equally reluctant to abandon the fields for looms
and spinning wheels.[28]

Belknap and Morse's words also indicate that the Oneidas were buying
food from other Indians. Quaker missionaries were trying to redefine gender roles and also to persuade Natives to raise foodstuffs and manufacture
goods such as cloth that the Indians already obtained through the market.
The Oneidas' documented interest in leasing their lands and selling fish
suggests that many Oneidas found that these cash-generating ventures were
more compatible with traditional economic activities and therefore were more
acceptable and efficient ways to obtain clothes, food, and liquor. An 1803 visitor to Kanonwalohale observed that the Natives supplied the tavern where
he stayed "as well as those in the Neighborhood, with Fish, Indian Corn
&c."[29] Although the game population was still declining, enough remained
to supplement their income. Peter Smith still collected pelts, including beaver, marten, mink, raccoon, and bear. Deer also remained common. Oneida
men and women collected and scrubbed ginseng, which they gave to Smith,
Van Eps, and other traders, who sent the roots to East Asia. Participation in
the market on these terms appeared more lucrative and less tedious than the
tasks of ploughing and spinning that were part of the Quakers' plan. Furthermore, hunting, fishing, gathering, and traditional agriculture were less
disruptive of gender roles.[30]

The 1798 Treaty

The attorney Thomas R. Gold had been appointed by the state to oversee
the filing of claims by whites living on the lands ceded in the 1795 treaty. He
was to determine who was eligible to receive legal titles directly from the

state. By offering a first shot at legal titles to Smith's tenants, as well as others who leased lands from Oneidas directly, the state rewarded citizens who had come and taken their chances on Native lands. George Embree, a Quaker, had accompanied the 1795 treaty commissioners to meet the settlers. He wrote, "Some . . . appeared to be well meaning men, and came to that country not fully informed of the true situation of the Indian affairs." Others, however, were "very hostile to the poor Indians." "One of them," he said, "remarked that he believed the Almighty had decreed that those heathens should be driven out of the land, and that the white people should inherit it."[31] Settlers of both kinds continued to press on to the reservation in the months and years that followed. Unfortunately for the Oneidas, the agent was not inclined to discriminate. Chapin had told the secretary of war that he believed land sales made the Indians more dependent on the whites and therefore "more faithful allies" of the United States. In the absence of any government officials interested in helping them, the Oneidas had only the Quakers. Thus, it fell to Clark to draft a letter "to warn off some bad tenants, who had settled on their land contrary to law."[32]

Gold's job placed him in an excellent position to gauge the course of economic development around the Oneida reservation, and it was not long before he suggested to Schuyler that another treaty be held "for the purchase of the Land contiguous to the Genesee Road on each side of the Onida, within a mile or two of the same[.] Without this every foot of the road must be causway'd." The "Genesee country" was located south of present-day Rochester and west of the Finger Lakes, and therefore, as its name implies, the Genesee Road was one of the principal arteries to western New York. The Genesee country was an early magnet for settlers, but it was inaccessible, Gold pointed out, when travelers found "their horses . . . drenched in the mire to the hips and shoulders." The legislature authorized a treaty in early 1798 "for the extinguishment of [the Oneidas'] claim to such part of the lands reserved for their use that may be convenient for public roads and suitable settlements for accommodations."[33]

The negotiations, which had been prompted by the appearance of several Oneidas in Albany during the winter, set the terms of the treaty that would be signed at the reservation in June. The composition of the delegation is not known, and its authority was questionable. According to the Quakers, it "caused much uneasiness amongst numbers of the Nation as the[y] . . . think it will prove very Injerious to have such spots cut out of their land."[34] Enclaves with Euro-American "accommodations" would be nodes of subversion, exponentially increasing the Oneidas' exposure to settlers and their beverages. Surprisingly, the Oneida delegates used the state's desire for road frontage as leverage to sell roughly the western fifth of the reservation as well. The delegates may have been desperate to quickly raise as much cash as possible. Hunger was a likely reason. Before leaving Albany, state officials gave the Oneidas three hundred dollars of a future annuity payment "to answer their immediate occasion." In April, two Quakers, Jacob Taylor and Jonathan Thomas, reported that the Oneidas requested food aid because "the[y] expect to be short this summer." The decision to sell lands on the western side of the reservation may also have reflected the Oneidas' unease with their continued ability to hold on to Canaseraga, over which a whiff of dispute still hung. A traveler named Timothy Bigelow observed that "the country to the westward . . . had begun to be settled some time before," and an adjacent tract had already been purchased by a well-informed and well-connected investor, Richard Varick, mayor of New York.[35]

Internal politics also appear to have been at play. The tract sold was home to the Oneida mixed-blood Doxtator and Denny families, who were of Palatine and French extraction, respectively. Louis Denny was a former French captive from the Mackinac region now married to an Oneida woman. Members of these families lived somewhat differently than other Oneidas. They were more likely to be literate. According to Kirkland, the Oneidas at Canaseraga were "decent *Indian farmers*." "At a moderate estimate," he reported, "that small village has for several years past raised more than one thousand bushels of wheat & pease. Few taverns west of Whitestown are more plentifully furnished with forage than *Indian John's (so-called)* in this village." Although the Oneida delegates requested that the Oneidas at Canaseraga not be ousted from the parcels on which they lived, a group of Canaseragas, including Jacob Doxtator, went to Albany in March to announce their ignorance of, and their opposition to, the proposed sale.[36]

Governor Jay made good on his assurances that he would abide by the Trade and Intercourse Act. A federal commissioner was present at Kanonwalohale for the treaty signing in June (as was Mayor Varick). The commissioner was Joseph Hopkinson, a Philadelphia lawyer whose other achievement in 1798 had been to write the lyrics to the first national anthem, "Hail, Columbia!" In his instructions to Hopkinson, Pickering did not request versifying, only certifying. Pickering had reviewed the terms of the treaty and left Hopkinson little discretion; he was merely to attend the transaction, sign it, and transmit it to the State Department. Hopkinson also conveyed a declaration signed by John Skenandoah, Anthony Shonoghriyo, Paul Te-havwengaroreno, and Jacob Reed that the Oneida national council had decided to strip John Denny and Lewis Denny of provisions allowing them to retain tracts in the ceded lands, a clear sign of antagonism toward the two men. A visitor reported that John Denny had been "banished" and threatened with violence by fellow Oneidas as a result of "his attachment to the whites." Some whites, and powerful ones at that, must have become attached to Denny as well: in addition to the modification of the treaty to exclude him, the state legislature became his patron by granting him 250 acres for a dollar an acre.[37]

Nativist Revival

The Quaker mission limped along through 1798 and 1799. Having spent approximately two thousand pounds at Oneida, and considering the more promising prospects at the Seneca mission that had begun in 1798, the Quakers decided to withdraw. Leaving ample supplies behind, they told the Oneidas that it was now time for the nation to put them to good use on its own.[38] The correspondence between the missionaries and the Philadelphia Quaker Indian Committee indicates they had little confidence that the Oneidas would do so. Nor did the pagan party's farewell speech imply they would. The pagans made a half-hearted promise to reform but openly stated the more pressing reason they wanted the Quakers to remain—and possibly one of the reasons they welcomed them in the first place. The pagans' speaker said, "The White People now live very near us and are growing very numerous and we think your living here has a Tendency to prevent Trouble and Difficulty between us and them. We think it is likely when they know you are gone they will be more severe towards us, and perhaps you may hear of Trouble in this way before you arrive at Home and some of us may loose our Lives by them." They were not exaggerating. A month later, Kirkland recorded in his diary that an Oneida chief, "a very peaceable man, had been beaten with a pair of fire tongs by a white man, & that his head was so broken they despaired of his life."[39]

The pagans acknowledged the failure of the mission to meet its sponsors' expectations. They took the blame on themselves, stating, "We have not improved the opportunity as we ought to have done." They also blamed the Christian party, noting that "the other part of the Nation have always tried to Discourage us." Indeed, the two parties fell to bickering over the house and barn, about twenty acres of cleared land, and farming and carpentry implements. According to Kirkland, "This property has laid the foundation for such a division & mutual jealousy among the Indians as I fear will do them more injury than twice the value of the property." Wemple promptly seized the metalworking tools left behind by the Quakers.[40]

The Quakers' departure coincided with a nativist revival. One night in 1799, a Mohawk at the Grand River lapsed into a trancelike state. In that condition, he met the Upholder of the Skies, who demanded the revival of the White Dog ceremony. This ritual, originally part of the sacred Midwinter Ceremonial, involved the strangling of at least one spotless white dog and its display atop a pole, accompanied by feasts, dances, and the playing of the sacred bowl game. It had been thirty years or more since the White Dog feast had last been held among the Oneidas, but when Blacksmith, the leader of the pagan party, learned of the developments at Grand River, he reinstated the ritual. He also warned participants that they must not "drink any Rum for ten days," or they would "pollute the Sacrifice," a proscription that even he was unable to observe.[41]

The nativist revival that took place in 1799 also epitomized the synthesis of Christian and Indian beliefs that had developed. Strikingly indicative of the importance of Christianity to Oneida religious discourse was that, in reintroducing the White Dog ceremony, Blacksmith felt compelled to explain it to the hundred or so Oneidas present in terms of Christian ritualism. According to Kirkland, he "informed his adherents that the eating the flesh of the roasted dog in that ancient rite was a transaction equally sacred & solemn with that which the Christians call the Lord's feast. The only difference is in the elements: the Christians use bread & wine, we use flesh & Broth." Blacksmith's explanation also suggests most Indians' this-worldly, traditional understanding of the efficacy of the Lord's Supper: "The Priest cuts a small piece & eats & by the assistance of his aids, the multitude are all served with a piece & profess themselves to be the dutiful subjects of the Upholder of the Skies, expecting to enjoy his protection and favor."[42] This privileging of Sapling made their faith more comparable to monotheistic Christianity, at the expense of the traditional wider pantheon of spirits.

Partition

In February 1802, roughly twenty Oneidas traveled to Albany in the company of Myndert Wemple to offer more land to the state. This delegation was led by the Christian party leaders Peter Bread and Martinus Rotshin. Although a petition was sent from the reservation signed by more than thirty Oneidas condemning Bread, Rotshin, and Jacob Doxtator for leasing land and selling timber to whites, the state did not pause the negotiations.[43] Instead, they worked out the details of yet another treaty, once again signed at the reservation in June. The Oneidas relinquished four thousand acres along Fish Creek and seven thousand acres south of the Genesee Road for nine hundred dollars and a three-hundred-dollar annuity. How did the state and its Oneida negotiating partners manage to win sufficient approval for the sale to permit its signing? Presumably support was generated by a sense of helplessness: Oneidas could take what was offered or risk getting nothing at all. In 1801, the Quaker schoolteacher John Dean noted, "There is a number of white people come on their land which they or some of them want off but cannot get them off." Dean also noted Chapin's indifference. The legislature granted members of the Denny family 320 acres along the Genesee Road after they complained that they were once again being run off their property. Cash payoffs helped win support as well. The New York surveyor general, Simeon DeWitt, distributed "donations" to individual Oneidas, including twenty dollars to John Skenandoah, twenty dollars to Jacob Doxtator, and one hundred dollars to Martinus. Presumably they used this money to gain the consent of others. The legislature also approved the sale of lands from the ceded territory to specific individuals for half their appraised value. Martinus Rotshin was granted 160 acres, and Honyost Onongsongetha and Isaac Shorewasken received 80 acres each. The first two were treaty signers; all three were Christian party members; Shorewasken was a student at Kirkland's academy. For his role in facilitating the transaction, Myndert Wemple was granted 100 acres for one hundred dollars.[44]

When DeWitt arrived at the Oneida reservation in January 1803 to distribute these "donations," the Oneidas refused to give up more land to provide for the Dennys. The 320 acres allotted to them would have to come from the cession. The Oneidas also told DeWitt that they wanted the legislature to order settlers to remove weirs and seines and dams that were obstructing the free passage of salmon up the Oswego River. In a strange way, the Oneidas could relate to the salmon's plight. As the state incorporated private companies to improve the principal road through the reservation, these companies erected tolls. Thus, the Oneidas had to request free passage for themselves as well. The Oneidas insisted that their surrender of land did not mean they had surrendered traditional prerogatives of fishing or movement.[45]

At least two members of the pagan party signed the 1802 treaty, but it was primarily a Christian party affair. In its wake, the pagan faction felt vulnerable. In addition to constituting a minority, they were keenly aware of the Christian party's ongoing efforts to deprive them of influence with the state. In 1802, Ann Mifflin, a Quaker visiting the pagans, reported, "The more corrupted majority [i.e., the Christian party] represented them to the New York government as Heathens because they did not embrace the forms of worship they were in." As one pagan put it in a speech in 1805, "Our party is small & could not do as we wish for the Christian party will not do the thing that is just for they think the title of Christian which they take upon themselves Screans them from Censure."[46] At the crux of the pagan minority's concern was the growing influence of a Frenchman, Angel de Ferrière, among the Christian party. A royalist exile from Niort, De Ferrière had married Polly Denny (fig. 7) and been adopted by the nation. The "head warriors" of the Christian party had agreed to allow De Ferrière "to take charge of their Mills" and one hundred acres of land. They did so over the objections of the pagans, who also accused Christian chiefs of misappropriating the federal annuity.[47]

In July, Kirkland observed that "the dispute" was "much increased between the Christian & pagan party." In mid-January, he reported, "A number of their Chiefs collected for farther conversation upon the situation of their affairs" determined "that a division of their Reserv[ation] should be made betwixt the Christian Indians & the pagans, or such as were for maintaining & preserving the traditions of the fathers, who sacrificed Animals & worshipped idols." The chiefs petitioned the state to secure a federal commissioner and assist them in the process, for which purpose two dozen Oneidas of both parties proceeded to Albany.[48] On March 21, 1805, twenty-five Oneidas signed an agreement to divide the reservation according to proportion of population. The Christian Party was assigned the Fish Creek reservation as well as the main reservation west of the Oneida Creek and north of a line parallel to the Genesee Road. The Pagan Party received a smaller tract south of the line. A hundred-acre tract passed out of the lands communally held by the nation when it was reserved for the Pagan chief Cornelius Doxtator and became his personal property. Angel de Ferrière witnessed the treaty. Despite their request to the governor that a federal commissioner be appointed, none was present, nor would one appear at any

Fig. 7. Polly de Ferrière (née Denny), portrait by Frederick R. Spencer, ca. 1850. Courtesy of the Madison County Historical Society, Oneida, N.Y.

subsequent treaty held under the auspices of the state. The 1805 partition turned the informal factions into legal entities with the power to alienate land.[49]

The Oneidas' Religious Era of Good Feelings

The names of the parties, and Kirkland's assertion that religious differences underlay the split, are misleading insofar as they suggest widening divisions in religious life. The Pagans sought to reconcile their beliefs and practices with those of Christianity. By 1807 Kirkland was able to say of the nativists,

"[They] have new modelled their mode of worship several times, they have adopted the Christian Sabbath, and were very zealous last summer to improve it, in pleasant weather. . . . They inculcate several moral precepts & social duties, & some almost in the very words of scripture." Kirkland added that the general religiosity of the Oneidas was gratifying "& affords a prospect of some happy fruit."[50]

The nativists countenanced such an engagement under the terms of a separatist theology that acknowledged that they shared with whites the same creator but emphasized that they were created for different purposes and with different strengths and weaknesses. Thus, missionaries had something to teach them about the creator but not necessarily about ways of life or worship. While they conceded a modicum of validity to Christianity, they used this relativism to demand at least an equal measure of respect in return. As Kirkland observed, some of the pagans argued "that no Christian minister . . . could prove that their traditionary system of morals & sacrifices was not equally adapted for the good of Indians & for their final happiness, as the Christian religion was for white people."[51]

Alcohol was understood in similar terms. During the spring of 1804, the Oneidas were again beset by a spike in the number of liquor-related difficulties. Young men of both parties had orchestrated the sale of large quantities of timber from the reservation to whites without tribal consent in exchange for liquor. This scandal was amplified by a brutal alcohol-related fratricide. When, in mid-March, a drunken Oneida made an attempt on the life of a white man, Pagan Peter told a mixed Indian-white audience, "I dont think it is right for the White people to give so much rum to the Indians when they know the weakness of Indians, & that they are not favored with that capacity, skill & resolution which some white people possess, who can make use of strong drink & do themselves no injury, neither disturb society." Lest any whites infer their superiority from such a statement, Pagan Peter observed: "If we Indians must bear this reproach of *loving Rum*, the White Man certainly *loves monney*. Which will deserve the heaviest punishment I presume not to determine." Indeed, Peter offered a fierce criticism of those who might conflate wealth—and race—with virtue: "The White Skin race as a body have become proud. . . . You glory in your riches, your great & commodious houses, your large fields & your abundance. You wear a white shirt & sometimes it is ruf[f]led. And you despise us Indians for our indigence, our poor huts, our scanty food, & our dirty shirts. . . . A foul spirit may be concealed on a body richly clothed & a pure heart may reside unseen

Fig. 8. *Indian Family* by Baroness Hyde de Neuville, 1807. This depiction of a woman (two views), man, and boy illustrates styles of dress that distinguished the subjects, who were very probably Oneidas, from their Euro-American neighbors. In addition to deerskin moccasins and leggings, they made use of European textiles but in distinctly Native American ways. Men continued to elongate and adorn their earlobes and wear scalplocks. Collection of The New-York Historical Society, accession no. 1953.215.

in another covered only with rags. God our Maker will judge right in respect to the worth of our souls, whatever complexion the bodies wear."[52] (See figs. 8 and 9 for contemporary representations of Oneidas by the French exile and noted watercolorist Anne-Marguerite Hyde de Neuville.)

Handsome Lake, the Seneca prophet whose doctrines were being disseminated at Oneida by Onondaga followers and others, reinforced the temperance message on similar grounds: "God . . . made Rum & made it for the white people, to be used as a medicine to strengthen them after labor." But Handsome Lake's opposition to the White Dog ceremony led some Oneidas to oppose him and "plead for the traditions of the fathers, as the only proper religion for Indians." Although his doctrines gained an au-

Fig. 9. *Mary . . . of the Oneida Tribe* by Baroness Hyde de Neuville, 1807. Collection of The New-York Historical Society, accession no. 1953.207

dience among Oneida pagans and even some Christians, they did not gain the following they enjoyed among the Senecas during this period.[53]

"Injuries and Villainies"

The partition of the reservation was followed by a period of reduced inter-party tension because land cessions were now contested among members of the same party rather than between the two parties. The land transactions that followed partition are further proof that the division had more to do with the territorial ambitions of the Christian Party patron Angel de Fer-rière and Pagan Party leader Cornelius Doxtator than any theological dis-putes. Both men claimed their rewards in 1807. Removing the pagans from the treaty process smoothed the way for De Ferrière to receive 744 acres along the turnpike from the Christian Party in a treaty signed in Albany in March. The state bought 780 acres, 400 of which it granted to De Ferrière. In October, Doxtator collected a thousand dollars by selling the 100 acres set aside to him in the partition. The buyer was the trader and land speculator Peter Smith, who had been so active in their land affairs a decade earlier.[54]

In February 1809, the Christian Party relinquished 7,500 acres on Fish Creek. They reserved the usufructuary right "of taking fish in the said river with spears and with hooks and lines and not otherwise," and those who wished to stay could do so indefinitely, provided they limited themselves to a 640-acre tract. They were to receive eleven hundred dollars and an annu-ity of 6 percent on two thousand dollars. More important were the personal benefits that accrued to particular individuals. The state paid cash to ten Oneidas "for their services in negotiating a treaty." Bounties of eighty dol-lars each were given to John Skenandoah, Jacob Doxtator, Lewis Denny, and Oneidas named Anthony and Christian. Sally Hanyost received fifty dollars, Paulus twenty dollars, and Nicholas Sharp ten dollars. In exchange for 300 acres, Abraham Van Eps wiped clean the personal debts of all Christian Party members.[55] De Ferrière's roadside holdings were expanded by another 400 acres by this treaty.

In a second treaty that month, this one with the Pagan Party, the state used the same tactic, which Governor Tompkins referred to as "secret ser-vice money." A receipt issued on the day of the treaty indicates the state made roughly equal personal payments totaling $340 to four Oneidas: Cap-tain Peter, Henry Plattkopf, Peter Thonarogeah, and Cornelius Doxtator. It also designates tracts for individual members of the party: Dolly Denny,

Logan Cook (son of Colonel Louis), and John Cornelius. The party as a whole received less than $2,000 in exchange for about twelve thousand acres. In both 1809 treaties, the Oneidas parted with their land for less than a fifth of the sum for which the state might resell it. The 1809 Pagan Party treaty was the beginning of the sale of Kanonwalohale itself. Historically, this was the most densely settled part of the reservation, and its sale revealed that the geographic distinction between the parties had never been absolute, even if the partition had been predicated on that assumption. Thus, although the partition had brought a brief respite in factional strife over land, the partition itself now fueled the dispute. The tracts granted to Dolly Denny and John Cornelius turned out to be on the Christian Party side of the division. The Pagan treaty had also ceded lands occupied by the Christian Jacob Doxtator and some of his Euro-American tenants. More than a dozen Oneidas (some Christian, others Pagan) later petitioned for compensation for their improvements on this land and complained they were "not privy to said purchase." According to a survey, they collectively claimed 241 acres of land, eighty apple trees, twelve houses, and six barns. The Christians claimed that Pagans had sold land belonging to members of their party, and subsequent surveys indicated that they had.[56]

In early 1810, members of the Christian and Pagan Parties petitioned the legislature separately but with a common message: respect their land rights. The Pagans warned the state, "Our Brothers the Christian Partie inclines to sell . . . a goar of Land belonging to them" that actually ran into the heart of the Pagan settlement. They also sounded an alarm about Cornelius Doxtator, who, they said

> has become acquainted with the Inglis tongue and thereby is enabled to be in a great degree usefull of hurtful to us & unhappily for us that he makes use of his acquirements for our disadvantage . . . to promote his own interest and when he has been instructed to conduct our business it has been to our disadvantage by his keeping to himself whatever he could get into his own hands and now appears to be disposed to sell timber contrary to the will of the nation and to acquire an undue proportion of our annuity and make diversion and tumults amongst the people.[57]

The Christian Party conveyed their grievances to the "many good men in Albany, who not knowing our distresses, will be willing to do us justice, when they shall know." The petition was signed, and doubtless influenced, by Rev. William Jenkins, who had replaced the ailing Kirkland in 1806, and who, according to the Northern Missionary Society reports, had extremely bad relations with some local whites because of his concern about the fleecing of his flock. The Oneidas' petition complained of "many injuries and villainies we have suffered, for many years, from Wicked White men . . . who are now as busy as ever, in trying to destroy us, and our property." By this time, there were nearly seventy non-Native families residing on the reservation among eight or nine hundred Oneidas. According to the petition, "They . . . bring some thousands of Cattle every summer, to eat up all our pasture, often also these Cattle brake our fences, and eat up all our wheat and corn, which we have wrought hard to sow and plant. . . . [Furthermore,] white men . . . sell our land, live in our houses, use our land, take our money, and clothes, eat our pastures by their Cattle, and our grain, and not we ourselves."[58]

Both parties inveighed against the post-1795 practice of Oneida delegations visiting Albany to negotiate away lands. The Pagan petition urged that any future land purchases be made exclusively "at a Council in the presents of our Nation." Negotiating treaties in situ would "better enable us to ascertain the boundarys of the Land to be sold & you to ascertain quality of the land." Then there was the problem of influence of the Euro-Americans who took them to the capital, and the officials there. The Christian Party lamented, "Those white men we have employed to get our rights supported, or our property to us have often deceived us." They named De Ferrière and Wemple and asked that the legislators "not hear them." Furthermore, they asked, "[Would you] like that we should buy the town of Albany, from a few of any White men, we could perswade to sell it. And we, then come and take it, whether you be willing or not[?]" The Christian Party concluded by reminding the legislators of their common humanity: "Although we know not your law, we feel when we are hurt, just like white men."[59]

One member of the Christian Party, Peter August, felt compelled to travel to Albany himself. He carried with him a letter of introduction from James Dean, who wrote that August was suffering "extream anxiety lest Martinus [Rotshin] & others . . . should sell his plantation from under him." Dean praised August as "an example of Industry, frugality, and Economy so rarely found in a Native Indian," adding: "He informs me that it is now nine years since he quit the Chace [hunting] & has taken to labour. He has now a handsome improvement made on his farm a comfortable House and a good framed Barn, and has a competent supply of the Necessaries of Life, for his family, consisting of his Wife & five children." Something of Dean's personal attitude toward the Oneidas can also be gleaned from his encounter with the Quaker Dorothy Ripley in 1805. She recalled that he said, "Few know an Indian's heart, but I do; and I think they are not of the same species which we are." Dean's contempt reflected, perhaps, his frustration with the Oneidas' inability to prevail over their social, economic, and political woes—in other words, not following Peter August's example. Ripley hinted, however, that Dean's contempt was a rationalization for his own relationship to those problems. She wrote, "I smiled with contempt at his opinion, . . . for as soon as I saw him, it passed through my mind, that he was not a suitable person to administer spiritual comfort; he might do to make treaties, and receive of their lands a reward, if they were disposed to trust him so far."[60]

Dean's "othering" of the Oneidas helps explain the need for the Christian Party's appeal to a common humanity. It also helps explain why both petitions were apparently ignored. When a group of Oneidas arrived in Albany in February 1810, the Senate and Assembly jointly resolved that the governor "make such contract with the Agents of the Christian Party of the Oneida Nation of Indians now in this City for the purchase of a part of the Reservation belonging to the said Christian party of that nation on such terms as he shall judge advantageous to the state." "Advantageous to the state" would be a good description of the treaty that was signed on March 3. In exchange for $800 and a $257 annuity, the Oneidas ceded the last of their property on the south shore of Oneida Lake. The treaty granted 8,441 acres directly to the state, some of it already dotted with squatters. This acreage included the gore that the Pagans had pleaded not be taken. The treaty was also advantageous to De Ferrière: he received 200 acres. Most of the thirty-eight signers of the March treaty had not signed the February petition, although at least six—including Peter August—had. The legislature had probably secured his acquiescence by sparing his land, which was very close to, but not included in, the cession. Another treaty signatory was De Ferrière's father-in-law, Lewis Denny. According to the state senator and soon-to-be governor DeWitt Clinton, who visited the reservation in 1810, Denny was "quite proud of his opulent son-in-law." Clinton observed that the Frenchman owned "1700 acres of the best land—a great deal of it on the turnpike—[a] tavern . . . , a large two-story house, grist mill and saw mill on the creek, and distillery, and is supposed to be worth $50,000."[61]

On his visit, Clinton also reported seeing "Indians plowing with oxen, and at the same time their heads ornamented with white feathers; some driving a wagon, and the women milking and churning,—all the indications of incipient civilization." By 1810, individual Oneidas of both parties had been disabused of earlier expectations about the sustainability of their land base, natural resources, and way of life, in a landscape transformed by Euro-American settlers. Some began to make the adjustments the new reality apparently demanded: while women continued their horticultural activity and looked after small animals, some men took up large-animal husbandry and agricultural fieldwork. The men donned traditional headgear to put to rest any confusion about their race—or their gender. Clinton acknowledged the Oneidas' conservatism in his comment that they had "hitherto been opposed" to the cultivation of wheat rather than corn, and his observation that most remained committed to communal land ownership. But the Quaker missionary's platitude years earlier about his "labours . . . [not] lost or time spent in vain" had not proven entirely hollow after all.[62]

The Shadow of War

Almost precisely one year later, members of the Christian Party at Albany ceded 3,600 acres lying between the 1810 cession and Oneida Creek in exchange for $400 and a very modest annuity.[63] Just as in the early 1790s, however, the pressure on the Oneidas eased somewhat as new military conflicts were brewing in the Old Northwest and larger concerns took to the fore. The first matter at hand was the proposed removal of the Stockbridge and Brothertown Indians to Indiana Territory. Through the efforts of Capt. Hendrick Aupaumut, a Stockbridge Indian, they had secured an invitation from Delawares and Mahicans living there. State and federal policy makers alike hoped that in addition to reducing the Native population of New York, the proposed emigration would temper the sentiment of resistance from which Tecumseh's War had erupted. In April 1811, Governor Tompkins asked his attorney general whether the Oneidas still retained underlying title to the lands of the Stockbridge and Brothertown Indians. Although the opinion is not extant, the governor broke recent precedent and traveled to the Oneida reservation in July. There, he treated with the Oneida nation as a whole to purchase a quitclaim to all lands occupied by the Stockbridge and Brothertown Indians.[64]

Tompkins was moved by the plight of the Indians. Confronted with the reality of reservation life, he acknowledged the Oneidas' grievances in strong and personal terms. He wrote of cases that "come under my own observation" that "excited my sympathy for the persecuted individuals of that nation, who had been violently expelled from their huts, gardens & planta-tions by white people." In his 1812 annual address to the legislature, Tompkins called for new laws that would expedite the ejectment of "worth-less and unprincipled white persons, availing themselves of the ignorance of the Indians . . . [who] wantonly and boldly violate their individual posses-sions and national domain." Existing laws offered too many opportunities for delay and were generally ignored. As the federal Indian agent Erastus Granger had noted to Secretary of War Dearborn, "There exists in the minds of many white people a strong prejudice against Indians—they want to root them out of the Country, as they own the best of their land.—Those people are often on juries."[65]

Tompkins also heeded the complaints of the 1810 petitioners about treaty venues. In 1813, when a Christian Party delegation arrived in Albany offer-ing lands adjacent to the Stockbridge tract, Tompkins rebuffed them "on account of the dissatisfaction" attending previous transactions. He asserted that "all treaties for future purchases of lands would be made with a full council at some convenient place on the reservation." While the legislature gave Tompkins authority to treat with Oneidas, it also finally acted on the Pagans' concerns by giving them "exclusive use and occupation" of the dis-puted gore, and ordered it be kept free of intruders.[66]

The War of 1812 offered a brief hiatus in the Oneidas' dispossession. But whereas in the past the Iroquois had seized on rivalries among European powers to enhance their standing with both sides, now they were simply caught in the middle. The possibility of halting the westward expansion of the United States or of resurrecting the play-off system had dwindled to a nullity. Although the Iroquois confederacy was enjoying something of a po-litical revival in the wake of the spiritual one led by Handsome Lake, when sachems from the various Iroquois nations met to discuss the prospect of war, they were united in approaching it only as an opportunity to improve their standing with the United States—and hence (they hoped) their con-trol over their remaining lands. Official Iroquois rhetoric toward the United States took on an ingratiating quality. In proposing an alliance, they told President Madison, "We are few in number, and can do but little, but our hearts are good."[67]

In courting potential Iroquois allies, the Americans followed closely the pattern of the early years of the Revolution. The United States called only for Iroquois neutrality and embarked on a vituperative propaganda campaign that touted purported atrocities by Indian warriors in Britain's service. This rhetoric of British race treason had lost none of its effectiveness as a means of mobilizing American soldiers and sentiment since the Revolutionary War days of the martyred Jane McCrea. Hence the text of a broadside printed in 1812: "You have seen Indians, such as those hired by the British, to murder women and children, and kill and scalp the wounded. You have seen their dances and grimaces, and heard their yells. Can you fear *them?* No. You hold them in the utmost contempt." (As for the Euro-American population of Canada, the broadside assured U.S. volunteers, "Your weapons are longer.")[68]

The Oneida sachems went along with the other Iroquois nations in accepting neutrality. As long as the conflict stayed out of their territory, their interest in it was limited. But it is clear that the majority of Oneidas favored participation. Just as the sachems were charged by their offices to promote peace as long as circumstances permitted, the exigencies of traditional Iroquois masculinity continued to dictate that other men did not share that pacifism. Game depletion and the impossibility of pursuing intertribal wars in the midst of white settlements meant that by 1813 several generations of men who conceived of themselves as warrior-hunters had been thwarted in demonstrating their prowess. This pressure cut across the political spectrum, causing concern among the elders of both factions, as well as American officials. By September 1812, the secretary of war assented to Iroquois recruitment after Granger informed him that "the young men of the Six Nations [could] no longer be restrained, and that in case of the refusal on the part of the United States to accept their services they would join the Indians under the British standard."[69]

Handsome Lake went to Onondaga and met with Oneidas, Onondagas, Stockbridges, and Tuscaroras to urge their nonparticipation. He advised those present to embrace pacifism and European-style agriculture. But the council's ambivalent communiqué to the president bespoke the contrary pressures within the Indian communities. The council claimed it was "much surprised and disappointed . . . at being invited to take up the Tomahawk." Yet in the same breath they acknowledged the American claim that, "their chiefs" were "unable to restrain their warriors," adding, "Their young men are clamorous to be employed." With neutralism at risk, they demonstrated a prudent concern to avoid alienating the United States: "We are anxious to know your wishes respecting us as soon as possible because some of our young are uneasy, and we fear they may disperse among different Tribes and be hostile to you."[70]

Warriors remained largely inactive only in those communities where Handsome Lake's ideology had been most deeply imbibed, the Seneca reservations at Allegany and Tonawanda. Among the Oneidas, where Handsome Lake's code had received only belated acceptance and was always subject to local interpretation, few were deterred from going to war. As many as two hundred Oneidas were recruited at their reservation in early June 1813 to the Indian Volunteers regiment at Niagara. They served in companies led by Indians, including Oneidas Adam Skenandoah, Jake Antoine, and Pagan Peter (a.k.a. Peter Elm). Farmer's Brother, a Seneca, was the battalion colonel until he was replaced by Granger the following year. It would be the last time the Iroquois would fight in autonomous units under Iroquois leadership.[71]

Extant Oneida war-claims records provide only the barest facts about their subjects. The wide swath of Oneidas represented, as well as the total number of Oneidas engaged, suggests, however, that they went forward with the active support of the majority of the nation. Men of both parties participated. The twelve Oneidas whose pension documents survive were of both sexes and ranged widely in age. Though Oneida warriors as young as fifteen were present, the youngest warrior recruit listed was twenty-two years old. But without a doubt the oldest Oneida fighter was the Revolutionary War veteran Cornelius Sagoyountha, who was about eighty. It was not unprecedented for fit Iroquois elders to go to war, since their culture valued the contributions of the aged particularly highly.[72] Two of the twelve identifiable veterans were women who were engaged as cooks. Interestingly, one of them was named Polly Cooper, suggesting that either tribal oral traditions regarding her name have conflated the Revolution and the War of 1812 or this Polly Cooper was following closely in the footsteps of her namesake. Clearly, one measure of the Oneidas' accommodation to European ways of war was the adoption of camp following. In this way, Iroquois women extended their traditional role supporting war efforts through provisioning into a new context.

The largest contingent of Oneidas—in excess of a hundred—reached Upper Canada in late September or early October, by which time some Oneidas had already seen action near Fort Erie under Gen. Peter B. Porter. Porter had encouraged his Indian allies with promises that they could keep whatever cattle they could seize. For the Indians, the importance of capturing the enemy's animals was undiminished from the 1760s. But although Porter was correct in his assumption that the promise of plunder would sharpen the warriors' zeal, he miscalculated the views of his superiors. Thus, fourteen Oneida warriors were forced to return nineteen horses, a significant loss for them that was compounded by the death of two Oneidas in a September skirmish at Ball's Farm. And to this indignity was added the nonpayment of bounties and annuities promised them. The Seneca Red Jacket complained that the Americans merely "trifled with" their Iroquois allies.[73]

Nevertheless, if the large numbers of Oneidas who served the United States the following year are any indication, the Americans' disregard did not dampen the Oneidas' willingness to aid them. In May 1814, more than 80 Oneidas and a similar number of U.S. riflemen defended a convoy of American boats en route to Sacket's Harbor. Their spirited and successful action at the Battle of Sandy Creek cost one Oneida warrior his life and nineteen British soldiers theirs. In the wake of the defeat, the British gave up their siege of Sacket's Harbor, allowing the United States to maintain a strong position on Lake Ontario. Shortly thereafter, the Oneidas contributed up to 150 warriors and 20 women to the force of 500 Indians that accompanied a 5,000-soldier U.S. invasion of Canada in early July under Maj.-Gen. Jacob Brown. Although the force captured Fort Erie with ease, the British and their Indian allies, including Iroquois, proceeded to Chippawa to meet the American invasion. The engagement that followed took a heavy toll on the New York Indians: they reported 10 missing, 4 wounded, and between 9 and 12 dead. These included Cornelius Doxtator, who was reportedly tomahawked by an Ojibwe warrior who had seized Doxtator's two sons before being tomahawked himself by Oneida warriors who freed the boys. The Grand River Iroquois suffered far more mightily. The British Inspector-General's Office recorded 87 Grand River Iroquois casualties from the 300 who fought on their side.[74] It was the bloodiest and most extensive Iroquois-versus-Iroquois engagement since the Battle of Oriskany and, like Oriskany, it quickly sapped the Iroquois' desire to fight.

The wounds—physical and emotional—inflicted at the Battle of Chippawa resulted in a rapid decline in Iroquois participation on both sides of the conflict. Porter tried but failed to rally the warriors to reject the policies of reascendant peace chiefs. Many warriors were in fact already en route home.[75] Traditional Iroquois warfare abhorred casualties because Iroquois communities were small. Indeed, prudence figured prominently in Iroquois calculations of valor, and Iroquois belief predicted a troubled afterlife for those killed in battle. After Chippawa, there was simply too much to mourn. Two pro-American Senecas on a mission to exchange prisoners with some of their Grand River counterparts expressed the deep regret that persisted on both sides that they were "brought to fight" against their "Relatives and friends."[76] The realities of the Iroquois' nineteenth-century situation precluded the possibility of their seeking revenge against whites, which they had done with some success during the Revolution. For the Iroquois, the War of 1812 had ended.

Although Britain did not repeat its ignominious 1783 neglect of Indian interests at the 1814 treaty negotiations in Ghent, it settled for an American pledge to desist from punishing Crown-allied tribes that chose to remain within U.S. borders. This promise was enshrined in Article 9 of the treaty, but it was unenforceable and ultimately ignored.[77] Exactly as American war hawks had fervently and confidently hoped, the war broke the back of Indian military resistance east of the Mississippi. The borders of U.S. settlement once again jumped west, this time along the expanse from the Great Lakes to the Gulf of Mexico. Indiana, Illinois, Mississippi, and Alabama all achieved statehood between 1816 and 1819. The newly secured West became a destination for hundreds of thousands of U.S. citizens, and its peripheries quickly came to be seen by some as places to which Indians occupying desirable territory could be relocated.

In early 1795, the Oneidas had had reason to hope that they would be permitted to enjoy what lands remained to them. After all, the federal government had pledged its protection, and of their ancestral six million acres, they had relinquished all but a quarter-million of them. In itself, this diminution forced the Oneidas to undertake significant cultural and economic changes, which they pursued incrementally in a way that was simultaneously conservative and creative. These changes, however, did little to reduce the Oneidas' ongoing susceptibility to land loss. Pausing only for a war, the state facilitated land sales by recognizing unauthorized delegations, conducting negotiations in Albany, offering clandestine payments, and rewarding local whites who enjoyed the trust of at least some Oneidas, and who used that trust to urge cessions. Oneida land remained attractive to New Yorkers because of its productive capacity, but also because of its location.

The Oneida heartland was situated along the most direct level route between the Mohawk River and Lake Erie. And although Philip Schuyler's
navigation scheme never quite lived up to expectations, its successor would:
the Erie Canal. The canal would raise the economic value of all Oneida
land to new heights. This development stoked renewed demands for a radical solution: the Oneidas' outright removal.

6

The Nation in Fragments

Oneida Removal, 1815–1836

THE STORY OF the removal of Indians from the Southern states is well-known, since it involved relatively large tribes and exacerbated the sectional tensions that eventually set off the Civil War. There was, however, considerable irony in Northerners' loud denunciations of Southern removal, because they had pioneered the enterprise. When the Treaty of Butte des Morts, involving the Menominee and Ojibwe nations, was before the U.S. Senate during the winter of 1828–29, language supporting the emigration of the Iroquois to Michigan Territory was inserted at the behest of land speculators from New York, recently dubbed the "Empire State." Those with a direct hand in Oneida removal included the Michigan territorial governor Lewis Cass, a New Englander who went on to become Andrew Jackson's secretary of war. Cass's experience with the Iroquois helped frame his arguments for removal and informed his later activities.[1]

The postwar years witnessed another upsurge in white immigration to central New York and pressure on the Oneidas to sell. In February 1814, twenty-six "chiefs and warriors" of the Christian Party warned the legislature that a delegation was en route to Albany. Among the signers was John Skenandoah, James Bread (briefly an influential chief before his untimely death later that year), and Peter Bread. In particular, they asked the government "not to pay any attention to the Petition of Angle DeFerier who has been in the habit of taking down Indians for the Express Purpose of cheating them out of their Land [because] as soon as the said Deferier gets our land he treats us with all the cruelty in his Power." A statement of support by "the wives and widows of the chiefs" accompanied the document. In June 1815, however, New York abandoned its policy against treaty making in Albany and consummated the deal. As the military threat dissipated, so did lawmakers' scruples; in the treaty, De Ferrière was even granted another fifty roadside acres. The Christian Party relinquished twelve hundred acres in four tracts, mostly along the turnpike. The one dollar an acre they received did not reflect even a tenth of the land's appraised value, let alone the symbolic value of the treaty's greatest prize, most of the remainder of Kanonwalohale. Indeed, the state thought the location at the confluence of Oneida and Skanado Creeks so propitious that it called in the surveyor John Randel Jr., who also laid out the grid of Manhattan Island, to divide "Oneida Castleton" into town lots.[2]

Digging In

By the summer of 1817, construction of the Erie Canal was under way. The location of the groundbreaking ceremony was none other than the town of Rome, on the Oneida Carrying Place. The Oneidas' blessing had become their curse. For centuries they had capitalized on the strategic significance of their territory, but this now only hastened efforts to dispossess them. Even if the Oneidas had already lost the lands through which the canal was being carved, the proximity of their remaining territory to "the great ditch" (and hence to vast new markets) put a premium on all reservation land. As one surveyor noted, the land "owned by the Indians which will soon become State property will be trebled in value."[3]

The demographic tide had turned against the Oneidas long before, but in the Canal Era they were truly swamped on the reservation itself. The population of the state had more than doubled since the beginning of the century, and non-Indians spilled onto the reservation with impunity. In 1816 the Oneida population was 1,031 and rose by about 100 over the next decade; by contrast, the combined non-Indian population of Oneida and Madison Counties rose from 70,000 to more than 95,000 between 1814 and 1825. The increase in overall population further inflated land values and added yet more luster to the usual glowing descriptions of Oneida land. A man traveling to Utica (to catch the canal boat *Oneida Chief*) described it as "a country so luxuriant as to require little labour to obtain all the necessaries of life." According to the Albany publisher Thurlow Weed, "none more fertile were to be found in the State."[4]

Less glowing were the descriptions of relations between Indians and whites in the neighborhood. In 1819, a downstate legislator, Abraham Haring, reported the results of the investigations made by his committee in response to Indian complaints. "The facts pretty conclusively show," he wrote,

> that they are incapable of protecting themselves, in consequence of being surrounded by the whites, and who have usurped nearly all of their possessions, and from thence pilfer every stick and stone which can be converted into money, highly injurious to the interests of the state; who frequently pilfer the personal effects of those unfortunate beings; that they are overreached by the aid of ardent spirits, and after illegally obtaining the possession of those lands, refuse to yield the possession; and when prosecuted, delay the trial until either the wants of the owner, or legislative provisions compel them to abandon justice and their rights; that most of those invaders are of the most abandoned cast . . . ; that hunger and cold have, in conjunction with spirits, deprived them of their young men, the hopes of their nation, and laid nearly all of them in the dust, while the whites raise themselves upon their ruin.

Haring's committee recommended the consolidation of different tribes on a single reservation, where they could more easily be protected and reformed.[5]

Surprisingly, the Oneidas' white neighbors also found cause for complaint in the situation. They considered it unfair that their counties should bear the expense of enforcing trespass laws. In a petition to the state legislators, the supervisors of Oneida County argued that "a settlement or residence on Indian land is not an offence against good morals nor does it militate against the general good. It is simply an infringement against the rights of Indians as declared by laws." The supervisors suggested the Indians had permitted many of these trespasses to take place and brought frivolous complaints in order to benefit from state support for indigent witnesses. Contesting Haring's characterization of the trespassers as persons "of the most abandoned cast"—a description echoed by most federal officials and missionaries—the supervisors described their constituents as "Farmers & a blessing to the Indians." Haring and the supervisors agreed about the scale of the problem, though the supervisors estimated that the trespassers on Oneida, Stockbridge, and Brothertown lands amounted to "about three Hundred families of white People, besides Negroes & mulattoes—the whole number . . . liable to be indicted is very little short of a thousand."[6] The Oneidas were quickly being relegated to a minority on their own reservation, and hopes for a remedy were dimming fast.

De Ferrière devised one further means of placing Oneidas in distress in the pursuit of profit. In 1819, he took six Oneida men (including the octogenarian veteran Cornelius Sagoyountha) and two women to France, where he abandoned four of them in the interior. Their purpose was to perform

Fig. 10. Oneidas in Paris, 1819. If accurate, the garb depicted here was likely to have been of French manufacture. Cornelius Sagoyountha would presumably be the man at left. He was described elsewhere as "a short, heavy man, thick neck, broad shoulders." He appears to be holding a water drum. Courtesy of the Bibliothèque Nationale de France, Paris.

various ceremonies and dances in theaters (fig. 10). At the outset, De Ferrière and Sagoyountha were probably inspired by the troupe of Senecas who went to Great Britain in 1818 and an Oneida quartet that went to London in early 1819. (According to an advertisement, the Oneidas were to take the stage at London's Royal Circus and Surrey Theatre between a romance, *The Heart of Midlothian,* and a brief comic opera, *Rather Too Bad.*)[7] The presence of these Natives in Europe contributed to an expanding transatlantic network of entertainment that included drama and exhibitions of animals and other natural curiosities and spectacles, but we know of the Oneidas' tour mostly through the documentation of its failure. While audiences were sufficiently large to cover their daily expenses, De Ferrière claimed not to have made enough money to send them back when they desired.

The stranded Oneidas eventually appealed to the U.S. consul in Paris, Albert Gallatin. In an effort to compel De Ferrière to pay for their return, Gallatin had him brought before a justice of the peace in Paris. To expedite the Oneidas' return, Gallatin reluctantly paid for some mattresses, ten pounds of tobacco, lodging for them at a port, and their passage to the United States. He sent De Ferrière the bill. Sagoyountha took ill between Paris and Havre but recovered (and lived until 1832) and the entire group was back at the Oneida reservation by the end of the year. De Ferrière may or may not have repaid Gallatin. He never received another grant of land from the Oneidas.[8]

Ominous Chatter

Faced with the challenge of supporting a slowly expanding population in a rapidly shrinking area, a minority of Oneidas came to accept relocation as their only real option. The war had intensified inter-Iroquois relations, and now some Oneidas considered seeking refuge from white settlers by moving in with the Senecas at Tonawanda and Buffalo Creek—more or less what Haring's committee had in mind. Though no specific plans were ever made or implemented, the idea of their moving in with the Senecas never went beyond discussion. The mere fact that discussion occurred provoked an angry reaction from the Ogden Land Company, which had purchased the right to buy Seneca land. (To get Massachusetts to drop its claim to Iroquois land, New York granted the Bay State the preemption right to six million acres in Seneca country. Massachusetts quickly converted this land into cash by selling its right to private interests for three hundred thousand Massachusetts pounds.) The company insisted that its rights barred the Senecas from making any such invitation to the Oneidas and stepped up its promotion of plans to remove the Iroquois as a whole to some distant western location. Although Oneida territory lay outside the Ogden Company's preemption, the Oneidas nevertheless became crucial to the Ogden strategy. Smaller and more vulnerable than the Senecas, the Oneidas could also acquire western lands in the name of the Six Nations or even all New York Indians. This combination made them an ideal wedge in effecting a more general removal of Natives from New York State.[9]

The governor threw his weight behind the removal idea in a letter to the president in 1815. Secretary of War Alexander Dallas responded favorably, but cautiously, to the governor, reminding him, "All transactions with the Indians, relative to their lands, are more or less, delicate, and a removal of them from one region to another, is critically so, as relates to the effect on the Indians themselves, and on the white neighbors to their new abode."[10] The federal government was hesitant to get in the middle of a dispute between its citizens in the east and west. First let the New Yorkers find a spot to which all parties might agree.

During the three years that followed, the Ogden Company, working with the federal Indian agents Jasper Parrish and Erastus Granger, quietly explored the options. They gave serious attention to lands where a party of Stockbridges were planning to relocate along the White River in Indiana. Cass admonished Ogden in 1818, however, that "the extinguishment of its Indian title & consequent sale, are anxiously wished for in that State." Indeed, the White River lands under consideration were ceded to the United States by the Miamis and Delawares that October, leaving as many as seventy-five Stockbridges who had begun to move there destitute and adrift. The Ogdens' attention then shifted to the Arkansas River, and they arranged a meeting between an unidentified Oneida and a Cherokee chief in Washington. But most Iroquois recoiled at the very thought because they believed that a removal to the Arkansas would cause them to "die with fevers & other diseases of the Southern climate." Returning to the map, the Ogdens suggested the Fox River in Michigan Territory.[11]

The Ogdens acknowledged the lack of support for removal among the Oneidas or Senecas. As plans took form, David Ogden counseled Parrish that "it might not be prudent to exhibit too strongly our desire to obtain the object we have in view." The company's lawyer, Robert Troup, similarly advised his clients "to lie perfectly still and to make no appearance whatever" at an upcoming Six Nations conference. He told them to "leave everything entirely in the hands of the Agents of the General Government; in full confidence that the Agents will do everything in their power, according to their instructions from the Government, to induce the Indians to *accept* of a *grant* of land *to the west*."[12]

For most of the Oneidas, ties to their ancestral homeland remained strong and gave strength to their resistance. The Oneidas may have lost the majority of their territory to non-Indians, but abandoning it entirely by moving to a distant land was to them something different still. From the whites' perspective the distinction between sale and abandonment may have been fine or even nonexistent, but from the Natives' it was neither. Earlier treaties had reserved Oneidas' rights to hunt and fish on ceded lands, and they continued to visit sacred places. Nearly all Oneidas remained committed to resisting the threat of the ever-rising tide of white occupation to wash them away, even though non-Indians had already, to use George Clinton's apt metaphor, "drowned" the Oneidas' lands by transforming the landscape and submerging many of its stories. As one Oneida put it: "We are determined that our bones shall be laid with those of our forefathers in the same spot of earth, which is rendered more dear to us by being mingled with their dust." While traveling a few years earlier, in 1815, Yale president Timothy Dwight recorded an Oneida origin story that bound the Indians even more closely to their homeland. The Oneidas, he noted, "pretend . . . to point out the place where their ancestors emerged from the ground."[13]

By late 1818, talk about removal increased, and it was even suggested that this removal might be coerced. Such rumors were certainly not dampened when Governor DeWitt Clinton (fig. 11) in an address to the legislature that year offered his approval of the emigration of New York Indians "to an extensive territory remote from white population."[14] Such talk emboldened local whites to step up their harassment of members of the Oneida nation to sell them land and increased pressure on individual Oneidas to sell quickly so that they might receive whatever pittance they could for their lands. Thirty-two eminent Oneidas, including the Pagan Cornelius Sagoyountha and Christians Peter Bread and Paul Powlis, petitioned the New York State Legislature and the president of the United States to back off. They complained of the efforts of "sundry individuals to poison the minds of your children [i.e., the Natives], and to make them discontented with their present residence and desirous of removal to the west." Such activities had "become the cause of much uneasiness and the source of many quarrels between the individuals of the nation." The petitioners repudiated any previous communications that might have left an impression that they wished to emigrate to the West. Invoking their Revolutionary War service, the Oneidas asked the president to remember "the obligations we humbly conceive the american people are under to this nation." He should therefore "not permit any steps to be taken for our immediate removal without our full and explicit assent to that effect. And also that no person be importuning us on that subject."[15]

The Apostle of Removal

The Mohawk catechist Eleazer Williams (fig. 12) never personally succeeded in convincing more than a small minority of Oneidas that it was in their interest to leave New York. But his handful of supporters provided the removal enterprise with a veneer of credibility in the eyes of whites that, however thin, was sufficient, along with Williams's extraordinary political machinations,

Fig. 11. DeWitt Clinton, portrait by George Catlin, 1827. Catlin, a celebrated portraitist of Native American chiefs, also painted prominent Euro-Americans. His portrait of Clinton celebrates the Erie Canal's contribution to westward expansion. Photograph by Glenn Castellano. Collection of the City of New York. Courtesy of the Design Commission.

to initiate a cycle of events that progressively undermined the ability of Oneidas to resist removal and initiated another, deeper fragmentation.

Kirkland's successor, Rev. William Jenkins, did not speak the Oneida language. He had an interpreter, but members of the Christian Party expressed

Fig. 12. Eleazer Williams, portrait by George Catlin, 1836. Courtesy of the Wisconsin Historical Society, WHi-3021.

dissatisfaction with him, complaining that the language barrier compromised their educational prospects and the singing that was at the center of their spiritual practice. In their appeal for a new missionary, the Oneidas noted, "Altho, they can sing now very well, . . . they wish to learn new tunes." A mixed-blood Kahnawake Mohawk, Williams was well prepared to replace Jenkins. His Indian kinship ties at both Kahnawake and St. Regis facilitated relations with the pagans. Williams and his father, Thomas, had been political allies of Col. Louis Cook, who maintained close contacts with the Oneida Pagan Party until his death in the War of 1812. Thomas and Eleazer Williams and Colonel Louis had all taken the American side in the recent conflict and had actively lobbied their Iroquois brethren to do so as well.[16]

Just as Williams's kinship ties helped him gain privileged entry into the Oneida nation, his kinship ties to white society yielded unusual opportunities there. Williams was the great-grandson of Eunice Williams, the renowned "unredeemed captive" taken during the 1704 French and Indian raid on Deerfield, Massachusetts. Eunice joined the Kahnawake Mohawks and refused to return to Euro-American society. Generations later, the white Williamses remained eager to reclaim Eunice's descendants to compensate for their famous inability to reclaim the woman herself.[17] With young Eleazer they were more successful. During his education among Massachusetts Congregationalists, he came to aspire to the ministry, although his later life suggests its principal attraction may not have been a calling from God but the status it conferred in white society.[18] Grandson of Eunice or not, as an Indian he had been denied high status by Euro-Americans during all his years among them. Indeed, though Eleazer found these elite Congregationalists willing to educate a young Indian man, he found them less inclined to ordain one. When his ministerial aspirations were thwarted by the indifference of his sponsors, Eleazer moved on to the Episcopal Church, under whose auspices he went to St. Regis and then to the Oneida reservation.

Williams's arrival among the Oneidas in 1816 helped revitalize worship among the Christian Party. Jacob Cornelius, an Oneida who would have been in his teens at the time, later recalled Williams's oratorical excellence. Williams had arrived at a portentous moment, amid literally darkening skies. The harvest of 1816 failed as a result of the massive eruption of Mount Tambora in the Indonesian archipelago. Ash in the upper atmosphere created the "year without a summer" across the northern hemisphere. Snow fell that June in upstate New York. Indeed, Williams's Oneida name, "Sky has been crossed," perhaps referred to the circumstance of his arrival.[19] This was also the year in which John Skenandoah died. Coveting the old chief's reputation and his relatively comfortable house, Williams acquired the latter and, he hoped, a little bit of the former with it. The Oneida church experienced a resurgence much like that which took place under Kirkland after the Revolution.

Williams's most notable accomplishment—one that he accomplished by trading on his kinship ties—was to widen the circle of self-professed Christians to include most of the Pagan Party. The most elderly members of the Pagan Party probably saw Williams as the heir to the Anglican mission undertaken during the middle decades of the previous century. That mission was supported by Sir William Johnson and well received by the sachems' faction of which the Pagan Party was a political descendant.[20] Williams's connection with Colonel Louis was doubtless also an important credential in the minds of the pagans. But even when Williams was at the zenith of his influence, his forging of religious unity among the Oneidas could not erase intratribal political antagonisms. Rather than join the ranks of the Christian Party, Williams's Pagan Party converts remained distinct, and became known as the "Second Christian Party."

The gap between the beliefs of Christian Oneidas and those of a more traditional religious bent had already narrowed considerably, as earlier chapters demonstrate. Members of the Pagan Party were familiar with Christian doctrine and had incorporated Christian motifs into their own worship. Ritual retained its place of prominence as a middle ground between indigenous religion and Christianity and Williams was keenly attuned to manipulating its possibilities. Williams had spent his early years (as well as the most recent ones) in Mohawk Catholic mission communities, and he was now serving in the Episcopal Church. The Catholics and the Episcopalians practiced more richly ritualistic variants of Christianity than had been available to the Oneidas for some time. As the ostensible supervisor of the Oneidas' education, Williams translated hymns and emphasized singing instruction even at the expense of literacy. Syncretism was evident in the sounds and sights a visitor to Williams's church described by in 1821: "The squaws sing delightfully & on Sundays dress in neat white short gowns fastened on the bosom with a broach. They wear no hats but throw their square cloth shawls which are fantastically ornamented with ribbons over their heads." In 1826, when the Quaker Thomas Shillitoe heard them, he had, he said, "not a doubt remaining in my mind (although I could not understand a word, it being in the Indian language) but that many of them felt the awful import of the words they uttered. The women appeared to take the most active part, the melodious sound, with the frequent gradual rise and fall of their voices, equalled in melody and solemnity any thing of the kind which I had before been a witness to."[21]

The treaty of 1817 was an early indication of Williams's impact on the Oneidas' land affairs. The state was used to working with him. He had visited Albany with his father in 1814 and 1815 at state expense, and New York contributed two hundred dollars to Thomas and Eleazer's tour to the "Senecas and other nations of western Indians" shortly after the peace treaty was signed. In 1816, Williams spent at least two weeks in Albany doing business involving the Oneidas and helping to orchestrate a land cession by the St. Regis Mohawks. Famine likely played a role in the St. Regis and Oneida treaties. The loss of the previous year's crop was still being felt in 1817, and to compound the loss, the Oneidas never received the pay they were promised for their wartime services. Speaking of the Iroquois as a whole, the federal agent Erastus Granger reported: "The situation of the Indians is truly deplorable. They have exerted themselves for the past year in trying to raise crops, but have failed in their expectations. . . . Their hunting ground is gone. . . . They are in fact in a state of starvation." On February 12, 1817, the legislature passed the "Act for the Relief of the St. Regis, Oneida, Onondaga, and Seneca Indians," which authorized disbursement of the annuity before its normal date of payment in early June.[22]

With Williams's help, New York came to terms with the Second Christian Party for 4126½ acres. The Oneidas were able to ransom the gore of which the Pagans had complained since 1810, but only at a cost of two acres for every one that was returned. Six hundred acres were given up to defray the cost of building a new church for Williams.[23] One hundred fifty acres were granted to Williams himself and two other non-Oneidas received grants of 50 acres. Abraham, John, Dolly, and Sally Denny were granted 450 acres in severalty. The Denny family had again demonstrated their acculturation and willingness to use their knowledge for private gain. Indeed, John received a $20 bounty payment from a state agent in July; Williams received $12.50 a few weeks earlier. These were probably secret "douceurs" for assistance in securing the treaty. After all the grants, only 1,470 acres were left for which the state had to pay, which it did at a rate of only $2 an acre. This rate was far less than the roughly $9 an acre that the surveyor who appraised the tract thought they could be sold by the state. All told, the Oneidas received about one-ninth the estimated value of the land.[24]

The Imperial Dream

The success Williams achieved in proselytizing the Oneidas may have been great, but the scale of his ambitions exceeded the conversion of any single tribe. He soon turned his attention to grander pursuits. DeWitt Clinton noted perceptively of Williams that "he aims at the same ascendancy among the Christian that the Shawanese prophet [i.e., Tenskwatawa, brother of Tecumseh] attained among the Pagan Indians."[25] But even Clinton's assessment fell short of the mark. Tenskwatawa merely preached intertribal cooperation. Williams aspired to multitribal removal and territorial consolidation under his personal direction. Williams's interest in Oneida removal was profoundly personal. He demonstrated a lifelong quest for admiration by whites that culminated in his amazing claim late in life that he was none other than the Lost Dauphin of France, Louis XVII. During the 1820s, Williams's involvement with Indian removal gave him entry into the highest ecclesiastical and political circles of white society. He worked with Bishop John Henry Hobart, Secretary of War John C. Calhoun, and President James Monroe. Rev. Jedidiah Morse, now a famed geographer, consulted Williams on an idea for a multitribal Indian state. According to Albert G. Ellis, a schoolteacher to the Oneidas and aide to Williams, the missionary metamorphosed that idea into a plan for an Indian empire—apparently only the first empire of which he fancied himself the leader.[26]

As a crucial first step, Williams took charge of plans to remove the Iroquois, Stockbridges, and Brothertowns when he visited Washington in 1820. He secured modest financial and logistical support from the U.S. government to travel with a small delegation to the western shore of Lake Michigan to scout for a new homeland and enter into negotiations with the Indians there. He was also supported by the Ogden Company. Accompanying him were the Oneidas John Brant (probably John Anthony or Antone), Daniel Bread (whose relationship to Peter is not known), Cornelius Beard and John Skenandoah (son of the chief John Skenandoah). The trip was unsuccessful. When they arrived at Detroit, the group learned that the U.S. agent at Green Bay had just purchased from the Menominees "that very tract of country" that Williams had sought.[27] This was just one of many missteps that reflected the federal government's conflicting goals of tamping down British subversion of Indian relations, developing the West for whites, and helping eastern states divest themselves of their Native populations. But Williams and the Ogdens had no such ambivalence. The Ogdens lobbied the government and

Williams returned to the West in 1821 with two Senecas, five Stockbridges, an Onondaga, and the same Oneidas as the previous year, except for Daniel Bread, who was replaced by Thomas Christian. Traveling with them was C. C. Trowbridge, the personal secretary of the territorial governor, Lewis Cass, but now acting (as he discreetly put it) "in the capacity of agent for certain gentlemen in the State of New York"—the Ogdens.[28]

Trowbridge's agency was no more shadowy than that of the Oneidas. It is nearly impossible to authenticate these individuals' status as bona fide Oneida leaders. To the extent that they were leaders, they had been recently elevated, with the possible exception of John Skenandoah.[29] Although they acted in the name of the Six Nations, they were at most delegates of the Oneida First Christian Party. A March 1822 message to the secretary of war expressing support for removal but requesting clarification of the government's position specified that it was of First Christian Party origin. But the reportedly angry reaction of many First Christians when the travelers returned suggests the delegates overstepped whatever mandate they may have possessed, and Williams's efforts alienated most of the Second Christian Party as well.[30]

Despite the absence of any authority to enter into agreements on behalf of the Oneidas, let alone the Six Nations, Williams completed treaties with the Winnebagos and Menominees in August 1821 and September 1822. To obtain these treaties, Williams and his party employed some of the very same tactics used to dispossess the Oneidas. The "New York Indians," as they were designated, negotiated with a delegation of Menominees and Winnebagos hardly more prominent than themselves. As the Menominee Great Wave recalled, the New York Indians told him, "[We] are pushed out of our own country, and we come here to take you by the hand!"[31] Their proposal of a cession prompted the Winnebago speaker, Dog's Head, to remind them that the land belonged not to them but to the Great Spirit and that that had "no power to sell the property of another." Equating market transactions with deceit, he declared, "Surely the great spirit would be angry if one Indian should cheat another." He chided them: "If they were our lands, do you think that God ever intended that an Indian should sell land to an Indian—no." To appease the visitors, the Wisconsin Indians present—who included only one chief among the six signers—agreed to give the New York Indians "a part of that country" amounting to 860,000 acres on "the same right which we have" (i.e., usufruct). Even though Dog's Head stated, if any exchange of goods took place, "we shall not receive it as payment for the lands, but as a token of your love for us & your desire to assist us," the treaty document described the transaction as an outright sale for the sum of two thousand dollars.[32]

Williams declared success, but his imperial designs required a still larger canvas than the one the Wisconsin Indians had offered him. The area was insufficient to relocate the entire Iroquois Confederacy, which was his goal, so Williams stayed on into 1822 to expand the cession. This time, he perpetrated the same ruse with a slightly more distinguished group of Menominees, of whom three of the nine signers were chiefs. Eliding the difference between European and aboriginal notions of land tenure, Williams persuaded the Menominees to let the New York Indians "come and sit down with them" over an expanse of nearly seven million acres. While the treaty document recorded another sale (this time for three thousand dollars), the Wisconsin Indians believed they were merely extending the area over which the New York Indians could cohabitate with them.[33] Debate over what had gone on during the negotiations, as well as the ultimate settlement arising from these treaties, would rage for a decade to come.

Backlash

While the first phase of Williams's career among the Oneidas had resulted in a greater degree of religious unity than they had experienced for quite some time, the second phase, committed to their removal, inadvertently created an unusual agreement in political sentiment—against him. According to local Baptist missionaries who filled the vacuum left by Williams when he went west, the Oneidas had made the "solemn determination in their Council in May 1820" not to remove. The Second Christian Party wrote to Williams's church superiors complaining that while he continued to draw from the funds dedicated to Oneida missionization, "He seems to have neglected us, and gone off on business of his own contrary to the will of the Nation." Shrewdly (but, one suspects, not particularly convincingly), they stressed their allegiance to Bishop Hobart and asked that Williams be directed to return to minister to their spiritual needs where they were or be replaced.[34]

Williams's actions had generated enough alarm that in August the Oneidas and Onondagas dispatched three "worthy young men" (two Oneidas, Moses Schuyler and Martin Denny, one Onondaga, John Brown) to see the president.[35] Having recently learned that Williams had shamelessly mistranslated an Oneida speech to Morse the previous year, they had a renewed appreciation of the potential perfidy of the translated, written word. Parrish had followed his instructions to discourage costly visits by Indian delegations to Washington, but the Indians justified their travel on the grounds that "sometimes our Letters are not answered and at other times we are not understood." Unfortunately for them, however, neither the president nor the secretary of war was in town when they arrived. With no better alternative, they left a written memorial stating that they would have nothing to do with Williams's plans "to have us settle among the wild Indians of the West, we don't know where." "We have made up our minds to stay here," they said, "and will not give it up. Our Reservation is already diminished to a very small space; but we calculate to keep what we have got, and we think much of it, we intend it shall go down to generations after us."[36]

Through the Baptists, the Oneidas received assurances from the secretary of war that they would not be forcibly removed. They thanked the president by letter but also warned, "If Mr Eleazer Williams our Missionary makes any communication to you, with respect to us, you may be sure that we are not agreed in it." They also made it clear that written correspondence simply would not do when important issues were at stake: "When we plan to emigrate we shall not apply to you by writing; you may expect to see the Chiefs, in person, and until you are applied to in this way, you may consider we are contented where we are." Among the signers of the Oneida remonstrance were Peter Bread and Jacob Doxtator, prominent leaders of the Christian Party, and Peter Summer and Job Anthony, prominent members of the Second Christian Party. A follow-up remonstrance to the president dated January 1822 asserted that the men accompanying Williams in the West were "bribed to his interest" and described Williams as "the Tool" of the Ogden Company.[37]

Oneidas Divided

Sentiment against removal was general but not unanimous. Williams's eventual Episcopalian replacement as Oneida missionary, Solomon Davis, acknowledged that when he arrived in 1823 "nearly all [the Oneidas] . . . were opposed to migration for a long time." News of Williams's success in expanding the 1821 cession reignited the debate over land, survival, and identity. Cracks in the opposition to removal appeared and then widened. These debates first fractured the First Christian Party, but the Second Christians divided over it later. Daniel Bread (fig. 13) emerged as the principal exponent of the initially unpopular removal option. But, as Davis saw it, Bread's "assiduity . . . , his kindness to his people, and his unbending integrity"—in other words, the classic characteristics of the ideal Iroquois leader—eventually persuaded over four hundred of them to remove.[38] With per capita land holdings at sixteen acres and falling, Bread could argue that the Oneidas' dispossession had left them in essentially the same position as poor non-Indians.

Fig. 13. *Bread, Chief of the Tribe*, portrait by George Catlin, 1831. Smithsonian American Art Museum, Gift of Mrs. Joseph Harrison Jr.

Survival dictated they do the same thing their white peers were doing in unprecedented numbers: migrate to the West.

Without a doubt, the backbone of opposition came from the more traditional Second Christian Party. When the Reverend Morse paid the Oneidas a visit in July 1821, they rejected the assimilationist logic by which he sought to give removal moral and intellectual legitimacy. Peter Summer, a principal chief of that party, asked Morse to "render our thanks to the Government of the U.S. for . . . wishing to raise us to the principles of freemen, and give us an equal rank in the nation with the Whites." "But," he added, "we do not desire it. We wish to walk by ourselves, and enjoy our own privileges in our own way."[39] Moses Schuyler became, in the words of the federal agent Justus Ingersoll, "a kind of Red Jacket among the Oneidas," a reference to the Seneca leader who became famous for his articulate defense of Seneca land and traditions. The debate was not a showdown between "progressive" and "traditionalist" ideals, because thoroughly acculturated, mixed-blood Oneidas were represented on both sides. Schuyler was the grandson of a German settler, and he was joined at the head of the opponents of removal by Martin Denny. Like Bread, Denny could read and write English. Indeed, in 1818, Surveyor General DeWitt described him as "much more civilized than the generality of his nation."[40]

Bread's argument was similar to the one the Stockbridge leader Capt. Hendrick Aupaumut had been making for decades, and the two hundred Indians who began preparations to move on learning of Williams's success were drawn about equally from the Stockbridges and the First Christians. The Stockbridges were already emigrants themselves. Having left their homeland and the dust of their forebears in New England decades before, they lacked strong roots in central New York, and Aupaumut had been trying to engineer their removal to the Midwest since the 1790s. About a hundred First Christians departed for Green Bay in 1823 and 1824 under the leadership of the Oneida Neddy Archiquette, a descendant of Peter Otsequette. Although many did not stay—in 1828 there were still only seventy Oneidas at Green Bay—this departure nevertheless began the tribe's ultimate fragmentation.[41]

The Oneida exodus did not end there because the pressure on the Oneidas from their neighbors only increased. Parrish's 1824 report to the Indian Office in Washington suggested that the state was still not enforcing laws against trespass. He observed of the Six Nations, "All their reservations are more or less surrounded by white settlements, in consequence of which there are frequent depredation, petty thefts, and trespasses committed between the whites and Indians (more frequently on the part of the former)."[42]

Other practical pressures emerged as the removal proceeded. Although both federal and state governments had assured the Oneidas that the Indians' acceptance of western lands would not "be in lieu, or exchange of that which they now hold in New York," the costs of the westward journey and reestablishment were considerable, and the government refused to bear them. That meant Oneidas wishing to emigrate had to finance their removal with their only asset: tribal lands. Beginning in 1824, the state accepted tracts of land proportional in size to the numbers of emigrants in exchange for the cost of travel and resettlement. The treaty of August of that year ceded two tracts amounting to roughly two thousand acres. Proceeds from the first tract went to Indians emigrating to Green Bay under the leadership of Daniel Bread, Neddy Archiquette, and Thomas Christian. Proceeds from the second tract were given to a group headed by Jacob Doxtator, William Hill, and Martinus Rotshin. The name of this group, "the Detroit party," suggested their intention to emigrate, but they did not. Never one to let an opportunity pass, Eleazer Williams secured a hundred-acre grant. Since not everyone residing on these tracts wished to emigrate, provisions were made permitting five to stay on for five years; in addition, Abraham and Martin Denny each received a hundred acres outright.[43]

To whites, this process of proportional dispossession seemed equitable enough, predicated as it was on their own assumptions of individual rather than collective ownership. But it conflicted with traditional Oneida values that were still very much in evidence. Distributing the annuity in 1831, Ingersoll observed that the proceeds of earlier land sales were not reckoned individually. Instead, the entire sum was given to the chiefs, who, he said, "are in the habit of giving more than an equal share to the poor, to the sufferers &c one year, and perhaps the next year these individuals are passed over, and given to others omitted last year. They have no grades, they consider all on a level, and all equally entitled to assistance, except the poor generally have more than their share. The mother, pregnant, therefore, according to their custom, counts as much as two chiefs."[44]

The effect on Oneida land tenure was devastating. A falling Indian population coupled with a diminishing land base intensified the pressure on the "remnant" population in New York, spurring the next wave of departures and land sales. And since the proceeds of the sales disappeared with the emigrants, those who remained did not even benefit from the annuities generated by the cessions. With fewer and fewer resources, the remaining Oneidas found themselves under even greater pressure to enter treaties.[45]

The Orchard Party

The recriminations and confusion surrounding the treaty purportedly signed with the Second Christian Party in Albany on February 1, 1826, underscored the destabilizing, fractionating effects of removal on Oneida politics and the state's ability to profit from it. That treaty ceded 1,640 acres for three dollars an acre. Paying roughly half the land's appraised value, New York was clearly increasing the sums it was willing to pay the Indians when it believed they were likely to leave state limits. By setting aside land for "Indians who do not assent to this treaty," the treaty itself also departed from the principle that the nation or party involved gave its assent as a whole, however grudgingly. The treaty was immediately challenged by the party in whose name it had been negotiated. A petition, dated February 17, enumerated the Second Christian Party's "great & intolerable grievances & complaints." Foremost among these was that "if any council was holden to determine on said sale & Treaty, such council must have been held in a great measure in secret, for our nation were not generally notified of any such council." To this, the petitioners added that signers had been bribed and that names appearing on their power of attorney were forged.[46]

The documentary record shows remarkable irregularities, beginning with a power of attorney that authorized delegates to act on behalf of the Second Christian Party. Signed a week before the treaty, the document announced it was an instrument of the First Christian Party, with an explanation near the end that "a part of the second Christian party is united with [them] . . . and they are now together called the first Christian party in the above power of attorney." Only seventeen of its thirty-three signers were actually members of the Second Christian Party. Similarly, only half the signers of the treaty were members of that party.[47] Although the treaty text gives no indication that the First Christian Party signers did not belong to the party in whose name it was negotiated, they should have been identifiable to state officials, if for no other reason than that at least three of them were designated as First Christians on the power of attorney. The authority of the six Second Christian Party signers was weakened further by their all signing the power of attorney, merely conferring authority on themselves. The First Christian Party was using its weight to widen a division in the

Second Christian Party and effect a land cession by them, and state was a willing partner in the effort.

Who were the six Second Christian Party signatories? Honyost John and Moses Cornelius were not chiefs and are not prominent in the documentary record prior to this treaty. War chief William Day had signed, but Mary Doxtator, a Philadelphia-educated Stockbridge woman married into the Oneida Doxtator family, stated in an affidavit that he had signed in exchange for a hundred dollars and a suit of clothes from a local white landowner named John Hadcock (who also happened to be De Ferrière's son-in-law). Hadcock, she contended, was in turn to receive a 66.66-acre kickback from Nathan Davis, the Stockbridge superintendent, who received 200 acres in this treaty.[48] Jacob Smith claimed to be a chief, but his name appears on few if any earlier documents. For the time being, the weightiest member of this group was William Cornelius, who accepted the Pagan Party annuity in 1810 and whose name appears on some earlier protests against Eleazer Williams. Their leader, however, was William Cornelius's literate and physically imposing twenty-four year-old son, Jacob.

The treaty's backers defended the treaty in a message from "the chiefs and warriors of the Second Christian Party," with the absurd qualification that "what is [here] called the Second Christian party . . . consists of the old 'Second Christian Party' & some of the First Christian party who sometime since united and now form one party called the Second Christian party."[49] This document bore the names of thirty-two persons identifying themselves as members of the Second Christian Party. They claimed that the council meeting called to plan the treaty had not been kept secret but instead had been boycotted by those who opposed it—which was a still a significant problem in a society where legitimate decisions were consensual ones. Nathan Davis denied the accusation about Hadcock and noted that the Indians sold the lands because it was the only way they "could procure funds sufficient to enable them to remove." A legislative committee that weighed the claims decided to uphold the treaty and offered the glib observation that no Indian treaty "has ever been effected with the unanimous consent of all the Indians interested."[50]

The six signers of the 1826 treaty constituted a new faction within the Second Christian Party that emerged around 1824 and would soon be recognized officially as the Orchard Party. The difference hinged on their attitude toward removal. The Orchards were more inclined to emigrate to Green Bay, pending the resolution of the dispute with the Menominee and

Winnebago over the size and status of the western grant. With the induce-
ment of treaty cash on the table, about 250 Oneidas, a little less than half the
Second Christian Party, declared for them. One year and one day from the
1826 Second Christian Party (so-called) treaty, New York formally recognized
the Orchard Party by entering into a treaty with them. This treaty gave up
264 acres, according to Simeon DeWitt, "for the purpose of relieving some
urgent wants" and probably also to fund Jacob Cornelius's reconnaissance
mission to Green Bay in that year. Included, too, was a 60-acre tract for John
Hadcock.[51]

Despite their alliance with the First Christians, the Orchards did not
merge with them. In 1828 or 1829, the Orchards effectively renewed their separate identity by accepting a Christian mission from Methodists. This development was probably related to the need for a new singing master since the
departure of Williams. The Methodists' relatively successful Indian missions
were aided by the 1827 publication of the *Collection of Hymns for the Use of Native Christians of the Iroquois* by Kahkewaquonaby (Peter Jones), a Mohawk-
speaking Ojibwe. The Methodists were able to claim over a hundred converts
at Oneida. They enrolled seventy-nine students in a school and provided a
Mohawk preacher for at least a short time.[52]

"Lingering in This State"

Despite these treaties, the Orchards—and the First Christians, for that
matter—had yet to emigrate in any substantial numbers. Indeed, even Jacob
Cornelius did not remove until 1834. One reason was an "extreme reluctance
to leave the homes of their ancestors and graves of their fathers."[53] In 1826,
twenty-five Orchards recanted their decision to accept the treaty and returned to the Second Christian fold. They offered to refund the partial payment they had already accepted from the state and wished their numbers
added to the Second Christian Party for calculating the acreage the Oneidas
would retain. The state refused, but the Second Christians accepted them
anyway. An indicator of the ill will that prevailed between those who actually left and those who recanted was the departees' refusal to provide these
defectors with their share of the remaining treaty payments. In 1829, eighty-
one First Christian defectors to the Second Christian Party complained of a
similar experience in trying to collect their portion of the annuity. By 1834,
there were roughly two hundred First Christians living among the Second
Christians.[54]

Emigration was also slow because self-financed removal had proven an expensive proposition. In December 1828, at the request of Daniel Bread, the First Christian Party sent a petition to Albany arguing that they could only afford to relocate if paid a fair price for their land. They offered to sell territory but noted, "The sum for each individual of their Tribe, after deducting contingencies for the sale of said lands, would be less than 70 dollars, which would be but a slender sum for the payment of the expenses of an individual in traveling to Green Bay together with procuring the necessary apparel for such a journey and also for his subsistence there from said time to harvest." Thus, according to Surveyor General DeWitt, "with a view of hastening and facilitating the emigration of the Oneida Indians," the legislature passed an act to pay the Oneidas a fair price for their lands. On February 13, 1829, Governor Martin Van Buren signed a treaty in which the First Christians were supposed to be compensated the appraised value of the land, which was determined to be eight dollars an acre.[55]

This treaty was a marked improvement over earlier ones but turned out to be considerably less than the twenty-two-dollar-an-acre sale price. Still, Daniel Bread departed with roughly 110 Oneidas that summer. In October, Lieutenant Governor Enos Throop presided over another treaty with the First Christians under the same terms. Cornelius Beard led another contingent, about the size of Bread's, the following year. After Throop signed another treaty with the Orchard Party for a thousand acres in April 1830, 72 party members left; New York agent Eli Savage reported that 198 Oneidas emigrated to the West in that year. For some lawmakers, the pace of removal seemed unfortunate. William Abbott Moseley of the Assembly's Committee on Indian Affairs acknowledged the Oneidas' "repugnance . . . to abandon the place of their birth" and expressed his "sympathy" toward "this once numerous and powerful race, wasting under the resistless operation of great moral causes, and eventually to disappear before the 'ceaseless pressure of civilization.'" Responding to First Christian Party complaints about the unfairness of the "fair price" proffered by the state, he proposed devoting the difference "to the removal and establishment at Green Bay of the remnant of their people yet lingering in this state."[56]

Another reason for the stop-and-go character of Oneida removal was the uncertainty of Oneida holdings in the West. Many Oneidas questioned the wisdom of moving to lands that the Native owners denied having ceded, and where neither the federal nor the territorial government had formally and unambiguously recognized their right to settle. The Oneidas were aware of the plight of the Stockbridges who had attempted to remove to Indiana in 1818, only to find the area closed to them. The dispute over the validity of Williams's 1821 and 1822 treaties defied numerous attempts at resolution. Negotiations between the federal commissioners Lewis Cass and Thomas McKenney with the Menominees, Winnebagos, and Ojibwes at the 1827 Treaty of Butte des Morts were complicated by a brewing U.S.–Winnebago war and counterclaims by Green Bay's Franco-Menominee Métis population to lands the New York Indians claimed as theirs.[57] Unwilling to push the Menominees too far, the treaty commissioners left the matter of the cession up to the president of the United States.

Only in 1830 did Andrew Jackson act, dispatching a three-member commission to investigate the issue of the New York Indians' holdings in Michigan territory. In setting forth their instructions, Secretary of War John Eaton warned the commissioners against granting the New York Indians "an over quantity" of land. Such an error, he said, could lead the Indians to "return again to the roaming and hunter state." This, he said, "is particularly to be guarded against."[58] Thus, the principal factor in determining how much the New York Indians were due was not the legitimacy of prior agreements between the Indians, or even the landscape and its natural resources, but rather the government's preconceptions about Natives in general and its commitment to their cultural transformation. The commissioners recommended allowing the New York Indians only about 300,000 acres. This was more than the Menominees and Winnebagos said they could part with, but only a third of what the New York Indians felt was rightfully theirs.[59] From the Oneida perspective, their failure to fully embrace European-style agriculture had been used as a rationale to dispossess them in New York, and now their practice of it was a rationale to deprive them of lands at Green Bay (as suggested by the strange phrase "over quantity"). There the matter remained until the following year, when Menominee, Stockbridge, Brothertown, and Oneida representatives haggled for five weeks at the War Office in Washington. The Menominees finally agreed to allow 500,000 acres to the federal government, which could determine how much (or how little) to grant the New York Indians. Further wrangling ensued over the location of the grant and the rules of its settlement. Finally, in October 1832, leaders of the New York Indians at Green Bay, including Daniel Bread, signed an appendix to a Menominee treaty with the United States. They did so grudgingly but also with a sense of relief over ending the "tedious, perplexing and ha-

rassing dispute and controversy." They settled for half a million acres secured by a document bearing the names of all the parties involved.[60]

One signature that was notably absent was that of Eleazer Williams. He
had remained in the West through the 1820s to press for the recognition of
the New York Indian tract, but his grand plans were doomed by the lengthy
delay. He was formally removed as the Oneidas' missionary in 1833 but had
abandoned them long before. Yet his legacy remained. In 1837, the federal
agent John F. Schermerhorn wrote, "Let us say & think of Williams what we
please, had it not been for him the New York Indians would never have had
the Green Bay country nor settled there." It had been fourteen years since the
first exploratory party had gone forth, but the Oneida presence at Green Bay
had now taken firm root. The solidification of their title prompted the emigration of about three hundred Oneidas in 1832, and about a hundred more
the following year. The number of Oneidas residing at Green Bay would
reach a rough parity with the reservation in New York around the time of the
Buffalo Creek treaty in 1838.[61]

The geographic relocation of the Oneidas to Green Bay bifurcated the
nation in a way that was even deeper than the 1805 Pagan-Christian split.
Because of the demonstrated propensity of the state and federal governments
to recognize as a leader anyone who would do their bidding, the break had to
be formal and decisive. In 1831, several Oneidas in New York warned Secretary of War Cass through a letter that Oneidas from Green Bay could not
speak on their behalf or that of the Six Nations. "Since their removal," the
New York Oneidas stated, "they have not been considered as forming a part of
our body."[62] Although Oneidas traveled back and forth, those who set down
roots in the West in general no longer signed treaties with New York. The
federal government treated the two Oneida communities as distinct entities
as well. And after an 1838 treaty limited the size of the Oneidas' Wisconsin
reservation, the migration of large numbers of New York Oneidas became
problematic. In the removal to Green Bay, a second Oneida nation had been
created.

The Wisconsin Oneidas

The two groups of Orchard Party members who emigrated in 1833 provided
rare glimpses of the actual removal experience. The Scottish farmer Patrick
Shirreff observed Oneidas standing on a Buffalo wharf in transit between

the canal packet and the steamboat that would take them on to Green Bay. "The poor creatures were standing in groups," he recalled, "dressed in their best attire, and many young and old of both sexes stupefied by intoxication."[63] The Episcopal bishop Jackson Kemper's description of the arrival of a similarly well-dressed contingent of the Orchard Party in July 1834 demonstrates that, although this mode of travel was not necessarily as taxing as an overland march, it entailed its own hazards. Fifty Oneidas were crammed on board a single schooner. Describing the "very filthy and offensive" conditions on board, Kemper said that the passengers "when sea sick, vomited whenever they were on deck, in the hold over the baggage &c." Soon after they landed, he noted, "some had premonitory symptoms of colera." Making matters worse, their susceptibility to disease was compounded by alcohol—a vice the Oneidas were in no way able to outpace by their relocation, as had been hoped. Indeed, Kemper noted disapprovingly that the arrivals "were met most imprudently by their friends . . . & a scene of great intoxication and degradation ensued." Celebration gave way to mourning soon enough. By late summer, the cholera outbreak had spread through the Indian settlements, killing at least fifty Oneidas and some Menominees.[64]

Before long, however, the Oneidas' lives stabilized. In contrast to the Oneidas who remained in New York, those in Wisconsin possessed enough land to lay the foundation for a viable farming community. A series of visitors charted the remarkable expansion of Oneida men's agricultural efforts from the late 1820s through mid-century. The Indian agent Samuel Stambaugh estimated in 1830 that the Oneidas already had 237 acres under cultivation and harvested fifteen hundred bushels of corn. Four years later, Jackson Kemper offered his own estimate that the Oneidas had cleared 400 acres. And Kemper did not just quantify their production, he tasted it; he partook of the bounty at a Fourth of July feast that he described as consisting of "2 dishes of pork & beans, 2 chicken pies, squashes, potatoes, peas & rice pudding afterwards." By 1840, the Indian agent George Boyd could report of the 700 Wisconsin Oneidas, "These people are all practical farmers" and an 1844 census indicated that 722 Oneidas had over 2,200 acres of land under cultivation. In addition they owned a hundred horses, five hundred head of cattle, and a roughly equal number of hogs.[65] As an overall assessment of Oneida architectural and agricultural achievements, the Quaker missionary Alfred Cope stated, "In all these respects they would bear pretty well to be put in comparison with most communities of whites of as recent date." Cope also wrote, "It was asserted that these people formed the most important part of the agricultural population of this vicinity, were quite superior as farmers in industry and productiveness to the farmers of French descent, and, in fact, brought to market more corn and beef than any body else."[66]

Paradoxically, it seems that the initial absence of a large white population in the vicinity committed to agriculture contributed to the Oneidas' willingness to take up a more Europeanized mode of subsistence. As the anthropologist Alex Ricciardelli has noted, removal facilitated the "crystallization of the male agriculture pattern."[67] Since the only proximate white settlements were those of the French community, who were primarily fur traders and only secondarily farmers, Oneida adoption of white agriculture did not blur the boundaries between Indians and whites. While most of the Oneidas who emigrated had experience with European-style agriculture before their removal, physical distance from whites reduced their inhibitions about becoming too much like them.

Nevertheless, in adopting more extensive agriculture and animal husbandry, the Oneidas did not accept the Euro-American model entirely. Rev. Henry Colman, who lived among them in the early 1840s, recalled that "every winter, companies would be gathered for a hunt of several days," although conflicts erupted with the Menominees over the sharing of game resources and sugarbushes. Moreover, according to an early twentieth-century missionary, "There was one task . . . that wives and mothers would not give up; they always worked in the corn-fields with the men, planting, hoeing, and harvesting the maize. This they considered their privilege of birthright, a holiday task bequeathed to them by their Konoshioni [Longhouse] mothers of bygone days."[68]

Indigenous adjustments were also visible in settlement patterns. Although the Oneidas constructed frame houses, they were situated in large clearings, as had long been the Iroquois norm. "Like the residences of most of the Oneidas," Cope wrote, "[the chief's] had not a tree to screen it from the noonday sun, nor a bush or vine to relieve the dazzling glare of its white sides." The settlement pattern conformed closely to the Iroquois pattern of semi-dispersal that had become common in the previous century. As Colman described it, Oneida houses were spread along a principal road, and "each Indian had cleared a portion, some more and some less, of the forest and was supposed to own back to the creek and east to the reservation limits."[69]

Most galling to Cope was that among themselves the Oneidas still held to a usufructuary, communal understanding of land tenure. This fact marred the missionary's opinion of their acculturation. The individual Oneida, Cope complained, "can never acquire a more secure tenure than the consent and continued sufferance of the chiefs and the longest usage of the nation give him."[70] Cope's statement about "secure tenure" referred primarily to internal distribution of land, but it was still ironic, if not perverse, against the backdrop of Oneida dispossession. From De Ferrière's delegations to Williams's dealings with Menominees and Winnebagos to the creation of the Orchard Party, the story of the Oneidas' dispossession had not really been a matter of the caprice of their chiefs or councils, although they were not without blame. It had more to do with the upheaval that attended the invasion of Iroquoia by Euro-American settlers. Indeed, to the extent that Oneida land loss had hinged on anyone's whim, it was that of officials of New York and the United States who in their dealings with Natives were willing to invent chiefs or accept impostors when doing so suited the broader dictates of expansion. The negotiations surrounding the Treaty of Buffalo Creek in 1838 would bring these practices, and their master practitioner, Rev. John Freeman Schermerhorn, into still sharper focus.

Diaspora and Survival, 1836–1850

THE 1835 TREATY of New Echota between the Cherokees and the United States ranks among the most infamous treaties in the history of the United States' relationship with Native peoples. That treaty, which paved the way for the Cherokee Trail of Tears, exchanged the Cherokees' southeastern homeland for lands in Oklahoma. It was signed at a council by only a minority of Cherokees. The majority boycotted the proceedings in protest, but the treaty commissioner, John Schermerhorn, did them one better by writing in the treaty's preamble that absence implied consent. The New Echota treaty was a fine example of how Schermerhorn operated. The treaty earned the Dutch Reformed minister from Utica the opprobrium of the Cherokees (who punningly nicknamed him "the Devil's horn"), as well as many Euro-Americans who had come to sympathize with the Cherokees' plight. The New Echota treaty precipitated a national political drama that Schermerhorn ducked by busying himself with a new project: getting Indians from New York to join the Cherokees in Indian Territory. The fruit of his labor was a treaty with the Six Nations signed in January 1838 at Buffalo Creek. This was the first federal treaty involving the Six Nations as a whole since 1794. But Schermerhorn was no Pickering, and the Treaty of Buffalo Creek was no Canandaigua. For the Senecas, the Buffalo Creek negotiations resulted in significant land loss. For them, the Tuscaroras, and some Cayugas and Oneidas as well, it also resulted in a deadly removal, this one to Kansas Territory. The historian Grant Foreman describes the story of this botched migration as "incredible" were it "not borne out by the frightful mortality . . . and the sickly and emaciated countenances of the survivors."[1]

The Buffalo Creek treaty's effect on the Oneida nation as a whole was more ambiguous. The treaty dimmed their view of the federal government and their future, prompting some to leave the United States for Canada. But it had no provisions binding on the New York Oneidas and did not mandate their removal. And, indeed, while New York treaties and laws of the 1840s increased pressure on the Oneidas still further—even imposing severalty on them—some Oneidas remained firmly seated on their homeland.

The Buffalo Creek treaty was another attempt by the Ogden Land Company to remove the Senecas and Tuscaroras from the area for which they had purchased the preemption right. Hundreds of Oneidas had gone to Wisconsin but, from the company's perspective, the new effort had been in vain because the Senecas, Tuscaroras, and Cayugas had not followed them. Schermerhorn, who was related to the Ogden shareholder Peter Schermerhorn, had begun laying the groundwork for a new effort to lever them from New York in 1836. He felt that Kansas (part of Indian Territory at the time) was a viable destination. Schermerhorn visited New York governor William Marcy to ask his support, which, he said, was "most cheerfully tendered." Then he wrote a letter to President Jackson in which he said, "I am . . . endeavouring to bring about a treaty with the New York Indians; I think it very doubtfull, whether we shall be able to succeed *to the full extent of your wishes* to get rid of this portion of our population." But he was determined to try.[2]

Schermerhorn was convinced that eliminating the Green Bay option was a prerequisite to getting the Senecas to emigrate to Kansas. The Oneidas were therefore implicated once again in the Ogden Company's efforts to push the Senecas from their lands. Schermerhorn departed for Green Bay even before receiving permission from the War Department. Although the Oneidas there "utterly refused" to sell all their Wisconsin lands, in the so-called Duck Creek treaty of 1836, they agreed to consider removal to Kansas and accept a smaller reservation at Green Bay if its boundaries were sufficiently generous and clearly defined. Limiting the size of the Green Bay reservation would effectively arrest further emigration to Wisconsin. In the face of these questions, Daniel Bread complained that the Oneidas "had hoped . . . the U. States would have been satisfied after taking away so much land from them, and let them keep in peace the little that they had left. They did not wish to sell it, but they saw how it was, all the Indians must go West, West, Mississippi, Mississippi. He hated the word Mississippi—he was sick of it. But he said he supposed if the U. States wished their lands they must go because they were in the power of the Government."[3]

Bread's fatalism may have been tinctured with cynicism, since he was alleged to be the principal beneficiary of a secret treaty stipulation, worth ten thousand dollars to him, that governed the distribution of a large sum from the treaty proceeds. According to Schermerhorn, this stipulation had been drawn up "at the sitting of the Council the last evening after the treaty was signed." Other Oneidas, as well as Rev. Solomon Davis, Albert Ellis, and the subagent George Boyd, were among the recipients. After some Oneidas complained publicly, Schermerhorn admitted to the existence of the secret clause. He portrayed himself as nothing more than an innocent by-stander, in trouble once again over Indian dealings for no other reason than "because in the division of the spoils they cut too deeply for themselves."[4] The U.S. Senate declined to vote on the Duck Creek treaty, despite the support of both New York senators. Senator Silas Wright explained that the Senate Committee of Indian Affairs found it too vague: it did not fix a time limit on the Indians' removal or the relinquishment of their lands, nor did it define the bounds of the tract to which they would emigrate. Moreover, Wright observed that "there was no evidence that some of the Bands of the New York Indians . . . had been in any way parties to the Treaties, or had given their assent to them."[5]

Taking the long view, Schermerhorn did not see the effort as a failure. He would later state, "That treaty to say the least of it, has proved an enter-ing wedge for one more satisfactory I trust to all concerned & which will eventuate in the removal of the New York Indians west of the Mississippi." Schermerhorn continued his efforts in 1837, raising a party of Six Nations Indians to scout for lands in Kansas with him that summer. Several Indians who accompanied Schermerhorn on his expedition to Kansas painted a very unflattering portrait of him. They accused him of being abusive, irreligious, and duplicitous. They also asserted that he provided them with liquor and large sums of money when he thought it would improve their reports of the Indian Territory.[6]

This delegation was itself disavowed in strongly worded memorials from the Oneidas and the Six Nations. On August 17, Moses and Abraham Schuy-ler complained to President Van Buren that they had rejected Schermerhorn's overtures the previous year, adding, "[We] were very much frightened on his return this summer especially when we learned that he was determined to force us to measures contrary to our views of the interest of the nation—but still we assembled a 2d time and gave him a deliberate hearing—and decided 'not to send delegates.' And we wish the President of the United States to know that. . . . we do not wish to remove from the lands given us by the good spirit and secured to us by different treaties." They insisted that any Oneidas in Schermerhorn's westward-bound company were not authorized by the Oneida nation. In early October, Van Buren received a similar message from the Six Nations. It bore the signatures of six Oneidas, most of whom were chiefs of the First and Second Christian Parties.[7]

Buffalo Creek

The federal government had withdrawn Schermerhorn's commission to treat with the New York Indians by the time he returned from the West in 1837, just weeks before the scheduled winter treaty council with the Six Nations at Buffalo Creek. With the May 1838 deadline for the removal of the Cherokees looming, a national antiremoval protest movement was gaining momentum. Hundreds of petitions protesting the New Echota treaty would arrive in Washington during the following months. The War Department understood that Schermerhorn's name affixed to any treaty would undoubtedly attract unfavorable attention, so they replaced him. The negotiations would be handled by Ransom Gillet, a former Democratic congressman from, fittingly, Ogdensburg, New York—a town named after the land company's founding family.

Schermerhorn was indignant over his ouster, but he was not passive. To the commissioner Cary Harris he expressed his "regret . . . that on the representations made for the purpose of avoiding objections in the Senate & soothing the irritated feelings of the Indians, the government felt bound to select another Commissioner." In a November 20 letter to Secretary of War Joel Poinsett, Schermerhorn pledged to "continue here, however mortifying it may be to my feelings . . . and see another reap the honors for which he never laboured nor merited." How could he stand it? He explained that his fortitude arose from "the great interest I feel in the future welfare of the New York Indians" and "a desire to see the benevolent policy of the Government in reference to the Indians finally accomplished." Schermerhorn also wanted to be reimbursed for his 1836 Green Bay junket and collect a handsome fee from the Ogden Land Company. The upcoming treaty still provided an opportunity to achieve these goals, especially since his replacement was unsure of himself. Gillet freely admitted his lack of experience in Indian affairs and his confusion with regard to Native politics and government.[8]

To compensate for his deficiencies, Gillet initially leaned on the two men most interested in the treaty's outcome: federal subagent James Stryker and Schermerhorn. Gillet would later express regret about both. Of Stryker he wrote, "My unlimited confidence in him soon failed when I caught him in conflicting statements & in doing several deceptive things." Indeed, Stryker had been promised a ten-thousand-dollar bounty by the Ogden Land Company, but only if the Senecas gave up all their reserved lands in the treaty, and he was eventually found to have embezzled years' worth of Indian annuities and other funds. Of Schermerhorn, Gillet said,

> I soon learned that he was not to be trusted, & that he was the paid representative of the pre[e]m[p]tionists [i.e., the Ogden Land Company]. He tried hard to have me give him some employment & especially to surrender to him the custody of the treaty, that he might get pay as the bearer of it even if he did not tamper with it. Before violating his honor in not paying a few hundred dollars, borrowed of me, I became convinced that he was a wily schemer who would not keep the faith with any one further than his own interests demanded.[9]

Ironically, the only people whom Gillet did not trust at the time were the Iroquois. Although he admitted finding "the task of endeavouring fully to understand all the various matters connected directly or remotely, with the subject committed to me, one of no inconsiderable magnitude," he did not proceed with humility. Instead, he let his sense of cultural superiority fill in the gaps, inspiring him with the confidence to say, "The Indians are not always accurate in their conclusions concerning what is most beneficial for them." Gillet was quick to dismiss Native grievances or concerns as irrational.[10]

The Buffalo Creek negotiations were complex and involved numerous agreements between different parties. The treaty between the U.S. government and Six Nations set aside a reservation of 1,824,000 acres in Kansas for the Six Nations while definitively nullifying the Six Nations' unconsummated claims to lands in Wisconsin.[11] The most devastating effects were felt by the Senecas, who relinquished more than 100,000 acres, including much of the modern city of Buffalo, in federally supervised side treaties with the Ogden Company and New York State. These transactions were debated furiously as allegations of bribery, alcohol use, and insufficient representation at the treaty were made and for the most part substantiated. Senate ratification of the Buffalo Creek treaty was delayed for more than two years and finally was achieved only through some serious twisting of Senate rules. Some of the land was even returned to the Seneca in the so-called compromise treaty of 1842. In retrospect, the decision to drop Schermerhorn had proven tactically sound: had the Buffalo Creek treaty been formally linked to the controversial minister, it probably could not have survived the ratification vote.

The only New York Oneidas present at Buffalo Creek were the First Christian Party chief Baptist Powless and Jonathan Jordan. Both signed the treaty. Each received a five-hundred-dollar bounty promised by the Ogden Company "in case the Seneca tribe of Indians shall accept the offers of the Government of the United States for their removal to the West."[12] The treaty also provided for a payment of four thousand dollars to "Baptista Powlis, and the chiefs of the first Christian party residing at Oneida, and the sum of two thousand dollars shall be paid to William Day, and the chiefs of the Orchard party residing there, for expenses incurred and services rendered in securing the Green Bay country, and the settlement of a portion thereof." But Day was not present and did not wish to remove to Kansas or Green Bay. Powless had not played a particularly significant role in the Green Bay removal; his presence and prominence had to do with his liaison with Schermerhorn rather than his stature among the Oneidas. Like the four Green Bay Oneidas who signed the Buffalo Creek treaty—John Anthony, Honyost Smith, Henry Jordan, and Thomas King—Powless had been handpicked by Schermerhorn because of his support of Kansas emigration. Indeed, within a day of signing their own contracts for five-hundred-dollar bounties, Powless, Anthony, and Smith put their names on a glowing report of the far West. As a related matter, five other Green Bay Oneida chiefs signed a treaty in Washington in February that was essentially a cleaned-up version of Schermerhorn's 1836 Duck Creek treaty. This treaty fixed the size of the Oneidas' Green Bay lands at one hundred acres a person on and around their existing settlements. The controversial stipulation dividing ten thousand dollars among various influential figures was absent.[13]

New York Oneidas did not consider themselves parties to the Buffalo Creek or Washington treaties, and Gillet acknowledged of all the Oneidas present at the negotiations that "none of them profess to have power conclusively to bind their nation." A memorial from the Second Christian and Orchard Parties repudiated the Buffalo Creek treaty, proclaimed "their unwillingness to emigrate," and noted, "They have delegated no power to any persons to make a treaty." The Second Christian Party chief Moses Schuyler later stated that he had "never been consulted to emagrate to the West."[14] Gillet's report to the Office of Indian Affairs lists only "a portion of the Oneidas" as signatories to the treaty. Moreover, Gillet reported that when he visited Oneida Castle in August 1838, he "most solemnly assure[d] them that the treaty does not & is not intended to compel the Oneidas to remove from their reservation in the state of New York . . . they need not go unless they wish to. When they wish to remove they can sell their lands to the Governor of the state of New York, then emigrate. But they will not be compelled to sell or remove."[15]

Canada

Gillet's assurances notwithstanding, the Buffalo Creek treaty and its effects on the Senecas contributed to the Oneidas' sense of insecurity. In January 1839, the Second Christian Party grew alarmed when it learned that a First Christian Party delegation, apparently under Baptist Powless's direction, had departed for Albany. They sent a message to Governor William Seward expressing their concern that the delegation meant "to sell out some portion of our reservation in a secret manner" and requested that this delegation be ignored. They explained that they had allowed Powless's faction of First Christians to settle among them "chiefly out of pity" but now, they said, "we fear that they have forgotten the favour." At the same council, the Second Christians wrote President Van Buren to deny any rumor that they supported removal west of Missouri. They declared they were "opposed to leaving the land of our fathers at present. We respectfully request of you to protect us in our possessions and in the enjoyment of our homes that we may lay our bones in peace upon our ancient possessions."[16]

Although the Second Christians claimed the moral high ground in relation to the First Christians among them, they had accepted payment from the First Christians for a share of the reservation. Everyone probably understood that state officials would allow the Powless faction to sell out sooner or later. Under these circumstances, most Oneidas concluded that prospects for any Iroquois to enjoy security anywhere in the United States were bleak. Moses Schuyler complained that the Oneidas felt "despised" by the people of New York. The absence of support from the federal quarter was evident not just in the Buffalo Creek turmoil but also in Stryker's embezzlement of annuities, for which he was never punished even after it came to light. By late 1839, Schuyler looked to Canada as a promising refuge. Whatever the Oneidas might receive from Great Britain seemed more then they were receiving from the United States. Upper Canada was closer than Green Bay and offered proximity to other Native communities, including other Iroquois. Although the number of white settlers in Upper Canada was growing, they were fewer in number. The Oneidas' decision to leave the United States was also made against the menacing backdrop of the Trail of Tears. The removal of the "Five Civilized Tribes" of the South to Oklahoma sparked a voluntary migration of more than two thousand Native people from the United States to Canada. A British Indian Department officer observed, "The policy of the [U.S.] Government in compelling [the Cherokees et al.] to remove to a strange country, the climate of which has already destroyed the greater part of the first division of them, which I have been informed was marched to the place of exile under a strong military escort is most keenly felt by them, and they have in consequence made repeated applications . . . to be allowed to seek asylum in Upper Canada and enjoy the protection of the British Government."[17]

Officials in Canada were surprisingly obliging. The superintendent of Indian affairs, J. B. Clench, assured the Oneidas, "You will be respected and kindly treated." Playing on the Oneidas' aggrievement, Clench proffered "the powerful protection of the British Government which protects all her subjects without distinction or reference to the Color of the skin." According to Hadcock, the Oneidas held "a grate counsel as I ever attended" to discuss the proposals and "the British Agent wrote a smoothe letter and gave the Indians all a pressing invitation." "Smoothe" and "pressing" indeed; Clench had written: "Brothers and Sisters! When you come and settle amongst us you will all . . . receive *Presents* and enjoy all the other priviledges which your Indian brethren enjoy in this Country: But you must not delay in secureing the good land you have fixed upon—if you do, there is no other land on the River Thames that can be had unless at six dollars an acre."[18]

Why were Canadian officials so supportive of the idea of an Oneida settlement? The British Indian Department was in the midst of a difficult transition as its raison d'être shifted away from managing military alliances to undertaking a paternalistic mission to transform Native peoples. The Oneidas contributed to that mission to the extent that their relatively greater exposure to Euro-American culture had had acculturative effects. Moses Schuyler and August Cornelius, the leaders of the delegation, certainly understood Euro-American agriculture: among the property attributed to them in New York were nearly two hundred cleared acres, framed houses, barns, and a share of a sawmill. Presumably they would have a good influence on the other Native inhabitants of the Thames Valley. But the British

Indian Department was also, in the words of one of its contemporary crit-
ics, "a repository of jobbery and corruption." To department functionaries,
every new group of Natives represented opportunity. Both Clench and his
superior, chief superintendent Samuel P. Jarvis, were eventually discovered
to have misappropriated large amounts of Indian funds destined for Native
peoples.[19]

In the winter of 1839 and spring of 1840, Schuyler headed Oneida delegations to identify suitable lands in Upper Canada. They decided on a 5,400-
acre tract on the Thames River near Ojibwe and Munsee communities. It was
three hundred miles directly west of their homeland. Canadian officials
agreed to purchase the lands for the Oneidas, provided the Oneidas sold their
lands in New York and turned over the proceeds to create an annuity. Since
Schuyler's plan was in direct and acrimonious competition with the Kansas
scheme championed by Powless, time was of the essence. Moreover, other
Oneidas expressed a desire to stay, while still others hoped to join family at
Green Bay. An 1840 message from the Green Bay chiefs strongly supported
the removal of New York Oneidas to Wisconsin.[20] For its part, New York was
willing to facilitate the departure of the Oneidas, whatever their destination.
A series of four treaties were undertaken between 1840 and 1842 to finance
the removal of most of the remaining Oneidas to points outside the state.

The treaties were so numerous because not all Oneidas could be persuaded to leave at any single time. The largest of these cessions was the 1840
treaty with the First and Second Christian Parties. The Oneidas yielded
about 3,100 acres and retained 1,400, approximating the proportion of emigrants (460) to nonemigrants (178). The lands ceded to the state included
some of the Oneidas' most densely settled areas along Oneida Creek. The
First and Second Christian lands bordering those of the Orchard Party were
relinquished; thenceforward the parties' reservations would no longer be contiguous. Many of the Oneidas who declared their intention to stay were displaced and now had to relocate elsewhere on the lands that remained part of
the reservation. The First and Second Christian Party reserve would become
known as the "Windfall." The state compensated 57 Oneidas for several hundred acres of cleared land and numerous houses, barns, and the above-
mentioned sawmill that Schuyler co-owned with Big Nicholas, William
Dockstader, and Abraham Sickles, who emigrated with him.[21] The state also
provided fifteen thousand dollars for the immediate removal to Canada of
Schuyler's "first emigrating party" made up of 23 First Christians and 219 Second Christians. The Oneidas' state-appointed attorney, Nathan Burchard, had

accompanied at least one of the exploratory missions to Canada, and his interest in emigration became apparent; in addition to payment for his presence, he exacted surcharges on all transactions. He also earned money back home as the surveyor who would plot the sale of land and appraise the value of improvements. Moreover, when the time for payment of individual Oneidas came, he charged a fifty-cent fee for each disbursement. Dubbing him their "lawless Lawyer Agent," the Oneidas claimed in a letter to New York governor William Seward in May, "All of the Improvement money fell short and yet he required us to sign receipts for the full amount."[22]

In March 1841, a Methodist minister informed the Indian agent that the Oneidas in Canada "are doing well, highly pleased with their lands &c.— quite content & happy in their new situation . . . [and they] have built a comfortable house for the double purpose of School & public worship."[23] In subsequent removals, most of the First Christians, including Baptist Powless, went to Green Bay; the Second Christians, including Peter Summer, to Canada. The majority of Orchard Party members who departed went to Canada as well. (Those who remained lived on a small tract that bore the same name as the party but was later called Marble Hill.) Like the Oneidas who moved to Wisconsin, the Oneida emigrants developed a dynamic agricultural sector. According to William H. Smith's *Canadian Gazetteer*, published in 1846, the Oneidas already had 335 acres under cultivation, 64 oxen, 61 cows, 27 heifers, 17 horses, 162 swine, 14 wagons and carts, 13 ploughs, 16 harrows, two sets of carpenter's tools, and 3 fanning mills. They had purchased houses and barns from old settlers. In 1850, an Indian Department official noted: "They have continued to . . . improve the lands for the last ten years. They have made excellent roads through the Tract at their own expense."[24] Like those used in Wisconsin, the land use patterns they adopted from the outset were more clearly oriented to Euro-American patterns than to the patterns of the Oneidas who remained in New York.

These Oneidas sought different ways to assert their Oneida identities; indeed, the Canada emigrants were culturally conservative by reputation and had stronger ties to the other Iroquois reservations. In 1850, they expected a large number of Tonawanda Senecas to join them. Of the six Oneidas who signed a Six Nations remonstrance against the Kansas plan at the Senecas' Buffalo Creek reservation in 1837, at least five eventually moved to Canada. Shortly after their arrival, the Oneidas were visited by an Iroquois delegation from Grand River (about sixty miles away) that performed a condolence ceremony, according to Clench, to "install chiefs and rekindle the Oneida council fire." To set the newcomers right as residents of Canada, Clench also reported the performance of "the ancient ceremony of burying the hatchet between the Six Nations and the Oneida who had shed each others blood at the instigation of the British and American governments."[25]

Each treaty generated a list of Oneidas who committed to moving beyond the boundary of the state, but many did not actually go. Some collected their quota of treaty cash, relinquishing their right to live on the reservation, but did not proceed to purchase a share in the Canadian tract or transport themselves to Green Bay. As the Green Bay leaders predicted, "It will not do to pay the money to individuals. If you do, many of them will never reach here." Some drank away the proceeds, while others simply preferred to seek refuge in larger Iroquois communities elsewhere in New York State. Family ties still united the Iroquois, as exemplified by the appearance on the Oneida emigration lists of the Onondaga surname LeFort, as well as claims by eight members of the Second Christian Party residing at Tonawanda to shares of Oneida treaty proceeds. In 1845, twenty-one Oneidas were living on the Onondaga reservation. Many intermarried with Onondagas, increasing the numbers of that nation. Others lingered there as landless residents, creating an enduring yet distinct population of Oneidas at Onondaga that numbered roughly eighty through the remainder of the century. About fifty Oneidas lived among the Seneca and Tuscarora as well. And some of those who had claimed to emigrate simply stayed at, or returned to, the Oneida homeland. Thomas Wells, a Quaker who visited the Oneidas in 1848, noted that some emigrants, "mostly aged women not feeling satisfied with their new homes, have returned, & are now living in old deserted cabins, & are in a destitute condition, dependent on their neighbors for a subsistence." The census taker in 1855 observed the Oneidas had "friends . . . residing among them who have no lands."[26]

"They will cease to be Indians, except in name": Severalty and Citizenship

In May 1841, New York governor William Seward wrote a letter to Moses Schuyler in response to the latter's request for assistance with the removal of a second wave of Oneidas to Canada. Seward wished him well and reflected on the deeper meaning of the Oneidas' migration, characterizing the Oneidas' departure as nothing less than "one of the most affecting events in our history." But he did not see it as the result of the state's expansionist policies.

Instead, he portrayed the state as a historic guardian of Oneida interests, whose good intentions had been undone by "firewater." Seward did not approve of the removal policy championed by his Democratic opponents, yet he naturalized, even sacralized, the departure of Iroquois from New York. It was evidence, he wrote in a second letter, "that a Providence overrules the action of white men and red men." Seward's secretary of state, John C. Spencer, was a little less philosophical. A visiting Quaker, Charles Marriott, reported Spencer's opinion "that the Oneidas were now greatly reduced by recent emigration to Canada, and he hoped some more of the looser sort would go, when the residue of the Lands might be divided amongst those left behind." Marriott countered that the state's measures were "better calculated for obtaining the Indians Lands from them by purchase, than for preserving their possessions to them" and "told him our object was to reform and retain, not to banish."[27]

Marriott's wry commentary aside, Spencer's reference to dividing lands alluded to the most striking element of the removal treaties signed in 1840 and 1841: they authorized the commissioners to set aside tracts to be held as private property by Oneida families. These families would relinquish their interest in the rest of the reservation but exercise complete control over the tract assigned them, including the right to sell. To qualify for possession of land in severalty, the family had to have sufficient numbers to entitle its members to more than fifty acres—about eleven people for the Orchard Party or seven for the First or Second Christian Parties. Families could, however, unite to meet this threshold. The treaties also stated that applicants had to satisfy the commissioners that they were "prudent, industrious & capable of managing & taking care of such lands" and that they had the consent of the remainder of the party. These provisions for the possession of land in severalty predated the infamous federal Dawes Allotment Act, their federal counterpart, by nearly half a century. Their effects were identical: near-total land loss as individual land sales created a checkerboard pattern of landholding which undermined communal life and promoted further land sales in turn.[28]

The Seward administration claimed the authority to introduce this practice of severalty on the basis of the 1839 "Act Relating to the Oneida Tribe of Indians," which granted broad discretion to the state's Indian commissioners in regulating land matters. The Quakers reported in their Yearly Meeting minutes that the governor had told them that "dividing their lands without making them citizens, would at present be most to their interest, and that he thought it had better be done quietly," adding, "He spoke of the strong prejudice that exist[s] even in this state against Caste and Colour, said it was general except among the most enlightened . . . [and that] if one applied to have the Indians made citizens, this prejudice would be strongly aroused, and probably defeat us." Seward and Spencer, both eminent Whigs with national reputations, did not see this kind of forced legal and economic assimilation as a complement to the removal policies championed by their Democratic rivals but rather as a more favorable and humane alternative. In the words of Lewis Henry Morgan, a Rochester Whig attorney whose books on the Iroquois would help create the modern field of anthropology, "The first step toward the amelioration of [the Iroquois'] condition . . . would be a division among themselves. . . . This would prepare the way for other changes," culminating in their possession of the "rights and privileges of citizens of the State. When this time arrives, they will cease to be Indians, except in name."[29] By Seward's and Spencer's own lights, severalty, like the 1842 compromise treaty with the Senecas (negotiated by Spencer's father, Ambrose), admirably balanced their obligation to protect the Natives with their commitment to commercial development. The resolution of the "Indian question" lay in the Oneidas' transformation into agrarian capitalists.

The state advanced the severalty policy by two great steps in April 1843. "An Act to Enable Resident Aliens to Hold and Convey Real Estate" included a provision allowing Indians to "take, hold, and convey lands and real estate . . . in the same manner as a citizen." It also made every male adult "liable on contracts, and subject to taxation and to the civil jurisdiction" of state courts "whenever he shall have become a freeholder, to the value of one hundred dollars." To hasten Oneidas down that road, the legislature promptly passed "An Act Relative to the Oneida Indians." This act restated the severalty provisions of the 1840 and 1841 treaties but extended them by permitting a local superintendent to oversee the sale of the Oneidas' lands to third parties. As for those lands still held in common, the superintendent was also authorized to oversee their disposal whenever "the majority of chiefs or head men" concurred. New York was getting out of the treaty business.[30]

The severalty provisions in the treaties and the 1843 statutes were milestones in the concerted effort of the Spencers and Seward to legally assimilate New York's Native American population to New York. John C. Spencer had been a lead attorney for the state in its 1821 prosecution of Tommy Jemmy, a Seneca who killed a Seneca woman on the Buffalo Creek reservation after a tribal council convicted her of witchcraft. A jury acquitted him because of the state's lack of jurisdiction over a case that did not involve non-Indians. The legislature intervened in the appeals process by pardoning Jemmy—but also pledged the state would exercise jurisdiction over the reservation thenceforth. In *Goodell v. Jackson,* an 1822 case that argued the validity of a deed to nonreservation land inherited by an Oneida man, Justice Ambrose Spencer had ruled the Oneida man was a citizen of New York. This decision was reversed by a higher court. Seward's backdoor strategy of making Indians citizens bore fruit, however, in 1876, when an Oneida, Abraham Elm, who had cast a ballot for a member of Congress, was convicted of illegal voting on the grounds that he was not a citizen. A federal judge ruled that Elm was indeed a citizen. He observed that although the Fourteenth Amendment did not automatically make Natives citizens, Elm and other Oneidas were citizens because they already possessed significant attributes of citizenship—and he cited the two April 1843 state statutes as benchmarks. These had been followed in 1847 by a law abolishing the office of Oneida attorney and permitting Oneidas to convey their lands through deeds witnessed by any justice of the peace. The state's 1849 "Act for the Benefit of Indians" offered severalty on any reservation with approval of its tribal government, making the Oneidas' situation general.[31]

Intriguingly, the state legislature apparently received a petition from the Oneidas in support of the 1843 severalty legislation. The petition probably burned in the 1911 fire at the state capitol; no copies are extant. The petition's content and its signers are unknown. Because of the history of Oneida communications to the state, we must wonder whether it was spurious, like the 1826 Second Christian Party petitions. But since some Oneidas did voluntarily divide their lands, they probably believed doing so had some benefit to them. They may well have perceived advantages similar to the 1805 division of the reservation into Christian and Pagan sections, at least in the short run. Dividing the land ensured that others did not surreptitiously sign away what little remained. Dividing the land also protected the title holders against the claims of Oneidas who had departed but who might return. Some may have adopted the individualist ethic, as Peter August had by in 1810. Finally, severalty permitted those who were considering emigrating to sell their lands without having to wait for another treaty. A Quaker visitor in 1848 reported that since the Oneidas' lands were divided, "most of them have sold their possessions, and emigrated to Canada, Green Bay, & other Western locations, joining other tribes." More than two dozen Oneidas who had recently indicated their intention to stay instead left for Canada in 1845.[32]

Whatever the Oneidas' intentions, severalty facilitated Oneida dispossession, just as the 1805 partition had. According to the 1892 extra census bulletin, Oneida reservation lands had been reduced by more than half, to 350 acres. Its author, the special agent Gen. Henry B. Carrington, commented, "The experiment of holding land in severalty only hastened their dissolution, without elevating their industry or their condition." After less than a decade of divided holdings, Daniel Skenandoah (fig. 14) observed that severalty made people disputatious and was attended by myriad practical difficulties. Before severalty, he said, "we prospered a great deal better [because] we could plant our corn, sow our wheat, and pasture our cattle, in the best places. If we wanted a stick of timber, we could cut a tree in the most convenient place. We were not obliged to build fences as we are now, to protect us from our neighbors." By depriving the Oneida nation of collective control over its land base, severalty also weakened its formal government. With nominal management of land affairs taken from the chiefs' hands, the official tasks Oneida chiefs performed relative to the United States and the state of New York were reduced to two: a regular one, the collection of federal annuity, and a sporadic one, the lodging of complaints over the failure of the state and federal governments to fulfill various obligations established by prior treaties.[33]

A Trail of Blood

In 1840, the federal government received correspondence in the name of the "Seneca, Onondaga, Cayuga, Oneida and Tuscarora Tribes of New York Indians," as well as the Oneidas in particular, expressing support for removal to Kansas. Federal officials saw little point, however, in actually moving the relatively small numbers of New York Indians who professed interest in going, especially after the 1842 compromise treaty restored the Senecas' Allegany and Cattaraugus reservations. Removals in the South had not gone smoothly, and no significant amount of land remained to be gained in New York. The commissioner of Indian Affairs reported, "It is not probable that many, if any of them will emigrate . . . and we shall save the greater part, perhaps the whole, of the money consideration . . . and all or the same proportion of the land in the west."[34] An appropriation was finally made in 1843, but it was contingent on the emigration of no fewer than 250 New York Indians. In his annual report of 1844, the commissioner of Indian affairs T. Hartley Crawford remarked, "I believe that neither the interests of the State of New

York nor of the United States will be promoted in any degree by the emigration of as many as wish to go, while the United States will be burdened with an expenditure utterly unproductive of benefit in any quarter, and of probable positive injury to the Indians. The best information I possess, moreover, leads to the belief that the idea of emigration has been or will be abandoned."[35]

It was not. Federal agent Stephen Osborne noted the existence of men "whose only object is to get something from the Government"—in this case, control over the 1843 removal appropriation.[36] Dr. Abraham Hogeboom of Pekin, New York, continued to agitate for Kansas removal. One of the Oneidas who went along with these plans was John Denny, who visited Kansas in 1845. On his return trip, Denny told Thomas Harvey, superintendent of the St. Louis Agency, that, in Harvey's words, "he was of the opinion that some two hundred of his band would remove to their new homes during the coming fall." Presumably these Oneida emigrants would have come mostly from Green Bay, where Baptist Powless now reunited with the deposed Green Bay First Christian chief John Anthony to press for removal to Kansas. Both men had collaborated with Schermerhorn on the Buffalo Creek negotiations. The emigration faction led by Powless appealed to the president to release the funds appropriated in 1843 to enable them to go. They presented themselves as a persecuted minority within the Six Nations who wished to fulfill the promises of the Buffalo Creek treaty.[37]

In November 1845, on being informed by Hogeboom that the requisite 250 New York Indians had enrolled, the Office of Indian Affairs in Washington released eleven thousand dollars to him. Osborne ascertained, however, that Hogeboom had overstated the size of the emigrating party. When the emigrants failed to set out before the waterways froze, Hogeboom was instructed by the Office of Indian Affairs to abandon the effort. The Office of Indian Affairs also called for a council to be held in June to clarify the situation.[38] Hogeboom preempted this council by ignoring his instructions and setting forth with a party in May. Although Hogeboom insisted he had 250 at the outset, Osborne counted only 153 people and speculated that anyone beyond that must have been illegally recruited from Canada. Apparently a few had been recruited from Green Bay. In 1848, agent W. P. Angel could account for 188 but acknowledged that he might be short "a few names" with regard to the Tuscaroras. Of those he counted, he identified 32 as Oneidas. Subagent Osborne's tally was 162, including only 3 Oneidas.[39]

The number of Indians who actually arrived in Kansas in mid-June was lower still, largely because of Hogeboom's mismanagement. Some had turned back, but many died en route or shortly after arrival. Hogeboom, a doctor, reported that "change of diet as well as Climate caused many of them during almost the whole journey to be afflicted with sickness, and especially the diarrhoea which prevailed among them to an alarming degree." "Nearly my whole time," he added, "was occupied in a professional capacity." The agent at Fort Leavenworth, Kansas, noted that Hogeboom "left no funds, nor did he make any arrangements whatever in regard to these people."[40] Notwithstanding his profession, the prevailing illness of his charges, and the lack of arrangements for their support, Hogeboom set out on his return to New York on June 16—one day after depositing them at their destination. Hogeboom reported arriving with 191. Angel's final tally was 74 dead, 89 returned, and 25 alive not returned. The Oneidas had at least 4 dead, 3 returned, and 5 alive not returned. The Denny and Doxtator families were particularly prominent in this removal, and a few of them remained in the West. A committee of the New York Senate condemned the affair as an "inhuman outrage" and said of Hogeboom that the emigrants' "blood lies at his door." The legislature passed a concurrent resolution asking the president of the United States to "cause the said remnant of the six nations now residing in the Country west of the Mississippi to be removed back to their friends in this State and that they be provided with the necessary means and agencies to ensure their comfortable transportation home."[41]

"Idiots, Lunatics . . . also Indians"

The 1845 decennial New York State census enumerated the combined population of the towns adjacent to the Oneida reservation lands, Lenox and Vernon, at 8,465. Natives appeared in the section titled, "Whole number of Idiots and Lunatics; distinguishing sexes, ages and circumstances: also the number of Indians in the county." Twenty-two male Natives and twenty-five female Natives were living in the fourth ward of the burgeoning nearby city of Utica, whose total population was roughly 15,000. Most of these were doubtless Oneidas, and they were probably working as domestics and helpers in the city's craft shops. The Oneida reservation population was stated to be 185.

Beginning in 1845, the state also began producing a separate, detailed census of the Native population within its bounds. It did so at the behest of Henry Rowe Schoolcraft, another founding father of modern anthropology. Schoolcraft was a former U.S. Indian agent in Michigan and a well-connected but underemployed New York Democrat. When the Democrats returned to

the governorship in 1844, Schoolcraft saw his chance and secured an appoint-
ment as Indian census marshal. The 1845 count offers a portrait—though a
partial one—of the Oneidas in New York at midcentury. Schoolcraft appointed his nephew, Richard U. Shearman, to canvass the reservation. Shearman revised the overall population figure downward to 157, explaining, "The
count of last winter, which made 180 souls was made with reference to re-
taining a certain amount of missionary funds."[42]

Shearman's own tabulations, however, have to be regarded with some
skepticism, because the Oneidas were wary of him and therefore not fully
forthcoming. Schoolcraft fulminated about Oneida fears that the census was
"a plan, on the part of the State authorities to extend their laws over them &
tax them," adding, "They are so suspicious & ignorant people, that the slightest, or most absurd reports, alarm them." Oneidas continued to guard their
rights. Three months later, Shearman complained of the subversion of "a bevy
of old women" who interfered with his tabulations relative to the last six families on his list: "After endeavoring for upwards of an hour to satisfy them that
there was no wrong in the matter, I left them and sought the information of
some of their neighbors who had before given answers on their own account.
Suspecting what was going on they followed me up, and attempted to stop
their neighbors while answering me. But after some delay and difficulty I finally got all that was to be told about them, as well perhaps as they could have
given it to me themselves."[43] Despite Shearman's judgment of his success, the
end of his reporting sheet seems to have numerous lacunae.

Another problem was the census design. The Indian census used the state's
standard form. This questionnaire, though sophisticated for its time, reflected
how state functionaries imagined their domain. Only the crops and activities
they deemed important to the development of the state economy as a whole
were counted. Thus, peas were counted, squashes were not. Schoolcraft recognized the problem when taking the Onondaga census. For that census he
qualified the category "value of garden & horticultural products, in dollars"
with the notation "peas, turnips, beans, field squashes & pasturage as well as
esculents upon which they are disposed to set a high value, & which serves, to
a considerable extent, for their subsistence in summer." The census design-
ers' concern with the marital status of women also developed from certain
culturally specific assumptions that did not apply to Iroquois families. Indeed, the very conflation of "family" with "household" in the census divided
the Oneidas into units that did not necessarily reflect the operative relationships in Oneida society.[44]

Schoolcraft's census included some additional material. such as Oneida names (e.g., Ti o ga wah, "The Paddle," Thomas Cornelius; Si ait kuh, "Ugly," William Jourdan), as well as the Oneidas' pronunciation of their English aliases (e.g., "Elee zo at" for "Elizabeth," "Ta wit" for David). These lists demonstrate continuity in Oneida naming practices and the Oneidas' ongoing unfamiliarity with English. Schoolcraft mixed his European assumptions with his ethnographic observation by adding to the questionnaire a column for market value of hunting activities, as well as a tabulation of "persons who adhere to their native religion" (133), as distinguished from "church members" (31). The 1845 census listed thirty-one separate families. The largest household consisted of 10 individuals; the average was 5 and the median was between 4 and 5. While only the person considered by the enumerator to be the head of household is named, fully half of these households may have extended beyond the nuclear unit of parents and children. Where Shearman observed, "In each of three houses I found two families," it is not clear whether these cohabiting Oneidas defined themselves as separate families or simply that Shearman did. He also noted that seventy acres were being cultivated in common by the families of David Johnson, Betsey Johnson, Abram Schuyler, Moses Day, and Henry George. In six of thirty-one cases, Shearman listed a woman as head of household. Was this figure based on their opinion or his? The answer was not recorded, and the data do not permit any further analysis.

In land use, there is evidence of continuity of long-term patterns. Not surprisingly, of all the crops the census taker was instructed to count, corn was almost uniformly present. With one-third of his thirty cleared acres devoted to corn, Job Antone had committed more land to his corn than any other Oneidas, and his 300-bushel harvest was also the highest per-acre yield. The twenty families that raised corn produced 1,458 bushels. Spread across the entire Oneida population, this harvest amounted to 8.9 bushels per person—exactly the per capita quantity that one anthropologist has calculated was required by seventeenth-century Iroquoians. It was processed in the same time-honored manner, using mortars and pestles fashioned from trees.[45] Oneidas also devoted land to peas, oats, potatoes, and beans. Because slightly fewer than half of the farms had ploughs, we can assume hoes were still very much in use. Wells, the Quaker, saw "all kinds of garden vegetables," and the census took note of gardening on the land of twelve households. Shearman systematically underestimated their importance by reckoning them in terms of cash value, with a maximum of twenty-five dollars attributed to Chris-

Fig. 14. Daniel Skenandoah and his son Isaiah, ca. 1878. Courtesy of the Madison County Historical Society, Oneida, N.Y.

tian Beechtree's household. Compared with non-Native farms in the neighboring town of Lenox, the Oneidas raised a narrower range of crops but had similar per-acre crop yields, with the exception of peas and potatoes (lower) and wheat (higher).

Almost half of Oneida households engaged in dairying, producing 1,140 pounds of butter but, unlike Euro-Americans, no cheese. Wells considered the Oneidas "very bare of stock." The Oneidas' involvement with horses, so visible in 1780, had withered away almost completely. About half the families had some sort of "neat cattle," meaning oxen or mules; thirteen households kept one or two or three cows, and only nine kept hogs. In the absence of a Native tradition of pastured herd animals or wool production, they raised no sheep, unlike the whites in the two adjacent towns, who owned twenty-eight thousand sheep.[46] It is clear that while some Oneidas, like Euro-American immigrants, were producing a surplus to sell beyond their community, most Oneidas were concerned with subsistence.

There was some correlation between a Europeanized pattern of agricultural production (as indicated by plough ownership and a relatively large number of cleared acres) and the presence of Christians in the household. This correlation raises the question whether Christianity actually promoted that form of agriculture or whether openness to plough agriculture led to openness to Christianity. The statistics show that numerous wholly traditionalist households were highly productive agriculturists in the European fashion, and agriculturist families comprising mostly Christians were not. There was no apparent difference in land use (or profession of Christianity) by those families cultivating in common.

Shearman described those "farmers who raised a sufficiency of produce for their comfortable support" as "the flower of the tribe." Doubtless he had in mind Thomas Cornelius, Daniel Skenandoah, and Christian Beechtree. Their families enjoyed considerable and conspicuous material prosperity. Shearman noted: "The houses of these Indians are generally much better than the log houses of the whites, being constructed of hewn, even joisted logs, with shingle roofs and good windows. There are three good frame houses belonging to them, one of these is a very handsome one, belonging to Skenado. I noticed in it, some tasty fringed window curtains, and good carpets."[47] Wells also took note of these houses, making the further observation that they were "divided into several apartments." This description is consistent with short longhouses and suggests an extended-family arrangement within the household. Not coincidentally, these three men were identified as chiefs for the purpose of receiving the tribal annuity. Power, wealth, and status continued to correlate, as they had in the Revolutionary War era. Daniel Skenandoah, Thomas Cornelius, Cornelius Wheelock, and William Jourdan were all prosperous farmers, and they all rented out parcels ranging from fourteen to thirty-two acres. The leasing strategy had not been abandoned.

Households also earned income through wage labor, hunting, and fishing. Shearman reported: "There are several heads of families in my list, who cultivate no land of their own, but gain a subsistence by chopping wood and performing farm labor for others." Schoolcraft acknowledged "semi-hunters," of which he counted six. Martin Powless's thirty dollars of hunting-related income was highest; members of Christian Beechtree's and Henry Jourdan's families counted twenty dollars. These figures seem low, perhaps reflecting the season in which the data were collected or their concern about taxation.[48] Thomas Cornelius, David Johnson, and Henry Jourdan also earned money as interpreters. Most Oneidas did not speak English, so the non-Iroquois visitor still needed a guide, though only a linguistic one.

Comparing the 1845 figures with those of 1855 is problematic, because 1845 is the only year for which the manuscript version, with its household-level data, survives. Thus, we can compare only the Oneidas' aggregate figures. However, the 1855 figures are even more dubious than the earlier ones. With an eye to securing greater Oneida cooperation, the state dispatched Nathaniel T. Strong, a Seneca, to perform the 1855 census among the Oneidas and Onondagas. Strong may have been a Seneca, but it was widely known that he had been the interpreter for, and was a signer of, the Buffalo Creek treaty. He had been a close associate of disgraced agent Stryker. Now residing at Cattaraugus, Strong encountered the same suspicion that a deeper state agenda relating to taxation was at work. A meeting with the leaders of the Windfalls resulted only in a decision to consult the Orchards—a fact that itself illuminated an ongoing relationship between the two groups. In the end, the Oneidas agreed to answer Strong's questions but only at an official public meeting. Strong admitted that he obtained "the statistical information of 'Oneida Indian Settlement' . . . without calling at a single house."[49] Thus, Strong did not see what he was supposed to count, and Oneidas' statements about their households were likely affected by the social context in which they were made and by the fear that the state was paving the way for taxation. According to the 1855 census, Oneida population at the two reservations remained relatively stable at roughly 160. Improved acreage had declined from 421 to 354, with agricultural production stable but declining in the production of potatoes, peas, and dairy products. This census added maple sugaring to the list of measured economic activities, though the Oneidas had been engaged in this traditional practice all along. Strong took note of the production of sixty pounds of maple sugar and seventy gallons of maple molasses. Probably there was more.

Peddling and Performing

Significantly, the 1855 census questionnaire expanded its area of interest to domestic manufactures. Although the Oneidas' activities were again tabulated imperfectly, the importance of Oneida crafts was acknowledged by the total valuation of beadwork at $530. Oneida women, sometimes with other family members, left the community to sell baskets and beadwork. In her 1850 book, *Rural Hours*, Susan Fenimore Cooper, daughter of James, described a trio of Oneida women at her door vending baskets. They had traveled some fifty miles to trade their wares for subsistence items, such as meat and bread, that traditionally existed within the purview of women's exchange and would have been easily overlooked by the census. Through their demeanor and dress, the women asserted their difference. Cooper wrote: "Only one of the three could speak English, and she seemed to do so with effort and reluctance. They were dressed in gowns of blue calico, rudely cut, coarsely stitched together, and so short as to show their broadcloth leggings worked with beads. Their heads were entirely bare, their straight, black hair hanging loose about their shoulders, and, although it was midsummer at the time, they were closely wrapped in coarse white blankets." Cooper visited the Oneidas' camp and witnessed how the seasonal itinerant economy enabled the family to travel and operate as a unit. While the women sold baskets, the men were "cutting bows and arrows for the boys of the village." Whites fetishized Indian material culture, especially the implements of war.[50]

Whites' fascination with Native objects commodified and trivialized Indian culture, but it also provided the Indians with a market by which to make a living and retain traditional artistic and motor skills. Among the constricted options a colonized people faced, this was still meaningful work. Just as production for non-Indian consumers had not despiritualized hunting in past centuries, it did not necessarily despiritualize craft work now. Craft skill had always been infused with a sacred element—an item's efficacy was commensurate to its spiritual endowment. And meaning inhered in the materials themselves. The physical properties of beads resonated with Iroquois ritual objects originally fashioned from shell and crystal and closely linked to concepts such as "good mind." Basket dyes were made from the juice of berries, which had sacred associations (although druggists' dyes would do in a pinch). Basketmaking and wood carving cultivated continued familiarity with the natural environment and the materials it supplied. This familiarity blended easily with related areas of traditional knowledge, such as pharmacology. As the anthropologist Beverly Gordon points out, "A clear boundary line between the motifs on objects meant for internal, tribal use and external, tourist use does not exist." Cooper's description of the Oneida women mentioned the beads that were part of their dress. Common patterns included elements with religious significance, such as trees, flowers, and the celestial dome. Thus, though basket manufacture had European roots, it became a "traditional" activity for Oneidas, just as it did for many other Native groups in the Northeast. As the anthropologist Anthony Wonderley has pointed out with regard to basketmaking, "oral and material traditions were learned and practiced in the same setting."[51]

The Oneidas sold baskets in the neighboring communities. By the mid-1840s they were selling to John Humphrey Noyes's utopian Christian settlement, which had settled on lands the Oneidas had given up in 1840, including Good Peter's burial place. Initially, the communitarian Protestants lived in some Oneidas' former homes and appropriated their name. The members of the "Oneida Community" took particular pride in the history of the location because, as they put it, the land had "passed from the community of nature to the community of civilization and grace, without any intervening defilement from selfish ownership, and exclusive title deeds."[52] Oneida women traded baskets, berries, and labor for foodstuffs and small amounts of cash. Sometimes this trade progressed to the point of leaving the sect "stocked, and overstocked" with baskets that ranged "from the coarse market basket to the fine and curiously-wrought fanciful work-basket fit for a lady's boudoir." At a festive 1852 gathering of the two peoples, a newspaper observed that Oneida men now dressed much like their non-Native peers (with "a gloss on their raven-black hair that the city fop might envy"), while women retained "the peculiarities of the Indian costume; skirts and pantlets of broadcloth, embroidered with beads, and decorated with gold and silver ornaments. In the place of a bonnet, they wear the primitive 'blanket,' now generally consisting of a broadcloth, and in some of the younger women, giving place to richly colored shawls." The differential in dress was reflected in language as well; though most of the Oneidas did not speak much English, women were in the majority of those who did not.[53]

The Oneidas also took advantage of their access to New York's key transportation corridor. Traveling along the Erie Canal in 1833, the Englishman Richard Weston had noticed Oneida children running alongside collecting pennies pitched from boats. In 1845, a traveler identified in *Godey's Lady's Book* as Miss Leslie observed Oneida hawkers at the Oneida railroad station.

> At the Oneida station-house, some Indian women in half-civilized costume came about the cars. There was one rather handsome squaw, having a large and elegant silk shawl, striped with various colours, pinned gracefully round her head and flowing square over her shoulders and far down her back. . . . The last remnant of the once powerful tribe of Oneidas is yet lingering in this neighbourhood. Their number is reduced to between two and three hundred, and they live by making and selling bead-embroidered moccasons, shot-bags, tobacco-pouches and other articles of Indian fashion [fig. 15].

As transportation grew more convenient and economic prosperity facilitated the development of a tourist infrastructure, the Oneidas also went to the travelers' destinations to sell their goods. In conjunction with fellow Native craftspeople, Oneidas helped develop the lively markets in Indian wares that began at Saratoga and Niagara Falls in the 1840s.[54]

By the 1830s, Natives were becoming a rarity in upstate New York, and they understood that that made their very presence commodifiable, as it had been in Europe. Cooper had noted "More than one member of our household had never yet seen an Indian" and "had long been so anxious" to do so. Of her own feelings, she said, "It is impossible to behold them without a feeling of particular interest."[55] Visual artists, dramatists, and novelists met and perpetuated this rising public fascination with Natives, and Cooper's father had capitalized on it recently with the publication of *The Pioneers* in 1823 and *The Last of the Mohicans* in 1826. The Oneidas sought to capitalize on it as well. An 1828 broadside advertising a public performance of an "INDIAN WAR DANCE" invited the "ladies and gentlemen" of New York and New England to gaze on a display of martial and cultural rites, with musical accompaniment by an Oneida violinist, admission twenty-five cents (fig. 16). Margaret Hunter Hall, an English visitor to Saratoga Springs in 1827, described a poster seemingly identical in its content and also the performance itself. Although Hall did not specify the tribal identity of the performers, a Saratoga paper hailed the arrival of roughly ten Oneidas at Saratoga that summer and predicted that "the

Fig. 15. Anonymous, beaded bag, ca. 1850. The floral design reflected a style associated with the Tuscaroras, but Oneidas produced similar work. Courtesy of the Oneida Indian Nation of New York.

chief and his party will be all the go at the Springs." Hall bore out that assessment. She noted, "This was of course too valuable an opportunity of gratifying curiosity to lose, and, accordingly, we swallowed our tea and set off forthwith to the appointed place." Hall was not disappointed. But she also was surprised.

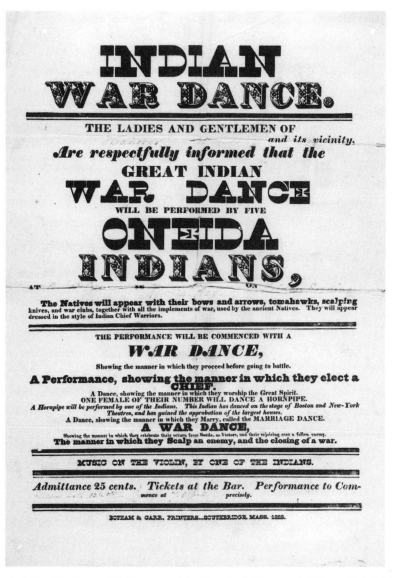

Fig. 16. *Indian War Dance*, 1828. Courtesy of the Rosenbach Museum & Library, Philadelphia, A828i.

The exhibition was certainly sufficiently savage and strange to be quite natural, but for the scalping part of it I confess that my nerves were not strong enough to admit of looking even at the mere pretence of this barbarous practice. We were told by the handbill that part of the entertainment was to consist of playing on the violin by an Indian, and this proved certainly not the least curious part of the scene, for this Indian, dressed in a surtout coat between the acts of their barbarous dances and war whoops, filled up the intervals by playing Scotch reels, Strathspeys, Paddy O'Rafferty, and such like civilized tunes.[56]

In the early 1850s, an Oneida "Indian Minstrel Company" also performed hymns in New York City.[57] Oneida performers played to the traditionally ambivalent expectations of the audience: the thrilling and frightening war dances of "bad" Indians and the affirming, reassuring hymn singing of "good" ones. The repertoire echoed the performances on the occasion of the Continental Army's visit to Kanonwalohale in 1776.

Peddling and performing marked the Oneidas' place at the margins of the economy of the dominant society and were important complements to their agricultural and horticultural production. They also provided a measure of cultural and personal pride. It should not be surprising that the Oneidas exploited this strategy as the tourist economy expanded. Summer fishing camps of the eighteenth century gave way to summer sales trips to places like Saratoga Springs, where Indian families thrilled tourists with their "exotic" wares—and their presence. They played on and, however modestly, profited from the trope of the vanishing Indian while implicitly refuting it by their presence, all the while maintaining a pattern of seasonal mobility. Through itinerant peddling and cultural performances, Oneidas in central New York asserted their cultural distinctiveness in a manner meaningful to them and acceptable to the dominant culture. An Oneida painting from the 1830s depicting three Oneida men of different periods (fig. 17) illustrates the Oneidas' ability to find continuity in change. This kind of painting was itself an appropriation of European representational practice and was likely destined for sale to a non-Oneida. In the painting, the man on the left is wearing contemporary, nineteenth-century ceremonial garb, in contrast to the other two, who represent a bygone era. But despite his coat with lapels, large cross, and Algonquian calumet, or peace pipe, the nineteenth-century Oneida man partakes of a traditional aesthetic.[58] As the painting shows, the symbols of their identity are the result of a symbiosis—however unequal—between colonizers and colonized. A visitor, identified only as T.C.M.,

Fig. 17. Anonymous (Oneida), *Three Iroquois Men,* ca. 1835. The artist depicted changing styles of Oneida male dress from the traditional to the contemporary. The painting was probably made for commercial purposes. Collection of The New-York Historical Society, accession no. X.521.

described the creation of these goods on a visit to an Oneida household in 1868.

> Opening a door, we beheld a curious scene. The room was small and—shabby, we white folks would call it; but if these people had been grandees in their palace they could hardly have received us with more complaisance. Not the least apology did they offer, nor did they apparently think one; but regarded us with a calm, benignant expression, as though we, and not they, were the be-nighted ones. Here is the picture photographed in our memories: Indian weaving bright-colored bits of worsted around the ends of cross-bows; squaw making bead-cushions, mats, and baby-slippers; young man sitting by the stove whittling arrows; grown-up daughter stirring a boiling kettle of hulled-corn; good-natured baby sprawling on a bed in the corner. There was an air of repose and satisfaction about the establishment quite anomalous. Not the least hurry.

> Time, indeed, seemed of so small account to them, that I was astonished to see a clock on the wall.[59]

This description evokes James Emlen's description of the Oneidas at Canandaigua as "masters of their own time." T.C.M.'s commentary aptly captures continuity in Oneida life, as well as the Oneidas' quiet resistance to the ideology of the dominant culture.

By 1840, the Oneidas had little land left to lose, and they received commensurately less attention from the state and federal governments. Those, like Abraham Hogeboom, who did attend to them sometimes did so from the most cynical motives. Others, like Seward, were more sympathetic, and even saw themselves as enlightened philanthropists. Ironically, the policies of the latter proved similarly detrimental to the Oneidas. Seward and Spencer were wedded to the notion that dividing and privatizing the Oneidas' landholdings would make the Oneidas prosperous while freeing land for their constituents. This "win-win" logic of severalty was seductive enough to obscure the more immediate cultural, social, and economic realities. Those realities suggested the Oneidas would simply lose, and lose they did. This drama would, of course, eventually be reprised on a grander stage when the Dawes Allotment Act made private property of tribal lands across the nation. President Theodore Roosevelt, in his 1901 State of the Union address, lauded allotment as a "mighty pulverizing engine to break up the tribal mass." Territorially, he proved largely correct. Culturally, however, as the Oneidas had already demonstrated, the "tribal mass" would prove more resilient.

Conclusion

B Y THE MIDDLE of the nineteenth century, the Oneidas had lost all but two tiny slivers of their ancestral homeland. It had been a rapid descent—all within the lifetime of any octogenarian. In 1770, traveling the length of Oneida territory took several days. In 1850, it took only several minutes. The loss of land constrained the Oneidas' ability to pursue the economic, political, social, and cultural patterns by which they had sustained themselves since time immemorial. They did not, however, disappear.

Faced with a rising tide of Euro-American settlers, the Oneidas at first attempted to divert it. At the 1768 Treaty of Fort Stanwix, the Oneidas spared themselves by shifting the problem to Natives in Pennsylvania and the Ohio Valley. The respite offered by this tactic would be brief, however. With the Euro-American population in the region increasing exponentially, the demand for western lands was too great. Although the notable events that culminated in the American Revolution—the fiery protests, the dumping of the tea—took place in colonial cities, nine in ten colonists were rural farmers. They were deeply frustrated with a British policy of territorial expansion that seemed to them insufficiently aggressive. In 1776, they took matters into their own hands. The Oneidas understood the danger and perceived that their interests lay in cultivating a favorable relationship with the Patriots. Their assessment was essentially correct, but the costs of acting on it were great. The Revolutionary War wrought great destruction on the Oneidas and the Iroquois Confederacy as a whole. Although it was not the "Iroquois civil war" that it has been made it out to be, the Oneidas' alliance with the Patriots contributed to their postwar alienation from the rest of the demoralized Six Nations. The benefits of the Patriot alliance to the Oneidas and the Six Nations generally were disappointingly meager. Not only were the Oneidas unable to influence the behavior of the new nation toward their fellow Iroquois in the wake of war, they were unable even to save their own lands. When the Patriot soldiers who invaded Iroquoia in 1779 returned as settlers and speculators, they successfully took hold of most of the Longhouse by 1789.

The new settlers enjoyed the active assistance of a state government that was anxious to refill its empty coffers and fend off the competing territorial claims of neighboring states and the jurisdictional claims of the federal government—compounded by British subversion from Canada. Treaties allowed the state to organize and control the process of levering the Natives off the land. The stereotypical view of treaties, at which unwitting Natives were plied with liquor and encouraged to put their marks on documents they did not understand, does bear some resemblance to reality, especially before 1780. Liquor did flow, but the Indians also faced the problem of surmounting linguistic and cultural barriers to understand the terms of the agreements into which they entered. Few Americans today comprehend fully their mortgage or credit-card contracts and would be hard-pressed if they tried. That challenge only begins to suggest those facing the Oneidas in the late eighteenth and nineteenth centuries who were presented with a strange artifact— the written contract—that used an alien language, mathematical system, and concept of territory.

The Oneidas turned to a succession of knowledgeable and, they hoped, trustworthy, individuals for help. They were disappointed again and again by men such as Livingston, Dean, Schuyler, Penet, Kirkland, and De Ferrière. These men may have been motivated by greed, but their actions were conditioned, and condoned, by a larger ideology of European cultural supremacy that conveniently supposed Indian dispossession to be in the Natives' best interest. In the Euro-Americans' model of how the world operated, Indians' landholdings were seen as ultimately impeding the Natives' "civilization," in particular their transformation into European-style farmers. The Indians' counterproposal to dispossession—that they become landlords—was therefore unacceptable. Leasing would deny Euro-Americans what they wanted and allow Native men to continue smoking and hunting. Even the Quakers, a group that took a self-consciously critical stance toward society, put more effort into their model farm at Oneida than into defending the Oneidas against unfavorable land deals. Timothy Pickering's hopes for Quaker success tempered his vigilance as well.

While ideology prevented the Oneidas from finding an effective advocate, demographic and ecological concerns dictated that the Oneidas did not usually have the option to say no to treaty commissioners. With tens of thousands of immigrants streaming into the Oneidas' strategically situated homeland from New England, The Natives' access to game and fish declined. They sold land to get cash to alleviate hunger when their subsistence cycle fell short, as well as to erase debts for goods they had previously manufactured themselves or paid for with income from hunting. Oneidas also sold land to get some compensation for acreage that had already been settled by whites, sometimes with a significant degree of Oneida complicity.

The Oneidas made serious efforts to better understand their predicament. These are most visible to us today in the accounts of their religious beliefs and debates. Most Oneidas pursued a synthesis of traditional and Christian practices and beliefs. Although most Oneidas considered whites' behavior to be morally objectionable, Oneidas hoped to tap into the source of their strength. They were particularly interested in Euro-Americans' ability to stave off the worst effects of alcohol consumption. Believing that prosperity was a function of effective relationships with spirit beings, the Oneidas sought to develop new ways of understanding and interacting with them. As a result, the Oneida hymn singers received the favorable notice of nearly every visitor. But Oneidas of all parties remained concerned with witchcraft and other traditional matters as well.

By 1850, dispossession, defeat, and disgust had spurred most Oneidas to go beyond the bounds of Iroquoia to secure their futures. By emigrating to Wisconsin and Canada, Oneidas renewed their access to land and regained relative freedom from molestation by whites, at least for a time. These moves made it economically feasible and psychologically easier for them to take up Euro-American land use patterns and develop stable, viable communities. Other Oneidas started west down the "ambassador road," but they traveled only as far as necessary to find refuge with other, more populous Iroquois communities. There were also those who remained hunkered down on their ancestral homeland. Although they had not gone anywhere, they had already completed a great journey. The landscape around them had been transformed as the forest had been felled, cleared, and converted to tilled fields. Deer had become fewer. Beaver had grown scarce indeed.

Sheep multiplied. Footpaths were erased by wagon roads and then turn-pikes, canals, railways. Surrounded by Euro-American immigrants, these Oneidas were now strangers, rather than masters, in their own land. As their landholdings dwindled, they took jobs as domestics and farm workers for whites. Although those residing on reservation lands remained outside the state's regimes of taxation and fishing and hunting regulation, their separa-tion from the broader society waned. Intermarriage became common by the twentieth century, and Oneidas submitted to state criminal jurisdiction on the reservation. Although some Oneidas attended state or federal boarding schools such as Thomas, Hampton or Carlisle, more went to local state-supported day schools.

Still, Lewis Henry Morgan was wrong: even after unilaterally being made citizens of New York and the United States, the Oneidas did not "cease to be Indians." Culturally, Oneidas passed down language and lore, family trees as well as family rivalries. These persist today—seemingly in roughly ascending order. The Oneida language in New York is perilously close to dying out and is not the mother tongue for Oneidas anywhere. Leg-ends, stories, and folk beliefs about spirits were transmitted in English, in which language they were extensively recorded in the twentieth century and are still being passed along in the twenty-first. The matrilineages, however, proved to be the crucial institutions of cultural survival across time and space. Throughout the nineteenth and twentieth centuries, as Oneidas were dispersed across New York State and beyond, the matrilineages sustained Oneidas' strong awareness of ancestral identity and rights.

Because of their reduced numbers and acreage, the Oneidas managed their affairs informally after the mid-nineteenth century. They needed to assert themselves formally only so far as they could garner serious attention from federal and state authorities. With respect to the federal government, the Oneidas continued to collect their treaty cloth annuity as well as compen-sation for the lands reserved to them, but never settled, in Kansas. Oneidas sporadically challenged state officials over one or another provision from their many treaties. In the 1860s and 1870s, Oneidas from New York and Wisconsin argued for, among other things, compensation for the dwindling value of their right to hunt and fish on ceded lands, as well as three half-mile squares on the north shore of Oneida Lake reserved to them but never ceded. They were rebuffed in these and other similar complaints.

The Oneidas' redemption came at the eleventh hour, or even somewhat past it. In 1909, having been forcibly ousted from the last thirty-two-acre parcel of the reservation for defaulting on a mortgage, the Oneidas challenged the legality of the ejectment. It took a decade for them to receive a decisive favorable verdict. This verdict illuminated, for the first time in the modern era, the problematic legality of New York's acquisition of Oneida lands arising from the state's defiance of federal authority and, later, even its own laws. Thus began a new phase in the struggle for Oneida lands in which the nation has managed to recoup control of some of its ancestral territory. Aspects of the Oneidas' legal challenges to their dispossession have been heard by the United States Supreme Court on three separate occasions. The process, however, has been, at best, halting: the litigation has now entered its second century. With regard to the Oneidas' land claims, the Iroquois dictum of thinking forward to the seventh generation when making decisions may fall short. It may take eight or nine generations for them to be resolved.

In the meantime, the preservation of a clearly defined Oneida nation territory eventually did make it possible for Oneidas to capitalize on their sovereign prerogatives. In the 1980s, with the understanding that the reservation was not subject to state laws, Oneidas opened a high-stakes bingo hall and sold tax-free cigarettes. These activities were controversial within and outside the nation. In fact, in 1988, the bingo hall was stormed and burned down—by Oneidas. This dissent was quelled, and in 1993 the Oneidas opened a major casino, Turning Stone, that became second only to Niagara Falls as a tourist draw to upstate New York. It is located about two miles from the "ambassador road" and closer to the newer east-west thoroughfare, the New York State Thruway. The prime mover behind the casino, the Nation representative Ray Halbritter, has written: "The casino is not a statement of who we are, but only a means to get us where we want to be."[1] Undoubtedly, it has been a means to other ends: Turning Stone has employed many Oneidas and underwritten myriad health, education, and cultural programs, new economic enterprises, and the outright repurchase of reservation lands, as well as more litigation.

Despite Halbritter's statement, however, the casino *is* a statement of who the Oneidas are and a potent symbol of how they survived. Turning Stone reminds the Oneidas' neighbors (to the great displeasure of many of them) of the Oneidas' sovereign immunity and their government-to-government relationship with the United States, which are rooted in the fact that the Oneida nation preceded the United States. There is also the materiality of the casino itself, which stands as a grand brick-and-mortar counterpoint to the seasonal "Indian Encampment" at Saratoga, where Oneidas sold "Indian wares" to passers-by and tourists in the nineteenth century. Like their fore-bears, Oneidas continue to make a living by commodifying their culture. While engaging the larger society that developed around them, Oneidas carved out an economic and cultural niche in whose shelter their identity might survive. The casino is just the most prominent—although not neces-sarily the most important—of many such creative adaptations, some mate-rial, some spiritual. It represents a process that allowed the Oneidas to de-fine themselves as a separate—and persisting—people.

Appendix

Selected Oneida Population Counts, 1763–1856

Year	Oneida territory	Wisconsin	Canada
1763	1,000		
1790	588		
1792	600		
1800	688		
1816	1,031		
1824	1,096		
1827	1,136		
1836	722	388	
1838		624	
1844		720	
1845	157		410
1853		978	
1855	161		
1856			519

Sources: *1763:* Sir William Johnson gave 250 as the number of warriors, and I have calculated the overall population at a ratio of 1:4. "Enumeration of the Indians within the Northern Department," Nov. 18, 1763, in Edmund B. O'Callaghan, *The Documentary History of the State of New-York* (Albany: Weed, Parsons & Co., 1850–51), 7:582. *1790:* Kirkland, "A General Statement of the Six Nations of Indians Living within the United States," Dec. 24, 1790, SKP. The decline in numbers is in part attributable to wartime dispersal, which was later partly reversed. *1792:* Israel Chapin to Timothy Pickering, Nov. 12, 1792, Henry O'Reilly Papers, vol. 8, New-York Historical Society, New York. *1800:* Kirkland to Alexander Miller, June 7, 1800, SKP. *1816:* Erastus Granger to W. H. Crawford, Sept. 17, 1816, M271, r. 1, NA. *1824:* Jasper Parrish, Oct. 11, 1824, Misc. Mss., New-York Historical Society, New York. *1827:* Jasper Parrish, Jan. 15, 1827, M234, r. 832, NA. *1836:* James Schermerhorn to Lewis Cass, July 12, 1836, M234, r. 583, NA. *1838:* Commissioner of Indian Affairs, *Annual Report,* cited in Laurence M. Hauptman and L. Gordon McLester III, *Chief Daniel Bread and the Oneida Nation of Indians of Wisconsin* (Norman: University of Oklahoma Press, 2002), 103. *1844:* Ibid. *1845:* Henry R. Schoolcraft, "Population Census of Indian Reservations, 1845," A1832, NYSA; British and Canadian Sessional Papers, cited in Jack Campisi, "Ethnic Identity and Boundary Maintenance in Three Oneida Communities" (Ph.D. diss., State University of New York, Albany, 1974), 324. *1853:* Commissioner of Indian Affairs, *Annual Report,* cited in Hauptman and McLester, *Chief Daniel Bread,* 103. *1855:* Nathaniel T. Strong, "Appendix," in *Census of the State of New York for 1855* (Albany, N.Y.: Charles Van Benthuysen, 1857), 500. *1856:* British and Canadian Sessional Papers, cited in Campisi, "Ethnic Identity and Boundary Maintenance," 324.

Abbreviations

Notes

Chapter 1. A Place and a People in a Time of Change

1. William A. Starna, "The Oneida Homeland in the Seventeenth Century," in *The Oneida Indian Experience: Two Perspectives,* ed. Jack Campisi and Laurence M. Hauptman (Syracuse, N.Y.: Syracuse University Press, 1988), 16–18; Anthony Wonderley, "An Oneida Community in 1780: Study of an Inventory of Iroquois Property Losses during the Revolutionary War," *Northeast Anthropology* 56 (1998): 19–41; Margaret C. Rodman, "Empowering Place: Multilocality and Multivocality," *American Anthropologist* 94 (1992): 640–57; Keith Basso, *Wisdom Sits in Places: Landscape and Language among the Western Apache* (Albuquerque: University of New Mexico Press, 1996); Anthony Wonderley, *Oneida Iroquois Folklore, Myth, and History* (Syracuse, N.Y.: Syracuse University Press, 2004), 78, 80.

2. Charles A. Huguenin, "The Sacred Stone of the Oneidas," *New York Folklore Quarterly* 8 (1957): 16–22; Wonderley, *Oneida Iroquois Folklore,* 1–14, 24–31; quotation by Shickellamy from James H. Merrell, *Into the American Woods: Negotiators on the Pennsylvania Frontier* (New York: W. W. Norton, 1998), 147.

3. J. N. B. Hewitt, *Iroquoian Cosmology* (1899–1900; 1925–26; repr., New York: AMS Press, 1974); John Mohawk, *Iroquois Creation Story* (Buffalo, N.Y.: Mohawk Books, 2005), 1; Barbara A. Mann, *Iroquoian Women: The Gantowisas* (New York: Peter Lang, 2000), 89–94; William Beauchamp, *Aboriginal Place-Names in New York State* (Albany: New York State Education Department, 1907), 44; *David Cusick's Sketches of Ancient History of the Six Nations* (Lewiston, N.Y., 1828), 18; Wonderley, *Oneida Iroquois Folklore,* 67 (quotation), 70, 74, 94–101, 104–6.

4. Kurt Jordan, *The Seneca Restoration, 1715–1754* (Gainesville: University Press of Florida, 2008), 34–42; Henry Rowe Schoolcraft, *Notes on the Iroquois; or, Contributions to American History, Antiquities, and General Ethnology* (Albany, N.Y.: Erastus H. Pease, 1847), 174–77; French visitors quoted in Alan S. Taylor, *The Divided Ground: Indians, Settlers, and the Northern Borderland of the American Revolution* (New York:

Knopf, 2006), 35–36; Nathan Burchard, "Tioniunt; or, The Oneida Stone and the Remains of Indian Antiquities in Its Vicinity" (paper presented to the New-York Historical Society, Apr. 3, 1849), New-York Historical Society, 20, 26, 28 ("remains"), 30 ("admirably piled"), 31, 33 ("cellars"), 34, 37 ("astonished ploughman"); Richard Smith, *A Tour of Four Great Rivers: The Hudson, Mohawk, Susquehanna, and Delaware in 1769*, ed. Francis W. Halsey (New York: Charles Scribner's Sons, 1906), liv.

5. William A. Starna, "Oneida Homeland," 9–22; Starna, "Aboriginal Title and Traditional Iroquois Land Use: An Anthropological Perspective," in *Iroquois Land Claims*, ed. Christopher Vecsey and Starna (Syracuse, N.Y.: Syracuse University Press, 1988), 31–48; Lewis H. Morgan, *League of the Ho-De-No Sau-Nee or Iroquois* (New York: Dodd, Mead, 1901), 1:40–43; Franklin B. Hough, *Proceedings of the Commissioners of Indian Affairs of the State of New York* (Albany, N.Y.: J. Munsell, 1861), 1:41; Beauchamp, *Aboriginal Place-Names*, 142, 168; "Journal of Warren Johnson," in *In Mohawk Country: Early Narratives about a Native People*, ed. Dean R. Snow, Charles T. Gehring, and Starna (Syracuse, N.Y.: Syracuse University Press, 1996), 261; Proceedings at a treaty held by Sir William Johnson with the Six Nations, Nov. 6, 1768, *NYCD*, 8:127.

6. George S. Snyderman, "Concepts of Land Ownership among the Iroquois and Their Neighbors," in *Symposium on Local Diversity in Iroquois Culture*, ed. William N. Fenton (Washington, D.C.: U.S. Government Printing Office, 1951), 13–34; William N. Fenton, "This Island, the World on the Turtle's Back," *Journal of American Folklore* 75 (1962): 298 ("whose faces"); Jeffrey J. Gordon, "Onondaga Iroquois Place-Names: An Approach to Historical and Contemporary Indian Landscape Perception," *Names* 32 (1984): 231n1; Starna, "Aboriginal Title," 34–37.

7. Schoolcraft, *Notes*, 71; Gordon, "Onondaga Iroquois," 221; Burchard, "Tioniunt," 35.

8. Michael Recht, "The Role of Fishing in the Iroquois Economy, 1600–1792," *New York History* 76 (1995): 5–30; Francis Adrian Vanderkemp, "Extracts from the Vanderkemp Letters from the Hudson to Lake Ontario in 1792," *Publications of the Buffalo Historical Society* 2 (1880): 67.

9. James Smith, "An Account of the Remarkable Occurrences in the Life and Travels of Colonel James Smith . . . ," in *Indian Captivities; or, Life in the Wigwam*, ed. Samuel G. Drake (Auburn, N.Y.: Derby and Miller, 1851; repr., New York: AMS Press, 1975), 198; Pickering, "Account of Losses Sustained by Oneida Indians," TPP, 62:157–66A; Wonderley, "Oneida Community," 25; Thomas Eliot Norton, *The Fur Trade in Colonial New York* (Madison: University of Wisconsin Press, 1974), 101–2; Starna, "Aboriginal Title," 31–33.

10. Elisabeth Tooker, *Ethnography of the Huron Indians, 1615–1649* (1964; repr., Syracuse, N.Y.: Syracuse University Press, 1991), 100; *Cusick's Sketches*, 21; Wonderley, *Oneida Iroquois Folklore*, 76–80; Samuel Kirkland, Journal, May to Aug. 12, 1788, 4, Lothrop Family Papers, microfilm, P-292, Massachusetts Historical Society, Boston.

11. *Citizen Soldier: The Revolutionary War Journal of Joseph Bloomfield*, ed. Mark E. Lender and James Kirby Martin (Newark: New Jersey Historical Society, 1982), 91–92; *Along the Hudson and Mohawk: The 1790 Journey of Count Paolo Andreani*, ed.

and trans. Cesare Marino and Karim M. Tiro (Philadelphia: University of Pennsylvania Press, 2006), 61–62; Wonderley, "Oneida Community," 25, 39.

12. A Meeting with the Six Nations, Sept. 13, 1762, *JP*, 10:512; James Taylor Carson, "Horses and the Economy and Culture of the Choctaw Indians, 1690–1840," *Ethnohistory* 42 (1995): 500–501; James Smith, "Account of the Remarkable Occurrences," 199–200; Jordan, *Seneca Restoration*, 50.

13. Paul A. W. Wallace, *Indian Paths of Pennsylvania* (Harrisburg: Pennsylvania Historical and Museum Commission, 1965), 1–14; Marino and Tiro, *Along the Hudson and Mohawk*, 55; Richard Smith, *Tour of Four Great Rivers*, 71.

14. Matthew Dennis, *Cultivating a Landscape of Peace: Iroquois-European Encounters in Seventeenth-Century America* (Ithaca, N.Y.: Cornell University Press / New York State Historical Association, 1993), 34–36.

15. *Parker on the Iroquois*, ed. William N. Fenton (Syracuse, N.Y.: Syracuse University Press, 1968), 1:36, 89–109; Carol Cornelius, *Iroquois Corn in a Culture-Based Curriculum: A Framework for Respectfully Teaching about Cultures* (Albany: State University of New York Press, 1999), 91–118; Anthony F. C. Wallace, *The Death and Rebirth of the Seneca* (New York: Knopf, 1970), 51.

16. George Hamell, "Strawberries, Floating Islands, and Rabbit Captains: Mythical Realities and European Contact in the Northeast during the Sixteenth and Seventeenth Centuries," *Journal of Canadian Studies* 24 (1986–87): 78; Wallace, *Death and Rebirth*, 13; Christopher Miller and George Hamell, "A New Perspective on Indian-White Contact: Cultural Symbols and Colonial Trade," *Journal of American History* 73 (1986): 322–23; Fenton, *Parker on the Iroquois*, 1:96–99.

17. Richard Smith, *Tour of Four Great Rivers*, 64–67 ("paltry," 66); Fenton, *Parker on the Iroquois*, 1:23–24, 30–32; Jane Mt. Pleasant, "The Science behind the Three Sisters Mound System: An Agronomic Assessment of an Indigenous Agricultural System in the Northeast," in *Histories of Maize: Multidisciplinary Approaches to the Prehistory, Linguistics, Biogeography, Domestication, and Evolution of Maize*, ed. John E. Staller, Robert H. Tykot, and Bruce F. Benz (Amsterdam: Academic Press, 2006), 529–37; Frederick Cook, *Journals of the Military Expedition of Major General John Sullivan* (Auburn, N.Y.: Knapp, Peck, and Thompson, 1887), 23, 27, 48, 305.

18. James Smith, "Account of the Remarkable Occurrences," 197; Pickering, "Account of Losses," 155–66A; Roy L. Butterfield, "The Great Days of Maple Sugar," *New York History* 39 (1958): 151–53; Wonderley, "Oneida Community," 24.

19. David D. Smits, "The 'Squaw Drudge': A Prime Index of Savagism," *Ethnohistory* 29 (1982): 281–306; Parker quoted in Fenton, *Parker on the Iroquois*, 1:31; *A Narrative of the Life of Mrs. Mary Jemison*, ed. James E. Seaver (1824; repr., Syracuse, N.Y.: Syracuse University Press, 1990), 31–32; Joy Bilharz, "First among Equals? The Changing Status of Seneca Women," in *Gender and Power in Native North America*, ed. Lillian A. Ackerman and Laura F. Klein (Norman: University of Oklahoma Press, 1995), 101–13; Diane Rothenberg, "The Mothers of the Nation: Seneca Resistance to Quaker Intervention," in *Women and Colonization*, ed. Eleanor Leacock and Mona Etienne (New York: Praeger, 1980), 66–70; Elisabeth Tooker, "Women in Iroquois Society," in *Extending the Rafters: Interdisciplinary Approaches to Iroquois Culture*, ed. Michael K.

Foster, Jack Campisi, and Marianne Mithun (Albany: State University of New York Press, 1984), 109–24; Mann, *Iroquoian Women,* 162–69.

20. Jack Campisi, "Fur Trade and Factionalism of the 18th Century Oneida Indians," in *Studies on Iroquoian Culture,* ed. Nancy Bonvillain (Rindge, N.H.: Franklin Pierce College, 1980), 38–39; Loskiel quoted in Judith K. Brown, "Iroquois Women: An Ethnohistoric Note," in *Toward an Anthropology of Women,* ed. Rayna R. Reiter (New York: Monthly Review Press, 1975), 250.

21. Bruce G. Trigger, "The Road to Affluence: A Reassessment of Early Huron Responses to European Contact," in *Affluence and Cultural Survival: Proceedings of the 1981 American Ethnological Society Conference,* ed. Richard Salisbury and Elisabeth Tooker (New York: American Ethnological Society, 1981), 13.

22. "Rev. John Ettwein's Notes of Travel from the North Branch of the Susquehanna to the Beaver River, Pennsylvania, 1772," *Pennsylvania Magazine of History and Biography* 25 (1961): 214; Georg Henry Loskiel, *History of the Mission of the United Brethren* (London: The Brethren's Society, 1794), 172; Campisi, "Fur Trade and Factionalism," 39; David B. Guldenzopf, "The Colonial Transformation of Mohawk Iroquois Society" (Ph.D. diss., SUNY-Albany, 1986), 131–51.

23. Kirkland to Eleazar Wheelock, Apr. 25, 1770, 8b, SKP; Campisi, "Fur Trade and Factionalism," 41–44; *Kirkland Journal,* 67–68.

24. Kirkland to Jerusha Kirkland, Aug. 5, 1772, 32b, SKP; Tagawaron quoted in *Kirkland Journal,* 73; Kenneth M. Morrison, *The Solidarity of Kin: Ethnohistory, Religious Studies, and the Algonkian-French Encounter* (Albany: State University of New York Press, 2002), 134. In his study of Seneca Christian hymns, Thomas McElwain has noted the translation of "heaven" as "sky." "The Rainbow Will Carry Me," in *Religion in Native North America,* ed. Christopher Vecsey (Moscow: University of Idaho Press, 1990), 99.

25. *Kirkland Journal,* 77.

26. Steven West to the Oneida Converts, June 25, 1773, 42e; Samuel Dunlop to the London Board of Correspondents in Boston, July 2, 1773, 43a; quoted in Kirkland to Jerusha Kirkland, Mar. 24, 1773, 39e; Aaron Crosby to Kirkland, Jan. 25, 1774, 47c, all SKP.

27. *Kirkland Journal,* 94–97 ("puppet-shows," 94); David Fowler to Eleazar Wheelock, June 15, 1765, in *The Letters of Eleazar Wheelock's Indians,* ed. James Dow McCallum (Hanover, N.H.: Dartmouth College, 1932), 94 ("great pleasure"); Fowler to Wheelock, Sept. 23, 1765, in McCallum, *Letters of Wheelock's Indians,* 97; Christine Sternberg Patrick, "The Life and Times of Samuel Kirkland, 1741–1808: Missionary to the Oneida Indians, American Patriot, and Founder of Hamilton College" (Ph.D. diss., SUNY-Buffalo, 1993), 113 ("Surprized"), 118.

28. David Avery, Address to Indians, June 20, 1772, 30d, SKP; Wallace, *Death and Rebirth,* 59–78.

29. Patrick, "Life and Times of Samuel Kirkland," 127.

30. *Kirkland Journal,* 73; Lender and Martin, *Citizen Soldier,* 66; Wonderley, "Oneida Community," 22.

31. Laurence M. Hauptman, "Refugee Havens: Iroquois Settlements in the Eighteenth Century," in *American Indian Environments: Ecological Issues in Native American History*, ed. Christopher Vecsey and Robert W. Venables (Syracuse, N.Y.: Syracuse University Press, 1980), 130.

32. Beauchamp, *Aboriginal Place-Names*, 110; Richard Smith, *Tour of Four Great Rivers*, 65.

33. Harmen Myndertsz Van den Bogaert, *A Journey into Mohawk Country, 1634–1635*, ed. Charles T. Gehring and William A. Starna (Syracuse, N.Y.: Syracuse University Press, 1988), 13; Dean R. Snow, "The Archaeology of Iroquois Longhouses," *Northeast Anthropology* 53 (1996): 61–84.

34. Daniel K. Richter, *The Ordeal of the Longhouse: The Peoples of the Iroquois League in the Era of European Colonization* (Chapel Hill: University of North Carolina Press, 1992), 260–62; Jordan, *Seneca Restoration*, 11–18; Patricia M. Lambert, "The Archaeology of War: A North American Perspective," *Journal of Archaeological Research* 10 (2002): 226–28; Colin G. Calloway, *The Western Abenakis of Vermont, 1600–1800: War, Migration, and the Survival of an Indian People* (Norman: University of Oklahoma Press, 1990), 89; Wayne E. Lee, "Fortify, Fight, or Flee: Tuscarora and Cherokee Defensive Warfare and Military Culture Adaptation," *Journal of Military History* 68 (2004): 713–70.

35. Pierre Bibeau, "Les Palissades des sites iroquoiens," *Recherches amérindiennes au Québec* 10 (1980): 194–96; Peter P. Pratt, *Archaeology of the Oneida Iroquois* (George's Mill, N.H.: Man in the Northeast, 1976), 11–12. Bruce Trigger, *The Children of Ataentsic* (Montreal: McGill-Queen's University Press, 1976), 358; William A. Starna, George R. Hamell, and William L. Butts, "Northern Iroquoian Horticulture and Insect Infestation: A Cause for Village Removal," *Ethnohistory* 31 (1984): 197–207; Jordan, *Seneca Restoration*, 198–224.

36. Jon Parmenter, "At the Woods' Edge: Iroquois Foreign Relations, 1727–1768" (Ph.D. diss., University of Michigan, 1999), 8; idem., "The Iroquois and the Native American Struggle for the Ohio Valley, 1754–1794," in *The Sixty Years' War for the Great Lakes*, ed. Larry L. Nelson and David Skaggs (East Lansing: Michigan State University Press, 2001), 109; Richter, *Ordeal of the Longhouse*, 119–20.

37. Jelles Fonda's Account, July 1770, *JP*, 7:836–37; Johnson to James Abercromby, May 17, 1758, *JP*, 9:903–4.

38. Peter C. Mancall, *Deadly Medicine: Indians and Alcohol in Early America* (Ithaca, NY: Cornell University Press, 1995), 86–91; Maia Conrad, "Disorderly Drinking: Reconsidering Seventeenth-Century Iroquois Alcohol Use," *American Indian Quarterly* 23 (1999): 6–9; *Kirkland Journal*, 83, 85; Kirkland to Andrew Elliot, Nov. 19, 1773, 45c, SKP; Richter, *Ordeal of the Longhouse*, 266; Jordan, *Seneca Restoration*, 199.

39. "A Letter from Gideon Hawley of Marshpee, Containing . . . a Narrative of his Journey to Onohoghwage," *Collections of the Massachusetts Historical Society*, 1st ser., 4 (1795): 63.

40. *Kirkland Journal*, 53–54 ("like a dog"), 83, 85, 97 ("few hearers"); Patrick, "Life and Times of Samuel Kirkland," 114.

41. Richard Smith, *Tour of Four Great Rivers*, 65–66; Jordan, *Seneca Restoration*, 237–38.

42. Kirkland to Elliott, Nov. 19, 1773; Francis Whiting Halsey, *Old New York Frontier* (New York: Charles Scribner's Sons, 1901), 276; Lender and Martin, *Citizen Soldier*, 84; quoted in *Kirkland Journal*, 83–84.

43. Lender and Martin, *Citizen Soldier*, 66 ("good house"); Wonderley, "Oneida Community," 26–27; Guldenzopf, "Colonial Transformation," 133; Joseph-François Lafitau, *Customs of the American Indians Compared with the Customs of Primitive Times*, ed. and trans. William N. Fenton and Elizabeth L. Moore (Toronto: Champlain Society, 1974), 1:310–12.

44. George Hamell, "From Longhouse to Log House: At Home among the Senecas, 1790–1828" (paper presented to the Native Americans in the Early Republic Symposium, United States Capitol Historical Society, Washington, D.C., Mar. 4–5, 1992).

45. William N. Fenton, "Locality as a Basic Factor in the Development of Iroquois Social Structure," in Fenton, *Symposium on Local Diversity in Iroquois Culture*, 41n2.

Chapter 2. Narrowing Paths

1. *Kirkland Journal*, 71; Joseph Bloomfield, *Citizen Soldier: The Revolutionary War Journal of Joseph Bloomfield*, ed. Mark E. Lender and James Kirby Martin (Newark: New Jersey Historical Society, 1982), 65.

2. James H. Merrell, "Shickellamy, 'a Person of Consequence,'" in *Northeastern Indian Lives, 1632–1816*, ed. Robert S. Grumet (Amherst: University of Massachusetts Press, 1996), 232; C. A. Weslager, *The Nanticoke Indians: Past and Present* (Newark: University of Delaware Press, 1983), 149; Laurence M. Hauptman, "Refugee Havens: Iroquois Settlements in the Eighteenth Century," in *American Indian Environments: Ecological Issues in Native American History*, ed. Christopher Vecsey and Robert W. Venables (Syracuse, N.Y.: Syracuse University Press, 1980), 129–31; Ted J. Brasser, *Riding on the Frontier's Crest: Mahican Indian Culture and Culture Change* (Ottawa: National Museums of Canada, 1974), 66–71; Peter Mancall, *Valley of Opportunity: Economic Culture in the Upper Susquehanna* (Ithaca, N.Y.: Cornell University Press, 1991), 31–39; Colin G. Calloway, *The American Revolution in Indian Country: Crisis and Diversity in Native American Communities* (New York: Cambridge University Press, 1995), 108–28.

3. Frederick Post quoted in Anthony F. C. Wallace, *King of the Delawares: Teedyuscung, 1700–1763* (1949; repr., Syracuse, N.Y.: Syracuse University Press, 1990), 48.

4. J. Leitch Wright, *The Only Land They Knew: The Tragic Story of the American Indians in the Old South* (New York: Free Press, 1981), 117–21; David Landy, "Tuscarora among the Iroquois," in *Northeast*, ed. Bruce G. Trigger, vol. 15 of *Handbook of North American Indians*, ed. William C. Sturtevant (Washington, D.C.: Smithsonian Institution Press, 1978–), 518–21; Ian K. Steele, *Warpaths: Invasions of North America* (New York: Oxford University Press, 1994), 160; Indian Proceedings, Sept. 5, 1766, *JP*, 12:183.

5. Philip Otterness, *Becoming German: The 1709 Palatine Migration to New York* (Ithaca, N.Y.: Cornell University Press, 2004), 141–45; A. G. Roeber, *Palatines, Lib-*

erty, and Property: German Lutherans in Colonial British America (Baltimore, Md.: Johns Hopkins University Press, 1993), 1–15; Walter Allen Knittle, "The Early Eighteenth-Century Palatine Emigration: A British Government Redemptioner Project to Manufacture Naval Stores" (Ph.D. diss., University of Pennsylvania, 1936); Paul A. W. Wallace, *Conrad Weiser: Friend of Colonist and Mohawk* (Philadelphia: University of Pennsylvania Press, 1945), 3–16.

6. Warren Hofstra, "'The Extension of His Majesty's Dominions': The Virginia Backcountry and the Reconfiguration of Imperial Frontiers," *Journal of American History* 84 (1998): 1281–1312; Report on the Board of Trade on the Plans for Settling the Palatines, Dec. 5, 1709, *NYCD*, 5:117; Governor Burnet to the Lords of Trade, Oct. 16, 1721, *NYCD*, 5:634; quoted in Report of Board of Trade Respecting the Palatines, Aug. 30, 1709, *NYCD*, 5:88.

7. David L. Preston, *The Texture of Contact: European and Indian Settler Communities on the Frontiers of Iroquia, 1667–1783* (Lincoln: University of Nebraska Press, 2009), 181–89, 201–15; Doris Dockstader Rooney, *The Dockstader Family: Descendants of Georg Dachstätter Palatine Emigrant of 1709* (n.p., n.d.), 9–10, 29–30; Ann Laura Stoler, "Tense and Tender Ties: The Politics of Comparison in North American History and (Post) Colonial Studies," *Journal of American History* 88 (2001): 836.

8. Jon Parmenter, "At the Woods' Edge: Iroquois Foreign Relations, 1727–1768" (Ph.D. diss., University of Michigan, 1999), 378–83; Otterness, *Becoming German*, 159; Summary Narrative of the Conduct of the Oneida Indians, in O'Callaghan, *Documentary History of the State of New-York*, 1:520–22; quoted in George Croghan to William Johnson, Dec. 3, 1757, *JP*, 9:861; French Descent on the German Flats, in O'Callaghan, *Documentary History of the State of New-York*, 1:515–22; Robert W. Venables, "Tryon County, 1775–1783: A Frontier in Revolution" (Ph.D. diss., Vanderbilt University, 1967), 27–32; Preston, *Texture of Contact*, 178–80, 189–90.

9. "Extract of a Letter from Albany," May 22, 1758, in O'Callaghan, *Documentary History of the State of New-York*, 1:337; Otterness, *Becoming German*, 161–63 (quotation on 163); Peter Silver, *Our Savage Neighbors: How Indian War Transformed Early America* (New York: W. W. Norton, 2008), 114–22, 303–5; Jane T. Merritt, *At the Crossroads: Indians and Empires on a Mid-Atlantic Frontier, 1700–1763* (Chapel Hill: University of North Carolina Press, 2003), 267–304; Krista Camenzind, "Violence, Race, and the Paxton Boys," in *Friends and Enemies in Penn's Woods: Indians, Colonists, and the Racial Construction of Pennsylvania*, ed. William Pencak and Daniel K. Richter (University Park: Pennsylvania State University Press, 2004), 204–16.

10. Robert B. Roberts, *New York's Forts in the American Revolution* (Rutherford, N.J.: Farleigh Dickinson University Press, 1980), 414–17; John F. Luzader, "Construction and Military History," in *Fort Stanwix: History, Historic Furnishing, and Historic Structure Reports*, ed. Luzader, Louis Torres, and Orville W. Carroll (Washington, D.C.: National Park Service, 1976), 6–8; Speech of Conoghquieson, Dec. 10, 1758, *JP*, 10:67.

11. Johnson to Thomas Gage, June 27, 1766, *JP*, 12:116. For an earlier, identical complaint about the coming of settlers, see Conoghquieson's speech on behalf of the Oneida and Tuscarora, in Niagara and Detroit Proceedings, July 7, 1761, *JP*, 3:432–33.

12. Lender and Martin, *Citizen Soldier*, 65; William Johnson to the Lords of Trade, Nov. 13, 1763, *NYCD*, 7:577; F. H. Roof, "Johannis Rueff," *Transactions of the Oneida Historical Society*, 1881, 96–99; D. E. Wager, "Forts Stanwix and Bull and Other Forts at Rome," *Transactions of the Oneida Historical Society*, 1885–86, 70–71; Nellis M. Crouse, "Forts and Blockhouses in the Mohawk Valley," *Proceedings of the New York State Historical Association* 16 (1915): 83–90; Johnson to Gage, June 27, 1766, 116 ("springs").

13. John Campbell to Johnson, July 6, 1763, *JP*, 13:287; Francis Nartloo to John Bradstreet, Nov. 16, 1764, *JP*, 11:468 ("Flock"); Johnson to Thomas Gage, Dec. 18, 1764, *JP*, 4:626 ("Encampments"); John Galland to Johnson, Aug. 11, 1767, *JP*, 5:613, Galland to Johnson, Sept. 9, 1767, *JP*, 5:663; Virginia deJohn Anderson, *Creatures of Empire: How Domestic Animals Transformed Early America* (New York: Oxford University Press, 2004), 236–37, 241.

14. Conoghquieson quoted in Proceedings of a General Congress of the Six Nations, Mar. 12, 1768, *NYCD*, 8:40; Indian Proceedings, June 3–29, 1766, *JP*, 12:121–26.

15. Robert S. Grumet, "The Minisink Settlements: Native American Identity and Society in the Munsee Heartland, 1650–1778," and John C. Appel, "Colonial-Native Relations in Northeastern Pennsylvania, 1727–1787," in *The People of Minisink: Papers from the 1989 Delaware Water Gap Symposium*, ed. David G. Orr and Douglas V. Campana (Philadelphia: National Park Service, 1991), 175–250, 251–66. The murder of the unidentified Oneida man was reported in the *Pennsylvania Gazette*, Apr. 17, 1766; see also Alden Vaughan, "Frontier Banditti and the Indians: The Paxton Boys' Legacy, 1763–1775," *Pennsylvania History* 51 (1984): 13–17; *New-York Journal, or, The General Advertiser*, Jan. 8, 1767 ("Vagabond"); Indian Proceedings, May 24–27, 1766, *JP*, 12:95 ("firm friend").

16. Johnson to Thomas Gage, Apr. 17, 1766, *JP*, 12:74 ("resentment"); Johnson to William Franklin, May 3, 1766, *JP*, 5:198; William Franklin to Col. Low Jr., Dec. 9, 1766, *JP*, 5:420–22; *Pennsylvania Gazette*, Apr. 17, 1766, Apr. 24, 1766. Silver has noted that the populace was agitated by the question of judicial venue when the government proposed trying him in Philadelphia. Silver, *Our Savage Neighbors*, 355–56.

17. Johnson to Magistrates of Minisink, Sept. 8, 1766, *JP*, 5:418–19.

18. Richard White, "'Although I am dead, I am not entirely dead. I have left a second of myself': Constructing Self and Persons on the Middle Ground of Early America," in *Through a Glass Darkly: Reflections on Personal Identity in Early America*, ed. Ronald Hoffman, Mechal Sobel, and Fredrika Teute (Chapel Hill: University of North Carolina Press, 1997), 404–18; Alan S. Taylor, *The Divided Ground: Indians, Settlers, and the Northern Borderland of the American Revolution* (New York: Knopf, 2006), 28–33; Daniel K. Richter, *The Ordeal of the Longhouse: The Peoples of the Iroquois League in the Era of European Colonization* (Chapel Hill: University of North Carolina Press, 1992), 32–33, esp. 33n7.

19. Indian Proceedings, June 3–29, 1766, *JP*, 12:121; New Jersey Council Proceedings, Nov. 8–Dec. 11, 1766, *JP*, 5:418–22 (quotation on 419); Richard White, *The Middle Ground: Indians, Empires, and Republics in the Great Lakes Region, 1650–1815* (New York: Cambridge University Press, 1991), 76–81, 92; White, "Although I am dead," 414–18.

20. *Pennsylvania Gazette,* Jan. 1, 1767 (quotations); Johnson to Charles Read, Feb. 14, 1767, *JP,* 13:417; New Jersey Council Proceedings, *JP,* 5:418–22; Johnson to Henry Moore, Oct. 22, 1767, *JP,* 5:741; Johnson to John Watts, Oct. 22, 1767, *JP,* 5:743; William Franklin to Johnson, Apr. 15, 1766, *JP,* 12:72–73; Indian Proceedings, May 24–27, 1766, *JP,* 12:95; Johnson to the Magistrates of Minisink, Sept. 8, 1766, *JP,* 12:170. For a different interpretation of Seymour's trial and execution, see Silver, *Our Savage Neighbors,* 148–55.

21. Sheila L. Skemp, *William Franklin: Son of a Patriot, Servant of a King* (New York: Oxford University Press, 1990), 71–80, 101–4; Carl Raymond Woodward, *Ploughs and Politicks: Charles Read of New Jersey and His Notes on Agriculture, 1715–1774* (New Brunswick, N.J.: Rutgers University Press, 1941), 193; Albert Volwiler, *George Croghan and the Westward Movement, 1741–1782* (1926; repr., New York: AMS Press, 1971), 248.

22. Shaw Livermore, *Early American Land Companies: Their Influence on Corporate Development* (New York: Octagon, 1968), 111–13; Advantages of an Illinois Colony, July 10, 1766, *JP,* 5:320–30; Circular Letter from the Earl of Shelburne to all the Governors in America, Sept. 13, 1766, *New Jersey Archives,* 1st ser., 9:569; William Franklin to Shelburne, Dec. 16, 1766, *New Jersey Archives,* 1st ser., 9:574.

23. Johnson to Charles Read, Feb. 14, 1767, *JP,* 13:417; Samuel Wharton to B. Franklin, Dec. 2, 1768, 1109, American Philosophical Society, Philadelphia, Pa.; Conference proceedings, Oct. 25 and Nov. 5, 1768, *NYCD,* 8:117, 134.

24. "Journal of Indian Affairs," Oct. 5–17, 1767, *JP,* 12:370.

25. William Tryon to Johnson, June 15, 1766, *JP,* 13:391–92; "Journal of Indian Affairs," Dec. 18, 1766, *JP,* 12:240.

26. Johnson to Henry Moore, Oct. 22, 1767, *JP,* 5:741 (quotation); Johnson to Thomas Gage, July 20, 1768, *JP,* 12:553. For early calls for the first boundary, see Merritt, *Crossroads,* 251.

27. Thomas Gage to Johnson, May 8, 1768, *JP,* 12:493–94; Peter Marshall, "Colonial Protest and Imperial Retrenchment: Indian Policy 1764–1768," *Journal of American Studies* 5 (1971): 1–17.

28. Congress at Fort Stanwix, Sept. 15–Oct. 30, 1768, *JP,* 12:617–29; William Johnson to the Earl of Hillsborough, Oct. 23, 1768, *NYCD,* 8:104–5; Mary Druke, "Linking Arms: The Structure of Iroquois Intertribal Diplomacy," in *Beyond the Covenant Chain,* ed. Daniel K. Richter and James H. Merrell (Syracuse, N.Y.: Syracuse University Press, 1984), 34–35; Indian council proceedings, Oct. 29, 1768, *NYCD,* 8:124 ("disagreeably circumstanced").

29. Congress at Fort Stanwix, Sept. 15–Oct. 30, 1768, *JP,* 12:629; Druke, "Linking Arms," 35; Ray Allen Billington, "The Fort Stanwix Treaty of 1768," *New York History* 25 (1944): 182–94; Proceedings of Sir William Johnson with the Indians at Fort Stanwix, Oct. 24, 1768, *NYCD,* 8:112–13; Taylor, *Divided Ground,* 42–45; William N. Fenton, *The Great Law and the Longhouse: A Political History of the Iroquois Confederacy* (Norman: University of Oklahoma Press, 1998), 533–47.

30. Proceedings of Sir William Johnson, Oct. 29, 1768, *NYCD,* 8:124.

31. Ibid., 123.

32. Ruth V. Higgins, *Expansion in New York, with Especial Reference to the Eighteenth Century* (Columbus: Ohio State University, 1931), 58–59; Edith M. Fox, *Land Speculation in the Mohawk Country* (Ithaca, N.Y.: Cornell University Press, 1949), 33; Venables, "Tryon County," 54; Johnson to Goldsbrow Banyar, Nov. 24, 1768, *JP*, 12:657 ("greatest trouble"); Proceedings of Sir William Johnson, Oct. 29–31, 1768, *NYCD*, 8:123–25.

33. Proceedings of Sir William Johnson, Nov. 6, 1768, 127.

34. Ibid., 125 ("several Fees"), 127 ("valuable Country"), 129; Johnson to Goldsbrow Banyar, Nov. 24, 1768; Samuel Wharton to Benjamin Franklin, Dec. 2, 1768, in *Papers of Benjamin Franklin*, ed. Leonard W. Labaree (New Haven: Yale University Press, 1959–1999), 15:277 ("large Present").

35. Johnson quoted in Johnson to the Earl of Hillsborough, Nov. 18, 1768, *NYCD*, 8:110; Proceedings at a Treaty Held by Sir William Johnson, Nov. 6, 1768, 121; the historian Michael N. McConnell suggests the Ohio Indian delegates at Fort Stanwix may have been shown a different line on the map. "Peoples 'In Between': The Iroquois and the Ohio Indians, 1720–1768," in Richter and Merrell, *Beyond the Covenant Chain*, 110–11; Croghan quoted in Volwiler, *George Croghan*, 223–24.

36. Venables, "Tryon County," 183; Schuyler quoted in Paul David Nelson, *William Tryon and the Course of Empire: A Life in British Imperial Service* (Chapel Hill: University of North Carolina Press, 1990), 110.

37. Proceedings at a Treaty Held by Sir William Johnson, Oct. 28, 1768, *NYCD*, 8:120.

38. Margaret Connell Szasz, *Indian Education in the American Colonies, 1607–1783* (Albuquerque: University of New Mexico Press, 1988), 253–57; Laura J. Murray, *To Do Good to My Indian Brethren: The Writings of Joseph Johnson, 1751–1776* (Amherst: University of Massachusetts Press, 1998), 54–59, 168–74; David Fowler to Eleazar Wheelock, May 29, 1765, in *Letters of Eleazar Wheelock's Indians*, ed. James Dow McCallum (Hanover, N.H.: Dartmouth College, 1932), 90; Thomas Cummock, "Sketch of the Brothertown Indians" (1859), *Collections of the State Historical Society of Wisconsin* 4 (1906): 292; John Wood Sweet, *Bodies Politic: Negotiating Race in the American North, 1730–1830* (Baltimore, Md.: Johns Hopkins University Press, 2003), 320; Kirkland to Andrew Oliver, Nov. 12, 1770, 12b, SKP ("no white people").

39. "Proclamation," Oct. 4, 1774, *JP*, 13:683–84 ("much streightened"); William deLoss Love, *Samson Occom and the Christian Indians of New England* (Syracuse, N.Y.: Syracuse University Press, 2000), 207–30; Paul R. Campbell and Glenn W. LaFantasie, "Scattered to the Winds of Heaven: Narragansett Indians, 1676–1880," *Rhode Island History* 37 (1978): 67–83; Kevin McBride, "'Ancient and Crazie': Pequot Lifeways during the Historic Period," in *Algonkians of New England: Past and Present*, ed. Peter Benes (Boston: Dublin Seminar for New England Folklife, 1993), 64–73; Murray, *To Do Good*, 30–50.

40. McBride, "Ancient and Crazie," 72–73; Anderson, *Creatures of Empire*, 212–18; William S. Simmons, "Red Yankees: The Narragansetts in the First Great Awakening," *American Ethnologist* 40 (1983): 253–71; David J. Silverman, *Faith and*

Boundaries: Colonists, Christianity, and Community among the Wampanoag Indians of Martha's Vineyard, 1600–1871 (New York: Cambridge University Press, 2005).

41. Extract from the Proceedings with the New England Indians (Mohegans) on their way to Oneida, Mar. 25, 1775, RG10, 1834:95–97, National Archives of Canada, Ottawa.

42. Kirkland to Andrew Oliver, Nov. 12, 1770, 12b, SKP; Gregory Evans Dowd, *A Spirited Resistance: The North American Indian Struggle for Unity, 1745–1815* (Baltimore, Md.: Johns Hopkins University Press, 1992), xix, 39 ("harnessed"); Daniel K. Richter, *Facing East from Indian Country: A Native History of Early America* (Cambridge, Mass.: Harvard University Press, 2001), 194–98; *Kirkland Journal*, 24 ("like negroes"); Dowd, *Spirited Resistance*, 39.

43. Daniel R. Mandell, "Shifting Boundaries of Race and Ethnicity: Indian-Black Intermarriage in Southern New England, 1760–1880," *Journal of American History* 85 (1998): 466–501; Proclamation, Oct. 4, 1774 ("shall not be possessed"); Sweet, *Bodies Politic*, 320. Murray points out that some Algonquians expressed a wish to separate from the racially mixed element among themselves. Murray, *To Do Good*, 173.

44. Joseph Johnson to the New York Congress, June 21, 1775, in *American Archives*, ed. Peter Force (Washington, D.C., 1837–53), 4th ser., 2:1047 ("cornfields"); Oneidas to Joseph Johnson, Jan. 22, 1774, in McCallum, *Letters of Eleazar Wheelock's Indians*, 170 ("ever ready"); Address of Oneida headmen to Avery and Kirkland, June 5, 1772, ibid., 282 ("despised").

Chapter 3. The Dilemmas of Alliance

1. The Cooper story was recounted by Amelia Cornelius at "Oneida Journey," a conference held in Oneida, Wis., June 1998, and in Gloria Halbritter, "Oneida Traditions," in *The Oneida Indian Experience: Two Perspectives*, ed. Jack Campisi and Laurence M. Hauptman (Syracuse, N.Y.: Syracuse University Press, 1988), 145; see also Anthony Wonderley, *Oneida Iroquois Folklore, Myth, and History: New York Oral Narrative From the Notes of H. E. Allen and Others* (Syracuse, N.Y.: Syracuse University Press, 2004), 203–10.

2. In an Apr. 7, 1778, letter to Marinus Willett, Louis de Tousard reported, "We are at present in plenty of Corn, which we received from the Indians them selves, who made a prohibition to receive any money for it, and every-day they carry Corn much more than we want for fitting our horses." Thomas Bailey Myers Collection, New York Public Library. In 1878, John Hadcock, a neighbor of the Oneidas since 1811, recalled seeing a "handsome belt," which he understood had been given by Washington to the Oneida war chief Peter Bread for his services at Saratoga. Hadcock to Lyman C. Draper, Feb. 6, 1878, Draper Manuscripts, 11U:265, State Historical Society of Wisconsin, Madison.

3. The Oneidas' participation in the American Revolution has been narrated in detail elsewhere. For this account, the most useful studies have been Barbara Graymont, *The Iroquois in the American Revolution* (Syracuse, N.Y.: Syracuse University

Press, 1972); Joseph T. Glatthaar and James Kirby Martin, *Forgotten Allies: The Oneida Indians and the American Revolution* (New York: Hill and Wang, 2006); David J. Norton, *Rebellious Younger Brother: Oneida Leadership and Diplomacy, 1750–1800* (DeKalb: Northern Illinois University Press, 2009), 72–110; William N. Fenton, *The Great Law and the Longhouse: A Political History of the Iroquois Confederacy* (Norman: University of Oklahoma Press, 1998), 564–622; Alan S. Taylor, *The Divided Ground: Indians, Settlers, and the Northern Borderland of the American Revolution* (New York: Knopf, 2006), 77–119. For broader perspectives, see Colin G. Calloway, *The American Revolution in Indian Country: Crisis and Diversity in Native American Communities* (New York: Cambridge University Press, 1995).

4. Karim M. Tiro, "A 'Civil' War? Rethinking Iroquois Participation in the American Revolution," *Explorations in Early American Culture* 4 (2000): 148–65; idem, "Ambivalent Allies: Strategy and the Native Americans," in *Strategy in the American War of Independence: A Global Approach,* ed. Donald Stoker, Kenneth J. Hagan, and Michael T. McMaster (New York: Routledge, 2010), 120–40.

5. The appeal for Iroquois support was so ill-conceived, the Oneidas did the New England rebels a great service by not passing it along. Provincial Congress of Massachusetts to Kirkland, Apr. 4, 1775, in *American Archives,* ed. Peter Force (Washington, D.C., 1837–53), 4th ser., 1:1349–50; Oneida declaration of neutrality, 57b, SKP; [Joseph Platt] Cooke to the Oneida Indians, July 1, 1775, 58a, SKP; James Sullivan, ed., *Minutes of the Albany Committee of Correspondence* (Albany: University of the State of New York, 1923), 96.

6. Anthony F. C. Wallace, "Origins of Iroquois Neutrality: The Grand Settlement of 1701," *Pennsylvania History* 24 (1957): 223–35; Tench Tilghman, *Memoir of Lieut. Col. Tench Tilghman* (1876; repr., New York: New York Times / Arno, 1971), 88 (quotation).

7. Samuel Kirkland to Philip Schuyler, Mar. 12, 1776, r. 172, i. 153, 2:97, PCC.

8. Abraham Yates to Clinton, Jan. 9, 1779, in *Public Papers of George Clinton, First Governor of New York* (Albany: State of New York, 1899–1914), 4:478–80.

9. On the Mohawks and their relations with Johnson and white settlers generally, see David Preston, *The Texture of Contact: European and Indian Settler Communities on the Frontiers of Iroquoia, 1667–1783* (Lincoln: University of Nebraska Press, 2009), 93–115, 190–215; Isabel Thompson Kelsay, *Joseph Brant, 1743–1807, Man of Two Worlds* (Syracuse, N.Y.: Syracuse University Press, 1983), 57–70; Taylor, *Divided Ground;* Calloway, *American Revolution,* 108–22.

10. James Duane to Philip Schuyler, May 25, 1778, in *Papers of George Clinton,* 3:356; Robert J. Surtees, "The Iroquois in Canada," in *The History and Culture of Iroquois Diplomacy: An Interdisciplinary Guide to the Treaties of the Six Nations and Their League,* ed. Francis Jennings et al. (Syracuse, N.Y.: Syracuse University Press, 1985), 68–72; Lawrence Ostola, "The Seven Nations of Canada and the American Revolution, 1774–1783" (M.A. thesis, Université de Montréal, 1989).

11. David B. Guldenzopf, "The Colonial Transformation of Mohawk Iroquois Society" (Ph.D. diss., SUNY-Albany, 1986), 135–37; Kirkland to Andrew Elliot, Mar. 28, 1774, 54b, SKP.

12. Proceedings of Guy Johnson with the Six Nations, Jan. 20, 1775, in *Ecclesiastical Records of the State of New York*, 6:4284–85 ("much trouble"); Guy Johnson to the Earl of Dartmouth, Mar. 16, 1775, *NYCD*, 8:548; Kirkland quoted in Kirkland to Albany Committee of Safety, June 9, 1775, in James Sullivan, ed., *Minutes of the Albany Committee of Correspondence, 1775–1778* (Albany: University of the State of New York, 1923) 1:86–87. The Albany Committee immediately granted Kirkland fifteen pounds and sent his report up the ladder. By September he was on the payroll of the Continental Congress. Christine Sternberg Patrick notes that Wheelock was also seeking funds for this purpose; Patrick, "The Life and Times of Samuel Kirkland, 1741–1808: Missionary to the Oneida Indians, American Patriot, and Founder of Hamilton College" (Ph.D. diss., SUNY-Buffalo, 1993): 285, 291–300.

13. Quoted in Provincial Congress of Massachusetts to Kirkland, Apr. 4, 1775.

14. Ashley had been married to Rebecca Kellogg, who died at Oquaga in 1757. A captive taken in the famous 1704 raid on Deerfield, Massachusetts, Kellogg had declined numerous opportunities to return and lived among the Kahnawake Mohawks for over two decades. Karim M. Tiro, "James Dean in Iroquoia," *New York History* 80 (1999): 391–99.

15. Gideon Hawley to Wheelock, Sept. 19, 1761, 761519, Dartmouth College Library, Hanover, N.H.; Hawley and Amos Tappan to Andrew Oliver, Oct. 20, 1761, typescript, James Dean box, Oneida County Historical Society, Utica, N.Y.; Eli Forbes diary, *Proceedings of the Massachusetts Historical Society*, ser. 2 (1891–1892), 7:384–99; Eli Forbes to Johnson, July 13, 1767, *JP*, 5:591.

16. James Dean, "Short Account of a Tour," box 13, Philip Schuyler Papers, New York Public Library.

17. Kirkland to Schuyler, Mar. 12, 1776, p. 99.

18. James Deane, "Extract of a Journal, Etc.," *American Archives*, ser. 4, 5:1100–1104.

19. Schuyler to Committee of Tryon County, July 4, 1777, Schuyler Family Collection, box 1, folder 13, NYSL; Patrick, "Life and Times of Samuel Kirkland," 109–10; David Levinson, "An Explanation for the Oneida-Colonist Alliance in the American Revolution," *Ethnohistory* 23 (1976): 265–89. On the morale of the Tryon County militia, see Schuyler's July 4 letter to the Committee of Tryon County; Albany Committee to Tryon County Committee, July 15, 1777, in *Mohawk Valley in the Revolution*, ed. Maryly Barton Penrose (Franklin Park, N.J.: Liberty Bell Associates, 1978), 121–24.

20. Proceedings of Guy Johnson with the Oneidas and Oughquageys, Feb. 11, 1775, *NYCD*, 8:550–51.

21. Pierre Van Cortlandt to the New York Delegates of the Continental Congress, Jan. 17, 1781, in *Correspondence of the Van Cortlandt Family of Cortlandt Manor, 1748–1801*, ed. Jacob Judd (Tarrytown, N.Y.: Sleepy Hollow Restorations, 1977), 2:399; Proceedings at two meetings with Guy Johnson, July 3–6, 1780, B119:96–99, Haldimand Papers, National Archives of Canada, Ottawa (hereafter cited as HP). Good Peter quoted in "Good Peter's Narrative of Several Transactions Respecting Indian Lands," TPP, 60:121v.; Proceedings of June 29, 1775 and July 3, 1775, in Penrose, *Mohawk Valley*, 19–21, 57; Proceedings of July 25 and 29, 1775, in Sullivan, *Minutes of*

the Albany Committee, 167–68, 172. A Mohawk chief in 1779 reported that the Oneidas claimed "they did not mean to quarrel with the Indians, & that it was merely for their own safety that they acted in favor of the Rebels." Quoted in Glatthaar and Martin, *Forgotten Allies,* 249.

22. Commissioners of Indian Affairs to Henry Laurens, Jan. 12, 1778, in *Indian Affairs Papers,* ed. Maryly Barton Penrose (Franklin Park, N.J.: Liberty Bell Associates, 1981), 103–4; Schuyler quoted in Graymont, *Iroquois,* 106.

23. Samuel Kirkland to Philip Schuyler, Jan. 14–17, 1777, r. 173, i. 153, 3:63–69, PCC; Washington to President of Congress, Mar. 29, 1777, in *The Writings of George Washington from the Original Manuscript Sources, 1745–1799,* ed. John C. Fitzpatrick, 39 vols. (Washington, D.C.: U.S. Government Printing Office, 1931–44), 7:328–29; Washington to Schuyler, May 15, 1778, in Fitzpatrick, *Writings of George Washington,* 11:389–91.

24. *The Literary Diary of Ezra Stiles,* ed. Franklin Bowditch Dexter (New York: Charles Scribner's Sons, 1901), 2:139–42; Washington to President of Congress, Mar. 29, 1777. Washington indicated the importance of diplomatic encounters like his with the six Oneidas in a message to the Massachusetts legislature, Sept. 28, 1775, that appears in Fitzpatrick, *Writings of George Washington,* 3:525.

25. *Citizen-Soldier: The Revolutionary War Journal of Joseph Bloomfield,* ed. Mark E. Lender and James Kirby Martin (Newark: New Jersey Historical Society, 1982), 79, 90–93; James Thacher, *A Military Journal of the American Revolutionary War* (Hartford, Conn.: Hurlbut, Williams & Co., 1862), 114–15; Claude Blanchard, *Guerre d'Amérique, 1780–3: Journal de Campagne* (Paris: Librairie Militaire de J. Dumaine, 1881), 49; *Memoirs of the Marshall Count de Rochambeau,* trans. M. W. E. Wright (New York: New York Times, 1971), 23; Howard C. Rice and Anne S. K. Brown, trans. and eds., *The American Campaigns of Rochambeau's Army, 1780, 1781, 1782, 1783* (Princeton, N.J., and Providence, R.I.: Princeton University Press and Brown University Press, 1972), 1:121–23.

26. Powless quoted in Draper Manuscripts, 11U:204.

27. Thomas S. Abler, *Chainbreaker: The Revolutionary War Memoirs of Governor Blacksnake* (Lincoln: University of Nebraska Press, 1989), 86–91; 128–30 (quotation on 128–29); Glatthaar and Martin, *Forgotten Allies,* 163–69; Graymont, *Iroquois,* 134–43.

28. Calloway, *American Revolution,* 123; Graymont, *Iroquois,* 142; Glatthaar and Martin, *Forgotten Allies,* 360n21.

29. Daniel Claus to William Knox, Nov. 11, 1777, in *Documents of the American Revolution,* ed. K. G. Davies (Shannon: Irish University Press, 1973), 14:251; Jelles Fonda to Commissioners of Indian Affairs, Apr. 21, 1778, in Penrose, *Indian Affairs Papers,* 134; Jemison quoted in *A Narrative of the Life of Mrs. Mary Jemison,* ed. James E. Seaver (1823; repr., Syracuse, NY: Syracuse University Press, 1990), 52–53; Graymont, *Iroquois,* 132.

30. Joseph Lee Boyle, ed., "From Saratoga to Valley Forge: The Diary of Lt. Samuel Armstrong," *Pennsylvania Magazine of History and Biography* 121 (1997): 246–47; *Revolutionary War Journals of Henry Dearborn, 1775–1783,* ed. Lloyd Brown and Howard Peck-

ham (1939; repr., Freeport, N.Y.: Books for Libraries Press, 1969), 107; Gates to Hancock, [Aug?] 12, 1777, Horatio Gates Papers, 5:1059, New-York Historical Society, New York; Hadcock to Draper, May 6, 1872 and Feb. 6, 1878, Draper Manuscripts, 11U:264 ("Brave men"); Graymont, *Iroquois*, 150, 155 ("ran off" and "great service").

31. Deane to Schuyler, May 25, 1778, in *Papers of George Clinton*, 3:356–58; Lafayette to Laurens, Mar. 20, 1778, in *Lafayette in the Age of the American Revolution: Selected Letters and Papers, 1776–1790*, ed. Stanley Idzerda (Ithaca, N.Y.: Cornell University Press, 1977), 1:364; George I. Denniston to George Clinton, Apr. 2, 1778, in *Papers of George Clinton*, 3:118; Washington to Schuyler, May 15, 1778, in Fitzpatrick, *Writings of George Washington*, 11:391; "Extract from the Minutes of a Board of Commissioners of Indian Affairs for the Northern Department held at Albany," Apr. 15, 1778, Gates Papers, 7:85.

32. Von Steuben quoted in Committee at Camp to Henry Laurens, Mar. 2, 1778, in *Letters of Delegates to Congress, 1774–1789*, ed. Paul H. Smith et al. (Washington, D.C.: Library of Congress, 1976–2000), 9:199–200; *Pennsylvania Gazette*, May 30, 1778.

33. Tousard to unidentified correspondent, May 23, 1778, r. 95, i. 78, 9:157–60, PCC ("hability"); Brown and Peckham, *Journals of Henry Dearborn*, 121; Glatthaar and Martin, *Forgotten Allies*, 208–15; Norton, *Rebellious Younger Brother*, 219.

34. Washington to Schuyler, May 15, 1778, in Fitzpatrick, *Writings of George Washington*, 11:389–91; James Dean to [Schuyler?], May 12, 1778, Historical Society of Pennsylvania, Philadelphia; Extract from the minutes of the Board of War, June 11, 1778, Gates Papers, 7:764.

35. Schuyler to Clinton, July 20, 1778, in *Papers of George Clinton*, 3:565; entries for May 28, July 30, Aug. 1, 1777, William Colbraith diary, Rosenbach Museum & Library, Philadelphia; Peter Gansevoort to Goose Van Schaik, June 1, 1777, Gansevoort-Lansing Collection, New York Public Library; Deposition of Frederick Helmer, July 17, 1777, in *Journals of the Provincial Congress, Provincial Convention, Committee of Safety and Council of Safety of the State of New York* (Albany: New York State Legislature, 1842), 1007. The Oneidas could also sound the all clear. Peter Gansevoort to Caty Gansevoort, July 21, 1778, Gansevoort-Lansing Collection.

36. Duncan Campbell to Frederick Haldimand, July 22, 1779, B111:136; Haldimand to Campbell, July 26, 1779, B113:69; Père Huguet to Duncan Campbell, Oct. 18, 1780, B111:239; Mathews to Daniel Claus, Oct. 19, 1780, B114:148; Campbell to Haldimand, July 30, 1779, B111:140, all HP.

37. Dean to Schuyler, Jan. 18, 1779; Washington to the President of Congress, June 21, 1778, in Fitzpatrick, *Writings of George Washington*, 12:99; Graymont, *Iroquois*, 178; Cornelius Van Dyck to George Clinton, Jan. 18, 1779, in *Public Papers of George Clinton*, 4:493 ("influence"); Kelsay, *Joseph Brant*, 226; Volkert P. Douw to Gansevoort, Nov. 13, 1778, Gansevoort-Lansing Collection. On prisoner exchange, see also Glatthaar and Martin, *Forgotten Allies*, 179–82.

38. Dean to Schuyler, July 4, 1778, Gates Papers (quotation); Dean to Schuyler, July 19, 1778, box 13, Schuyler Papers. The language that Dean employed in his correspondence suggests the limits of his identification with the Iroquois. He referred to

them as "cruel," "savage," and (ironically, in retrospect), "a people not to be bound by the Faith of Treaties."

39. Dean to Schuyler, Apr. 1–10, 1779, r. 173, i. 153, 3:440–41, PCC; Haldimand to Campbell, Apr. 8, 1779, B113:7, HP.

40. Washington to Schuyler, May 2, 1779, r. 169, i. 152, 7:287, PCC; Washington to Schuyler, Feb. 26, 1779, in Fitzpatrick, *Writings of George Washington*, 14:150 (quotations); Oneidas quoted in T. W. Egly, *Goose Van Schaik of Albany, 1736–1789* (n.p., 1993), 60–65; "Lieut. Erkuries Beatty," in *Journals of the Military Expedition of Major General John Sullivan against the Six Nations of Indians in 1779*, ed. Frederick Cook (Albany, N.Y.: Knapp, Peck & Thomson, 1887), 16.

41. Goose Van Schaik, "Minutes and Proceedings of the Onandaga expedition," Apr. 24, 1779, r. 187, i. 169, 5:259–63, PCC; idem, "A Return of Prisoners Taken and the Number Killed in the Onondaga Castle," Apr. 21, 1779, r. 169, i. 152, 7:264, 305–6, PCC; Extract of a Speech Delivered . . . by the Principal Chiefs and Warriors of the Six Nations, Dec. 11, 1782, B102:228, HP; Onondaga chief quoted in Calloway, *American Revolution*, 53; Clinton quoted in Anthony F. C. Wallace, *The Death and Rebirth of the Seneca* (New York: Alfred A. Knopf, 1970), 142; Van Schaik to Henry Glen, May 11, 1779, Gansevoort-Lansing Collection.

42. "The Particulars of a Conference held by a Deputation from Mr Lorrimiers Scout with a Party of Oneidas" July 29, 1779, B120:62–64, HP; "Extracts of Letters and General Orders Given to Van Schaik," Sept. 7, 1778, box 18, Gansevoort-Lansing Collection; Glatthaar and Martin, *Forgotten Allies*, 130.

43. Alexander Fraser to Frederick Haldimand, July 29, 1779, B120:56–57; Walter Butler to John Butler, Aug. 4, 1779, B105:126; Richard Houghton to Haldimand, Apr. 3, 1780, B111:188; Campbell to Haldimand, July 6, 1780, B111:213, all HP.

44. Sullivan to Oneidas, Sept. 1, 1779, Oneiga to Sullivan, Sept. 1779, Sullivan to John Jay, Sept. 30, 1779, in *Letters and Papers of Major-General John Sullivan*, ed. Otis G. Hammond (Concord, N.H.: New Hampshire Historical Society, 1939), 3:114–16, 135–36.

45. Sullivan quoted in *Sullivan Expedition Journals*, 303 ("vast quantity"), 305 ("single settlement"); British officer quoted in Richard White, *The Middle Ground: Indians, Empires, and Republics in the Great Lakes Region, 1650–1815* (New York: Cambridge University Press, 1991), 406.

46. Cook, ed., *Sullivan Expedition Journals*, 32, 91, 175, 188, 207, 236; "Journal of Lieut. Robert Parker, of the Second Continental Artillery, 1779," *Pennsylvania Magazine of History and Biography* 28 (1904): 14–17; Hammond, *Letters and Papers of Major-General John Sullivan*, 3:128–32nn50, 51. The Seneca account quoted is from Seaver, *Mary Jemison*, 55–57.

47. Quoted in Fraser to Haldimand, Sept. 10, 1779, B120:76, HP; Van Dyck to Van Schaik, Oct. 25, 1779, in *Papers of George Clinton*, 5:330; Haldimand to Campbell, Nov. 8, 1779, B113:101, HP.

48. Schuyler to Samuel Huntington, Feb. 5, 1780, r. 173, i.153, 3:503–10, PCC; quoted in English Minutes of Indian Affairs, Feb. 12, 1780, RG10, 1831:150–55, National Archives of Canada, Ottawa.

49. English Minutes of Indian Affairs, Feb. 14–16, 1780, 150–60; Glatthaar and Martin, *Forgotten Allies*, 269–70.

50. Morgan Lewis to Clinton, June 24, 1780 in *Papers of George Clinton,* 5:884 ("general invasion"); A Speech of the Oneida Chiefs to Colo. Van Dyck, June 18, 1780, in *Papers of George Clinton,* 5:883 ("move down"); Volkert P. Douw to Schuyler, Apr. 26, 1780, New-York Historical Society; Van Schaik to Clinton, June 24, 1780, in *Papers of George Clinton,* 5:882; Glatthaar and Martin, *Forgotten Allies,* 277.

51. Van Dyck to Van Schaik, July 3, 1780, in *Papers of George Clinton,* 5:912–14; Guy Johnson to George Germain, July 26, 1780, *NYCD,* 8:796–97; Schuyler to Lafayette, Aug. 18, 1780, and Van Schaik to Washington, July 29, 1780, George Washington Papers, Columbia University Library; Guy Johnson to Haldimand, Aug. 11, 1780, B107:104–5, HP; Clinton quoted in Graymont, *Iroquois,* 238–39.

52. Willett to Schuyler, Sept. 28, 1780, r. 17, Schuyler Papers; quoted in Schuyler to Huntington, Dec. 2, 1780, in Penrose, *Indian Affairs Papers,* 265–67. "List of Necessary Clothing for 406 Indian Men Women & Children," r. 173, i. 153, 3:545; Schuyler to Huntington, Jan. 18, 1781, r. 173, i. 153, 3:555; Richard Peters to Duane, Apr. 20, 1781, r. 173, i. 153, 3: 559; Schuyler to Pres. of Congress, Dec. 26, 1780, r. 173, i. 153, 3:589, all PCC.

53. Schuyler to Pres. of Congress, Dec. 2, 1780, r. 173, i. 153, 3:. 551, PCC ("dictates"); Schuyler to Robert Morris, Aug. 30, 1781, SC7002:8, Colonial Manuscript Collection, NYSL; Judd, *Van Cortlandt Family,* 2:400 ("naked"); Marquis de Chastellux, *Travels in North America in the Years 1780, 1781, and 1782,* ed. and trans. Howard C. Rice Jr. (Chapel Hill: University of North Carolina Press, 1963), 208 ("assemblage").

54. Schuyler to Huntington, Mar. 29, 1781, r. 173, i. 153, 3:547–49, PCC.

55. Cook, ed., *Sullivan Expedition Journals,* 8, 64 ("Civilization"); Fraser to Haldimand, May 30, 1780, B127:137, HP; Charles Patrick Neimeyer, *America Goes to War: A Social History of the Continental Army* (New York: New York University Press, 1996), 36–48; Abraham Hardenbergh to Goose Van Schaik, May 31, 1780, George Washington Papers, ser. 4, General Correspondence, Library of Congress, Washington, D.C.; Fraser to Haldimand, May 30, 1780; Gansevoort to Washington, Aug. 10, 1778, Gansevoort-Lansing Collection; quoted in Washington to the President of Congress, June 20, 1780, in Fitzpatrick, *Writings of George Washington,* 19:36–37.

56. Thomas McClellan to Gansevoort, Mar. 14, 1779, Gansevoort-Lansing Collection.

57. *Pennsylvania Gazette,* July 30, 1777; Robert Cochran to Gansevoort, Sept. 18, 1778, and Sept. 28, 1778, Gansevoort-Lansing Collection; Walter Butler to John Butler, Aug. 4, 1779. For a similar, earlier claim involving the Kahnawakes and Oneidas, see, in HP, Fraser to Haldimand, July 29, 1779, B120:56, and "The Particulars of a Conference Held by a Deputation from Mr. Lorrimiers Scout with a Party of Oneidas," July 29, 1779, B120:62.

58. Fraser to Haldimand, June 1, 1780, B127:139, HP; Van Dyck to Van Schaik, July 3, 1780 in *Papers of George Clinton,* 5:912–14 ("officious"); Fraser to Haldimand, Oct. 27, 1780, B127:184, HP; Haldimand to Germain, Oct. 25, 1780, *Documents of the American Revolution* (Shannon: Irish University Press, 1973–), 18:208–9 ("troublesome").

Governor Clinton cited the Oneidas' service as well. Glatthaar and Martin, *Forgotten Allies*, 277.

59. Glatthaar and Martin, *Forgotten Allies*, 285, 286; Claus to Mathews, Feb. 26, 1781, B114:170, HP ("fixed"); Schuyler to Huntington, Jan. 18, 1781, r. 173, i. 153, 3:555, PCC ("enemy"); Campbell to Mathews, June 7, 1781, B112:56, HP; Haldimand to Campbell, July 16, 1781, B113:213, HP; Haldimand to H. Watson Powell, Sept. 7, 1781, B104:232 ("much impede").

60. Abraham Wemple to Gansevoort, May 4, 1781, and Nov. 1, 1781, Gansevoort-Lansing Collection; Willett to George Clinton, June 28, 1781, Marinus Willett Letterbook, SC15705, NYSL.

61. Dean to Schuyler, Feb. 20, 1782, box 13, Schuyler Papers; Schuyler to the Inhabitants of the County of Tryon, May 1, 1782, BA9691:615, NYSL.

62. Speech by Oneidas, Tuscaroras, and "French Mohawks" to United States Commissioners, Sept. 9, 1782, HM 11621, Huntington Library, San Marino, Calif. ("Piece Meals"); Franklin B. Hough, *Proceedings of the Commissioners for Indian Affairs* (Albany, N.Y.: Munsell, 1861), 44, 73–74.

63. Pliny Moor to Noadiah Moor, Feb. 21, 1783, Miscellaneous Mss. M, Ontario County Historical Society, Canandaigua, N.Y.

64. Quoted in Conference with the Indians of the Six Nations, July 2, 1783, *IIDH;* Macdonald to Haldimand, May 18, 1782, B103:175–82; Maclean to Haldimand, May 11, 1783 B103:104; Speech of Schuyler to the Six Nations at the Council held at Tosisha, July 2, 1783, B119:184, all HP.

65. James Duane to George Clinton, n.d. 1784, quoted in Taylor, *Divided Ground*, 143.

66. "An Act for Indian Affairs," Mar. 25, 1783, New York Session Laws, chap. 48; Henry Glen et al. to Clinton, Aug. 29, 1783, *IIDH;* Hough, *Proceedings*, 33–36, 41–44, 47 (quotation), 59.

67. *The Writings of James Madison*, ed. Gaillard Hunt (New York: G. P. Putnam's Sons, 1901), 2:91–92; *The Writings of James Monroe*, ed. Stanislaus Murray Hamilton (New York: G. P. Putnam's Sons, 1898), 1:46–47; Hough, *Proceedings*, 21n.–22n.

68. Clinton quoted in Hough, *Proceedings*, 63; Wolcott, Nov. 23, 1784, in *IIDH;* Commissioners to Congress, Oct. 1784, i56:137–40, PCC; Richard Butler and Arthur Lee to Congress, Nov. 20, 1784, *IIDH;* Graymont, *Iroquois*, 278–79; Taylor, *Divided Ground*, 157–58.

69. Quoted in Neville B. Craig, *The Olden Time* (Pittsburgh: Wright & Charlton, 1847), 2:429.

70. Commissioners quoted in Craig, *Olden Time*, 425–26, *IIDH; Indian Affairs* 2:5–6.

71. "Journal of Griffith Evans, 1784–1785," ed. Hallock F. Raup, *Pennsylvania Magazine of History and Biography* 65 (1941): 211.

72. Doug George-Kanentiio, *Iroquois on Fire: A Voice from the Mohawk Nation* (Lincoln: University of Nebraska Press, 2008), 81–83.

Chapter 4. Misplaced Faith

1. Laurence M. Hauptman, *Conspiracy of Interests: Iroquois Dispossession and the Rise of New York State* (Syracuse, N.Y.: Syracuse University Press, 1999); Alan S. Taylor, *The Divided Ground: Indians, Settlers, and the Northern Borderland of the American Revolution* (New York: Knopf, 2006). See also Barbara Graymont, "New York State Indian Policy after the Revolution," *New York History* 57 (1976): 438–74; J. David Lehman, "The End of the Iroquois Mystique: The Oneida Land Cession Treaties of the 1780s," *William and Mary Quarterly*, 3rd ser., 47 (1990): 523–47; Anthony Wonderley, "'Good Peter's Narrative of Several Transactions Respecting Indian Lands': An Oneida View of Dispossession, 1785–1788," *New York History* 84 (2003): 237–73.

2. Quoted in Wonderley, "Good Peter's Narrative," 245; John Sergeant to Timothy Pickering, Jan. 3, 1795, TPP, 62:200.

3. Reply of the Oneidas, Aug. 8, 1795, r. 7, Philip Schuyler Papers, New York Public Library ("consumed to ashes"); Anthony Wonderley, "An Oneida Community in 1780: Study of an Inventory of Iroquois Property Losses during the Revolutionary War," *Northeast Anthropology* 56 (1998): 22; *Kirkland Journal*, 125 ("fish"); Kirkland to Jerusha Kirkland, Sept. 10, 1785, 97b, SKP ("depreciated").

4. Kirkland to Jerusha Kirkland, Sept. 10, 1785 ("thirty miles"); *Our Revolutionary Forefathers: The Letters of François, Marquis de Barbé-Marbois*, ed. Eugene Parker Chase (New York: Duffield & Co., 1929), 201–2; *Kirkland Journal*, 128, 132, 265–66; Christine Sternberg Patrick, "The Life and Times of Samuel Kirkland, 1741–1808: Missionary to the Oneida Indians, American Patriot, and Founder of Hamilton College" (Ph.D. diss., SUNY-Buffalo, 1993), 361; Kirkland to James Bowdoin, Mar. 10, 1784, 85c, SKP; Jack Campisi, "The Oneida Treaty Period," in *The Oneida Indian Experience*, ed. Campisi and Laurence M. Hauptman (Syracuse, N.Y.: Syracuse University Press, 1988), 60.

5. Charles M. Johnston, ed., *Valley of the Six Nations: A Collection of Documents on the Indian Lands of the Grand River* (Toronto: University of Toronto Press, 1964), 52; Draper Manuscripts, 11U:198, 205–6, 215, 217 (quotation), State Historical Society of Wisconsin, Madison.

6. Grant of land to John Harper, Nov. 20, 1784, *IIDH*; John Harper petition, Mar. 23, 1786[?], A1823, NYSA; Wonderley, "Good Peter's Narrative," 245 n21; Franklin B. Hough, *Proceedings of the Commissioners for Indian Affairs* (Albany, N.Y.: Joel Munsell, 1861), 78, 101.

7. Hough, *Proceedings*, 72–74, 77–81 (80, "perfect Translation"), 100–101 (100, "one Word").

8. Ibid., 83–84, 89–94 (quotations 92–93); Good Peter Memoir, TPP, 60:122.

9. Taylor, *Divided Ground*, 147–50; *Kirkland Journal*, 128, 132. The Oneidas threatened to revoke the Brothertowns' residency rights if they did not consent to live on a smaller tract or at large among the Oneidas. "Sam Occum's diary," ed. Julia Clark, in *The History and Archaeology of the Montauk Indians*, vol. 3 (2nd ed.), ed. Gaynell Stone (Stony Brook, N.Y.: Suffolk County Archaeological Association, 1993), 265–66, 274, 280; Hough, *Proceedings*, 230–31. John Pierce counted fifty-eight Tuscaroras in 1795.

Pierce "Notes, on a Visit to Several Tribes of Indians," 47–48, typescript, 11–12, FHL. The Oneidas also invited 360 Onondagas and Cayugas and 80 Delawares to settle within their boundaries, but they never came. All told, the Oneidas anticipated up to 1,000 arrivals to add to the combined Oneida and Tuscarora population in the area, which Kirkland estimated to be 800 in 1784. Patrick, "Life and Times of Samuel Kirkland," 361; Kirkland to James Bowdoin, Mar. 10, 1784, 85c, SKP.

10. As Patricia Cline Cohen asks, "Who among us recalculates the terms of a thirty-year mortgage to see that the bank's computer is charging the right monthly payment? Who refigures the FICA deduction that appears on the monthly paycheck? It is possible to live by the number without always knowing the derivation of important numbers." Patricia Cline Cohen, *A Calculating People: The Spread of Numeracy in Early America* (New York: Routledge, 1999 [1982]), 11–12 (quotation on 12).

11. Hough, *Proceedings,* 93.

12. Hough, *Proceedings,* 92–97; Good Peter Memoir, 122A–123. This episode is reminiscent of Edmund Morgan's classic description of Indian-hating at Jamestown, Virginia: "To be thus condescended to by heathen savages was intolerable." *American Slavery—American Freedom: The Ordeal of Colonial Virginia* (New York: W. W. Norton, 1975), 90.

13. Pickering, "Document about Treaty at Canandaigua," TPP, 60:26.

14. Taylor, *Divided Ground,* 164–65; Hough, *Proceedings,* 102–7 ("Friendship," 103, "last application," 106.); *Accounts of the Commissioners of Indian Affairs,* folder 2, folio 29, vol. 15, A0802, NYSA; Good Peter Memoir, 122A–123; Kirkland to Bowdoin, Aug. 23, 1785, *Collections of the Massachusetts Historical Society,* 7th ser., 6 (1907): 75–76.

15. Pickering to James McHenry, Oct. 13, 1796, TPP, 62:253; Washington quoted in James H. Merrell, "Declarations of Independence," in *The American Revolution: Its Character and Limits,* ed. Jack P. Greene (New York: New York University Press, 1987), 210; "An Act for the Speedy Sale of the Unappropriated Lands within this State," May 5, 1786, New York Session Laws, chap. 67.

16. George S. Conover transcript of Samuel Kirkland diary, 1–4, HM8884, Huntington Library, San Marino, Calif. ("utterly declined," 2); *Kirkland Journal,* 137; Hough, *Proceedings,* 362; Document related to Phelps lease, Nov. 12, 1787, Ayer 658, Newberry Library, Chicago; Isaac Carpenter to Philip Schuyler et al., [1795], r. 7, Schuyler Papers; indenture between Oneidas and Ebenezer Caulkins, June 21, 1793, Eleazer Williams Scrapbook, folder 18, Ayer 999a, Newberry Library.

17. Lehman, "End of the Iroquois Mystique," 546–47; Robert Berkhofer Jr., *Salvation and the Savage: An Analysis of Protestant Missions and American Indian Response* (Lexington: University of Kentucky Press, 1965), 125–51; Jack Campisi, "Fur Trade and Factionalism," in *Studies on Iroquois Culture,* ed. Nancy Bonvillain (Rindge, N.H.: N.p., 1980), 37–46.

18. Matthew Dennis, *Cultivating a Landscape of Peace: Iroquois-European Encounters in Seventeenth-Century America* (Ithaca, N.Y.: Cornell University Press / New York State Historical Association, 1993), 76–115; *Kirkland Journal,* 126 ("face"), 130 ("glass");

Christopher L. Miller and George R. Hamell, "A New Perspective on Indian-White Contact: Cultural Symbols and Colonial Trade," *Journal of American History* 73 (1986): 311–28, esp. 318–19, 322–24; George R. Hamell, "Strawberries, Floating Islands, and Rabbit Captains: Mythical Realities and European Contact in the Northeast During the Sixteenth and Seventeenth Centuries," *Journal of Canadian Studies* 21 (1986–87): 76–78.

19. Kirkland to Peter Thacher, June 30, 1792, 149m, SKP; *Kirkland Journal*, 311–14, 362; Joseph Sansom's Journal of a Tour to the Treaty of Newtown Point, 1791, Quaker Collection, Haverford College Library, Haverford, Pa. In 1806 an Oneida attributed to the Seneca prophet Handsome Lake the statement, "These ministers derive all their knowledge from the written holy book, and that he [i.e., Handsome Lake] receives his from the same source from which that originated." Quoted in Anthony F. C. Wallace, *The Death and Rebirth of the Seneca* (New York: Alfred A. Knopf, 1970), 279.

20. Taylor, *Divided Ground*, 151; *Kirkland Journal*, 130 ("apollus"), 134–35. Richard Cullen Rath, *How Early America Sounded* (Ithaca, N.Y.: Cornell University Press, 2003), 20; Jane T. Merritt, "Dreaming of the Savior's Blood: Moravians and the Indian Great Awakening in Pennsylvania" *William and Mary Quarterly*, 3rd ser., 54 (1997): 725. With the phrase "son [of] Thunder," Kirkland alluded to the divinely powerful preaching of the apostles James and John.

21. *Kirkland Journal*, 129; Patrick, "Life and Times of Samuel Kirkland," 396.

22. Aug. 19 entry ("scanty") and Sept. 2 entry ("ancient superstition"), Samuel Kirkland diary, June 1787–Mar. 1788, box 1, records of the Society for Propagating the Gospel among the Indians and Others in North America, Massachusetts Historical Society, Boston.

23. Ibid. For this style of artistic representation, see William S. Sturtevant, "Early Iroquois Realist Painting and Identity Marking," in *Three Centuries of Woodlands Indian Art: A Collection of Essays*, ed. J. C. H. King and Christian F. Feest (Altenstadt, Germany: ZKF Publishers, 2007), 139–40.

24. Sept. 2 entry, Kirkland diary.

25. Annemarie Anrod Shimony, "Conflict and Continuity: An Analysis of an Iroquois Uprising," in *Extending the Rafters: Interdisciplinary Approaches to Iroquoian Studies*, ed. Michael K. Foster, Jack Campisi, and Marianne Mithun (Albany: State University of New York Press, 1984), 153–64; Shimony, *Conservatism among the Iroquois at the Six Nations Reserve* (New Haven, Conn.: Department of Anthropology, Yale University, 1961), esp. 261–92; *Kirkland Journal*, 163.

26. Dec. 4 and 9 entries, Kirkland diary, June 1787–Mar. 1788.

27. Hough, *Proceedings*, 119–126n, Tayler quoted 141; James Axtell, *The Invasion Within: The Contest of Cultures in Colonial North America* (New York: Oxford University Press, 1985), 135–37.

28. Good Peter Memoir, 123A; Wonderley, "Good Peter's Narrative," 256; Lehman, "Iroquois Mystique," 529; Hough, *Proceedings*, 132, 133, 140–41. As Hough points out, the Genesee Company's shareholders included "a former Commissioner for holding

Indian Treaties, an acting State Senator, the Clerks of Albany and Columbia Counties . . . [and] eleven past, seven present and fourteen future Members of Assembly." Hough, *Proceedings,* 120.

29. Good Peter Memoir, 123A.

30. Quoted in Wonderley, "Good Peter's Narrative," 249.

31. Good Peter Memoir, 124–25; Hough, *Proceedings,* 124n.

32. Hough, *Proceedings,* 235; Good Peter Memoir, 125–26.

33. Hough, *Proceedings,* 141.

34. Tayler quoted ibid., 145, see also 149–54; Lehman, "Iroquois Mystique," 542; Samuel Kirkland diary, May 7, 1788–Aug. 12, 1788, Dartmouth College Library, Hanover, N.H.

35. Lehman, "Iroquois Mystique," 542; Good Peter Memoir, 125A ("drowned"); Hough, *Proceedings,* 126n., 129–30, 224 ("intention"), 242–44 ("themselves and their Posterity," 242).

36. Hough, *Proceedings,* 360–61; Good Peter Memoir 126–28.

37. Lehman, "Iroquois Mystique," 542–45; Wonderley, "Good Peter's Narrative," 264; Hough, *Proceedings,* 141, 224–25 ("annually forever").

38. Hough, *Proceedings,* 319, 358–62 (quotation on 361).

39. *Journal of the Assembly of the State of New York, at their twelfth session* (Albany, N.Y.: Samuel and John Loudon, 1789), 130; Taylor, *Divided Ground,* 65; Patrick, "Life and Times of Samuel Kirkland," 416–22; John Sergeant to Pickering, Jan. 3, 1795, TPP, 62:196.

40. Quoted in Patrick, "Life and Times of Samuel Kirkland," 426–27; Frenchmen quoted in Jean de la Mahotière to Pope Pius IV, Apr. 25, 1789, and May 17, 1790, America Centrale, vol. 2, fols. 564–69, Congregation for the Evangelization of Peoples or "de Propaganda Fide," Historic Archive, Università Urbaniana, Vatican City; see also Luca Codignola, "The Holy See and the Conversion of Aboriginal Peoples in North America, 1760–1830," in *Ethnographies and Exchanges: Native Americans, Moravians, and Catholics in Early North* America, ed. A. G. Roeber (University Park: Pennsylvania State University Press, 2008), 94–95.

41. Franklin B. Hough, *Notices of Peter Penet* (Lowville, N.Y.: N.p., 1866), 11, 15–16; *Kirkland Journal,* 176.

42. Morris quoted in "Correspondence of the Comte de Moustier with the Comte de Montmorin, 1787–1789," *American Historical Review* 8 (1903): 709.

43. Thomas Jefferson to John Jay, Feb. 4, 1789, in *The Emerging Nation: A Documentary History of the Foreign Relations of the United States under the Articles of Confederation, 1780–89,* ed. Mary A. Giunta et al. (Washington, D.C.: National Historical Publications and Records Commission, 1996), 3:922–23; James Madison to Jefferson, Dec. 8, 1788, in *Emerging Nation,* 3:896–97; Jay to Jefferson Nov. 25, 1788, in *Emerging Nation,* 3:881.

44. Hugues de Montbas, *Avec Lafayette chez les Iroquois* (Paris: Librairie de Paris, 1929), 111 ("troubles"), 113–14 ("assertion"); Chase, *Our Revolutionary Forefathers,* 191–93. The constitution appears in Hough, *Notices,* 24–31 and in manuscript, r. 15233,

73–75, Records of the Ministère des affaires étrangères, Library of Congress, Washington, D.C.

45. Hough, *Notices*, 24–31.

46. Nicolas Jourdain to Moustier, June 17, 1789, r. 15233, 96B, Records of the Ministère des affaires étrangères, Library of Congress, Washington, D.C.

47. Jourdain to Moustier, Aug. 27, 1789, r. 15233, 101, 105T; Moustier to unidentified correspondent, Aug. 14, 1789, r. 15233, 98; chiefs of the sovereign Oneida nation to Moustier, Sept. 15, 1789, r. 15233, 105B, all in ibid.

48. *Dunlap's American Daily Advertiser* (Philadelphia), Mar. 26, 1792, 3; *Kirkland Journal*, 206–7; Philip Lord Jr., *The Navigators: A Journal of Passage on the Inland Waterways of New York, 1793* (Albany: New York State Museum, 2003), 106–12; Thomas F. Powell, *Penet's Square: An Episode in the Settlement of Northern New York* (Lakemont, N.Y.: North Country Books, 1976), 166–67; Taylor, *Divided Ground*, 225.

49. Pomroy Jones, *Annals of Oneida County* (Utica: n.p., 1851), 125, 225, 272, 288, 713, 873; Elkanah Watson, *History of the Rise, Progress, and Existing Condition of the Western Canals* (Albany, N.Y.: D. Steele, 1820), 13, 339.

50. Taylor, *Divided Ground*, 90; Simeon DeWitt to Moses DeWitt, July 8, 1793, box 3, DeWitt Family Papers, Syracuse University Library, Syracuse, N.Y. For the Western Inland Lock Navigation Company's plans, see *The Report of a Committee Appointed to Explore the Western Waters in the State of New York . . .* (Albany, N.Y.: Barber and Southwick, 1792); "General Lincoln's Journal," *Collections of the Massachusetts Historical Society*, ser. 3, vol. 5 (1836): 120–21.

51. Dean to Phelps, July 6 1792, box 19, Phelps-Gorham Papers, NYSL; John Tayler to unidentified correspondent, May 9, 1792, Miscellaneous Manuscripts T, New-York Historical Society, New York; *Kirkland Journal*, 258. Clinton and Washington had purchased this land from Marinus Willett and his wife in 1783. Between 1787 or 1788 and 1793, they disposed of about four thousand acres; extant deeds indicate the per-acre prices of the land sold ranged from $2.00 to $6.79. *The Papers of George Washington, Presidential Series* (Charlottesville: University Press of Virginia, 1987–), 6:113–14.

52. Census of the Six Nations, Oct. 15, 1791, 140a, SKP.

53. *Kirkland Journal*, 167, 169–72.

54. Dec. 4 entry, Kirkland diary, June 1787–Mar. 1788; *Kirkland Journal*, 171.

55. John Pemberton to James Pemberton, Feb. 16, 1790, Incoming Correspondence, Papers of the Pennsylvania Abolition Society, Historical Society of Pennsylvania, Philadelphia; Hough, *Notices of Peter Penet*, 21–22.

56. *Kirkland Journal*, 172; Dec. 29 entry, Kirkland diary, Aug. 1788–Jan. 1789.

57. *Kirkland Journal*, 201, 205, 263; Arthur C. Parker, "The Indian Interpretation of the Sullivan-Clinton Campaign," *Rochester Historical Society Publications Fund Series* 8 (1929): 48.

58. Elisabeth Tooker, *An Ethnography of the Huron Indians, 1615–1649* (Syracuse, N.Y.: Syracuse University Press, 1991 [1964]), 39n.46; *Kirkland Journal*, 212.

59. Ker quoted in *Kirkland Journal*, 201–2; James Emlen, "The Journal of James Emlen Kept on a Trip to Canandaigua, New York," ed. William N. Fenton,

Ethnohistory, 12 (1965): 299–300; Thomas McElwain, "'The Rainbow Will Carry Me': The Language of Seneca Christianity as Reflected in Hymns," in *Religion in Native North America,* ed. Christopher Vecsey (Moscow: University of Idaho Press, 1990), 87–88; Michael McNally, "The Uses of Ojibwa Hymn-Singing at White Earth: Toward a History of Practice" in *Lived Religion in America,* ed. David D. Hall (Princeton, N.J.: Princeton University Press, 1997), 133–59.

60. *Kirkland Journal,* 263.

61. Quoted in Patrick, "Life and Times of Samuel Kirkland," 482.

62. *Kirkland Journal,* 203, 255–56; William N. Fenton, "A Further Note on Iroquois Suicide," *Ethnohistory* 33 (1986): 451–53; Fenton, "Iroquois Suicide: A Study in the Stability of a Cultural Pattern," *Bureau of American Ethnology Bulletin* 128 (1941): 79–140, esp. 124–25.

63. *Kirkland Journal,* 210.

64. Ibid., 265–66.

65. Ibid., 264.

66. Belknap and Morse, "Report," 11.

67. Lee Irwin, "Contesting World Views: Dreams among the Huron and Jesuits," *Religion* 22 (1992): 259–69; Kirkland and Hanwaleao quoted in *Kirkland Journal,* 362.

68. William A. Starna, "'The United States Will Protect You': The Iroquois, New York, and the 1790 Nonintercourse Act," *New York History* 83 (2002): 4–33; Washington quoted in "The reply of the President of the United States to the speech of the Cornplanter . . . ," Dec. 29, 1790, in *American State Papers: Indian Affairs* (Washington, D.C.: Gales & Seaton, 1832), 1:142.

69. Clinton to Knox, Apr. 27, 1791, in *American State Papers* 1:167; Washington to Hamilton, Mar. 24, 1791, in *The Papers of Alexander Hamilton,* ed. Harold C. Syrett (New York: Columbia University Press, 1961–87), 8:213; see also Hamilton to Washington, Mar. 27, 1791, in Syrett, *Papers of Alexander Hamilton,* 217, 218n.2.

70. Valuable studies of Pickering's efforts include Jack Campisi and Starna "On the Road to Canandaigua: The Treaty of 1794" *American Indian Quarterly* 19 (1995): 467–90; William N. Fenton, *The Great Law and the Longhouse: A Political History of the Iroquois Confederacy* (Norman: University of Oklahoma Press, 1998), 622–706; Edward Hoke Phillips, "Timothy Pickering at His Best: Indian Commissioner, 1790–1794," *Essex Institute Historical Collections* 52 (1966): 163–202; Taylor, *Divided Ground,* 242–94.

71. Pickering to Chapin, Apr. 29, 1792, *IIDH.*

72. Pickering to Knox, May 2, 1792, TPP, 62:31; Wonderley, "Good Peter's Narrative," 237–38; Gerald Clarfield, *Timothy Pickering and the American Republic* (Pittsburgh, Pa: University of Pittsburgh Press, 1980), 151.

73. Pickering, "Document about Treaty at Canandaigua," 217–41 (Captain John quoted on 219A); Isaac Rappelje affidavit, Jan. 24, 1793, Peter Smith Papers, Syracuse University Library.

74. Pickering, "Document about Treaty at Oneida," TPP, 60:224–27 (quotations on 224–25). On opposition to the Smith lease, see Reed to Smith, Feb. 25 and Mar. 21, 1793, Smith Papers.

75. Fenton, *Great Law and the Longhouse,* 687–89; Charles J. Kappler, ed. and comp., *Indian Affairs Laws and Treaties* (Washington, D.C.: Government Printing Office, 1904), 2:35–36 (quotation on 36); Irving Powless Jr., "Treaty Making," in *Treaty of Canandaigua 1794: 200 Years of Treaty Relations between the Iroquois Confederacy and the United States,* ed. G. Peter Schein and Anna M. Schein (Santa Fe, N.M.: Clear Light Publishers, 2000), 31.

76. Pickering to Kirkland, Dec. 24, 1793, 163a, SKP ("Something"); *Kirkland Journal,* 275–78 ("aggragate").

77. Kappler, *Indian Affairs,* 2:37–39.

Chapter 5. In a Drowned Land

1. Speech of Oneida and Stockbridge Indians to John Tayler, Feb. 27, 1806, Ayer 660, Newberry Library, Chicago.

2. Oneidas to State Legislature, Feb. 27, 1795, A1823, NYSA.

3. Capt. Israel Chapin to Timothy Pickering, Mar. 10, 1795, *IIDH;* Pickering to Chapin, Apr. 6, 1795, and Chapin to Pickering, May 6, 1795, Henry O'Reilly Papers, vol. 11, New-York Historical Society, New York.

4. "An Act for the Better Support of the Oneida, Onondaga, and Cayuga Indians, and for Other Purposes Therein Mentioned," Apr. 9, 1795, New York Session Laws, chap. 70; Barbara Graymont, "New York Indian Policy after the Revolution," *New York History* 57 (1976): 465; Commissioners to DeWitt Clinton, Apr. 10, 1795, r. 7, Philip Schuyler Papers, New York Public Library. On this treaty, see Alan S. Taylor, *The Divided Ground: Indians, Settlers, and the Northern Borderland of the American Revolution* (New York: Knopf, 2006), 302–9; Laurence M. Hauptman, *Conspiracy of Interests: Iroquois Dispossession and the Rise of New York State* (Syracuse, N.Y.: Syracuse University Press, 1999), 75–87; Hauptman, "Command Performance: Philip Schuyler and the New York State-Oneida 'Treaty' of 1795," in *The Oneida Indian Journey: From New York to Wisconsin, 1784–1860,* ed. Hauptman and L. Gordon McLester III (Madison: University of Wisconsin Press, 1999), 38–52; Jack Campisi, "New York-Oneida Treaty of 1795: A Finding of Fact," *American Indian Law Review* 4 (1976): 71–82.

5. William Bradford to Henry Knox, June 16, 1795, vol. 11, O'Reilly Papers; Pickering to George Washington, July 21, 1795, TPP 35:209–10; John Jay to Pickering, July 13, 1795, George Washington Papers, Library of Congress, ser. 4, fol. 245; Pickering to Jay, July 16, 1795, John Jay Papers, Columbia University Library; Jay to Pickering, July 18, 1795, George Washington Papers, Columbia University Library; "An Act to Amend an Act Entitled an Act Relative to the Indians Resident within This State," Mar. 5, 1795, New York Session Laws, chap. 17; Pickering to Chapin, June 29, 1795, and July 3, 1795 ("improper"), vol. 11, O'Reilly Papers; Schuyler speech to Oneidas, Aug. 6, 1795, r. 7, Schuyler Papers.

6. Simeon DeWitt to Moses DeWitt, July 8, 1793, box 3, DeWitt Family Papers, Syracuse University Library, Syracuse, N.Y.; Charles Maurice de Talleyrand-Périgord, *Talleyrand in America as a Financial Promoter: Unpublished Letters and Memoirs,* trans. Hans Huth and Wilma J. Pugh (Washington, D.C.: U.S. Government

Printing Office, 1942), 87; *The Report of a Committee Appointed to Explore the Western Waters in the State of New York*... (Albany: Barber and Southwick, 1792); Haupt-man, *Conspiracy of Interests*, 82–87; Philip Lord Jr., *The Navigators: A Journal of Passage on the Inland Waterways of New York, 1793* (Albany; New York State Museum, 2003), 126–27.

7. Captain John speech, Aug. 8, 1795, r. 7, Schuyler Papers; fish described in Pomroy Jones, *Annals of Oneida County* (Rome, N.Y.: n.p., 1851), 386.

8. Speeches of Aug. 10 and 11, 1795, r. 7, Schuyler Papers.

9. Oneidas to the Agents of the State of New York, Aug. 16, 1795, r. 7, Schuyler Papers; Karim M. Tiro, "James Dean in Iroquoia," *New York History* 80 (1999): 404; Dean to Schuyler, Aug. 16, 1795, r. 7, Schuyler Papers.

10. Speech of the Oneidas to the Commissioners, Sept. 12, 1795; Speech of William, Sept. 14, 1795; Comments of General Schuyler, Sept. 14[?], 1795; Commissioners' reply to the Oneidas, Sept. 14, 1795; draft of a speech to the Indians, Sept. 15, 1795, r. 7a, all Schuyler Papers; Kirkland to Pickering, Dec. 8, 1794, TPP, 62:121; *Whipple Report*, 244–46 (quotation on 245).

11. *Whipple Report*, 246–47; Simeon DeWitt, Jan. 10, 1797; Report of the commissioners to the State Legislature, n.d., both r. 7a, Schuyler Papers; "An Act to Provide for the Payment of the Annuities to the Indians Stipulated to Be Paid to This State," Apr. 1, 1797, New York Session Laws, chap. 83; Taylor, *Divided Ground*, 202.

12. Schuyler et al. to the State Legislature, n.d., HM 13491, Huntington Library, San Marino, Calif.; Dean to Schuyler, Aug. 18, 1795 ("active"); John Jourdain, money to Van Eps and who received it, Sept. 16, 1795, A0832, box 1, folder 5, NYSA.

13. John Sergeant to Pickering, Oct. 20, 1795, 184a, SKP; Washington to Pickering, July 27, 1795, in *Writings of George Washington*, ed. John C. Fitzpatrick (Washington, D.C.: U.S. Government Printing Office, 1940), 34:250–51; Pickering to Israel Chapin, Aug. 26, 1795, and Chapin to Pickering, Aug. 19, 1795, vol. 11, O'Reilly Papers.

14. Pickering to Arthur St. Clair, May 31, 1796, and Pickering to the Six Nations, Feb. 15, 1796, AA41, Quaker Collection, Haverford College Library, Haverford, Pa.

15. Israel Chapin to Pickering, Nov. 15, 1796, O'Reilly Papers, vol. 12; "The Journal of James Emlen Kept on a Trip to Canandaigua, New York," ed. William N. Fenton, *Ethnohistory* 12 (1965): 313; James Dean to Kirkland, July 11, 1785, 95aa, SKP; Merle H. Deardorff and George S. Snyderman, "A Nineteenth-Century Journal of a Visit to the Indians of New York," *Proceedings of the American Philosophical Society* 100 (1956): 586–87.

16. Quoted in John Pierce et al. to Philadelphia Yearly Meeting Indian Committee (PYMIC), July 1, 1796, AA41; minutes of articles of agreement with the Oneida Indians, June 25–30, 1796, AA44; Joseph Sansom to unidentified correspondents, June 28, 1796, Joseph Sansom letters, all Quaker Collection.

17. *A Journal of the Life, Travels, Religious Exercises, and Labours in the Work of the Ministry of Joshua Evans* (Byberry, Pa.: J. &. I. Comly, 1837), 128, 129.

18. Jeremy Belknap and Jedediah Morse, "Report on the Oneida, Stockbridge, and Brothertown Indians," in *Indian Notes and Monographs*, vol. 12 (New York: Heye

Foundation, 1955), 15; "Dr. Belknap's Tour to Oneida, 1796," *Massachusetts Historical Society Proceedings* 19 (1881–1882): 407; Israel Chapin to James McHenry, Sept. 4, 1796, O'Reilly Papers, vol. 11; *Joshua Evans,* 128; John Pierce, "Notes, on a Visit to Several Tribes of Indians," 25, 47–48, typescript, FHL.

19. Daniel D. Tompkins, Address to the Legislature, Jan. 1812, in *Public Papers of Daniel D. Tompkins* (New York and Albany: Wynkoop, Hallenbeck, Crawford, 1898–1902), 2:448.

20. James Dean to Pickering, Aug. 22, 1796, TPP 62:246; Tiro, "James Dean," 419–21; see also Taylor, *Divided Ground,* 317–22; *Kirkland Journal,* 332–33. For an example of traditional justice taking its course, see June 7, 1796 entry, John Sergeant journal, box 2, folder 26, Harvard University Corporation Records of Grants for Work among the Indians, Harvard University Archives, Cambridge, Mass.

21. *Kirkland Journal,* 314–15 ("maxims"); Pierce, "Notes," 28 ("live plentifully"); Kirkland to unidentified correspondent, Mar. 17, 1800, 209c, SKP ("widows").

22. Chapin to Pickering, Nov. 15, 1796; "Journal of James Emlen," 284, 333; Joseph Sansom to unidentified correspondents, June 20, 1796, Sansom letters, all Quaker Collection. See also Jacob Taylor et al. to PYMIC, Oct. 31, 1796, and Apr. 3, 1797, AA41; PYMIC minutes, Sept. 22, 1797, AA6.

23. Daniel K. Richter, "'Believing That Many of the Red People Suffer Much for the Want of Food': Hunting, Agriculture, and a Quaker Construction of Indianness in the Early Republic," *Journal of the Early Republic* 19 (1999): 616–17; Joseph Clark, *Travels among the Indians, 1797* (Doylestown, Pa.: Charles Ingerman, 1968), 18; Sahlins quoted in William Cronon, *Changes in the Land: Indians, Colonists, and the Ecology of New England* (New York: Hill & Wang, 1983), 79–80, 98.

24. Chapin to Pickering, Nov. 15, 1796; Jacob Taylor et al. to PYMIC, Oct. 31, 1796, and Apr. 3, 1797; PYMIC minutes, Sept. 22, 1797.

25. Chapin to McHenry, Sept. 4, 1796; Chapin to Pickering, Nov. 15, 1796; John Pierce, "Notes, on a Visit to Several Tribes of Indians, 1796," typescript, 25, FHL; Jacob Taylor and Jonathan Thomas to PYMIC, Oct. 9, 1797, AA41; Pierce, "Notes," 25; PYMIC to Thomas Eddy, Nov. 4, 1797, AA41.1; Thomas Eddy to PYMIC, July 20, 1797, PYMIC minutes, 1:58 (doc. 22), all Quaker Collection.

26. Jacob Taylor and Jonathan Thomas to PYMIC, Apr. 9, 1798, AA41; Thomas et al. to PYMIC, Apr. 23, 1797, AA41; John Drinker and John Sansom to unidentified correspondent, Jan. 18, 1797, AA41.1; PYMIC minutes, Aug. 18, 1797, AA6; Jacob Taylor and Jonathan Thomas to PYMIC, Oct. 9, 1797; Report of Jacob Taylor and others, Apr. 1797, AA42, all Quaker Collection; *A Brief Account of the Proceedings of the Committee, Appointed in the Year 1795 . . . for Promoting the Improvement and Gradual Civilization of the Indian Natives* (Philadelphia: Kimber & Conrad, 1806), 11.

27. Clark, *Travels,* 14; Jonathan Thomas and Jacob Taylor to PYMIC, June 18, 1798, and PYMIC to Oneidas, Apr. 12, 1798, AA41, Quaker Collection; *Kirkland Journal,* 314–15; "Extract of a Letter from Hannah Jackson to Jane Hough," Jan. 15, 1799, Historical Society of Pennsylvania, Philadelphia.

28. Pierce, "Notes," 14; Belknap and Morse, *Report,* 17, 23.

29. Richter, "Believing," 616. The Oneidas obtained some of these goods from the missionaries in exchange for work. PYMIC minutes, June 16, 1797, AA6, Quaker Collection; John Grew, *Journal of a Tour from Boston to Niagara Falls and Quebec, 1803* (n.p., n.d.), 43.

30. Friedrich Rohde, "Journal of a Trip from New Jersey to Oneida Lake," in *In Mohawk Country: Early Narratives about a Native People*, ed. Dean R. Snow, Charles T. Gehring, and William A. Starna (Syracuse, N.Y.: Syracuse University Press, 1996), 380; Julian Ursyn Niemcewicz, "Journey to Niagara, 1805," ed. Metchie J. E. Budka, *New-York Historical Society Quarterly* 74 (1960): 94, 96; J[ohn] J[acob] A[stor]'s Account of Peltry Received from Mr. Peter Smith," 1792, in *John Jacob Astor: Business Man*, ed. Kenneth Wiggins Porter (Cambridge: Harvard University Press, 1931), 365–67; Barent Sanders Journal, July–Aug. 1800, New-York Historical Society, New York; Brian L. Evans, "Ginseng: Root of Canadian-Chinese Relations," *Canadian Historical Review* 66 (2001): 10–26.

31. "An Act for the Better Support of the Oneida, Onondaga and Cayuga Indians, and for Other Purposes Therein Mentioned," Apr. 1, 1795, New York Session Laws, chap. 70; "An Act for the Relief of the Tenants of Peter Smith and others," Apr. 1, 1797, ibid., chap. 80; "An Act for the Sale of Lands in the Oneida Reservation to Persons Therein Named," Apr. 8, 1800, ibid., chap. 126; George Embree et al., "Some Account of a Visit Paid to the Indians . . . ," *Friends' Review* 5 (1795): 788–89.

32. Chapin to the Secretary of War, Oct. 18, 1797, O'Reilly Papers, vol. 12; "Joseph Clark's Account of a Journey to the Indian Country," *Friends' Miscellany* 1, no. 7 (1831): 370.

33. Thomas R. Gold to Schuyler, July 3, 1796, r. 18, Schuyler Papers; quoted in Lord, *Navigators*, 114; "An Act Authorizing the Governor to Appoint Commissioners to Treat with the Oneida Indians," Feb. 23, 1798, New York Session Laws, chap. 23.

34. Jacob Taylor and Jonathan Thomas to PYMIC, Mar. 13, 1798, doc. 27, minute book 1:74, Quaker Collection.

35. Egbert Benson, John Tayler, and Simeon DeWitt to Governor Tompkins, n.d., *ASPIA* 4/1:642; Jacob Taylor and Jonathan Thomas to PYMIC, Apr. 9, 1798, minute book, 1:76, Quaker Collection; Timothy Bigelow, *Journal of a Tour to Niagara Falls in 1805* (Boston, Mass.: John Wilson & Co., 1876), 25; Charles C. Brodhead and Robert Bardwell, "Valuation of Jacob Dockstedder's Improvements," A1820, 37:120–21, NYSA.

36. *Kirkland Journal*, 314; Doxtator's improvements are detailed in Brodhead and Bardwell, "Valuation"; Draper Manuscripts, 11U:191–92, State Historical Society of Wisconsin, Madison; petition of Oneidas and Tuscaroras, Mar. 5, 1798, *IIDH*.

37. Pickering to Joseph Hopkinson, May 5, 1798, TPP, 8:405; U.S. Senate Records, 5th Congress, 3d sess., report no. 87, Jan. 31, 1799; *Whipple Report*, 249; "Memoir of My Journey on the Western Circuit, 1798," James Kent Papers, vol. 6, journal 2, Library of Congress, Washington, D.C. ("banished"); "An Act for the Sale of Land to John Denny," Feb. 15, 1799, New York Session Laws, chap. 13.

38. *Kirkland Journal*, 314–15, 330, 332; *Brief Account*, 12–13; "Expended on the Settlement at Oneida &c," AA16, folder 3; PYMIC to Philadelphia Yearly Meeting, Apr. 21, 1800, AB40, Quaker Collection.

39. Oneidas to Jacob Taylor, Jonathan Thomas, and William Gregory, Jan. 6, 1800, AA41, Quaker Collection; *Kirkland Journal*, 350.

40. Conference with the Oneida Nation, Jan. 6, 1800, PYMIC minutes, 1:118, AA41, Quaker Collection; Kirkland to unidentified correspondent, Mar. 17, 1800, 29c, SKP; unidentified correspondent to David Bacon et al., Oct. 17, 1801, AA42, Quaker Collection.

41. Elisabeth Tooker, *The Iroquois Ceremonial of Midwinter* (Syracuse, N.Y.: Syracuse University Press, 1970), 114–18; Tooker, "The Iroquois White Dog Sacrifice in the Latter Part of the Eighteenth Century," *Ethnohistory* 2 (1965): 129–40; quoted in *Kirkland Journal*, 359–60.

42. *Kirkland Journal*, 360, 367.

43. *Otsego Herald* (Cooperstown, N.Y.), Mar. 4, 1802, p. 1; Oneidas to New York State, [ca. 1802], A1823, NYSA; U.S. Senate Report, 7th Congress, 1st sess., report no. 97, Mar. 10, 1802; New York Yearly Meeting Indian Committee (NYYMIC) Minute Book 2, May 22, 1830, FHL.

44. Joseph Annin, "Field Book of the Purchase Made of the Oneida Nation of Indians in the Year . . . 1802," A4019, vol. 13, NYSA; Charles Brodhead, "A Survey of Part of the Lands Purchased from the Oneida Indians in 1802," May 1805, ibid., vol. 16; John Dean to PYMIC, Oct. 19, 1801, AA41, Quaker Collection; Oneida petition, Jan. or Feb. 1802, *IIDH;* petition of Louis Denny et al., Mar. 13, 1802, Ayer 234, Newberry Library; "An Act Relative to the Unappropriated Lands of This State," Apr. 5, 1802, New York Session Laws, chap. 112; Simeon DeWitt, "Account with the State of New York," Jan. 13, 1803, A0832, box 4, folder 5, NYSA; "An Act for the Sale of the Unappropriated Lands, and for Other Purposes," Apr. 6, 1803, New York Session Laws, chap. 106.

45. Simeon DeWitt and Ezra L'Hommedieu, Jan. 13, 1803, A1823, NYSA; Simeon DeWitt and Jacob Tayler to DeWitt Clinton, Mar. 2, 1802, mss. 14591, NYSL; Oneida and Onondaga petition to Congress, Jan. 19, 1801 (also dated Feb. 13, 1802), Indian Committee mss. box 1, Haverford College, Haverford, Pa.

46. Ann Mifflin journal, 15–17, Logan-Fisher-Fox Papers, Historical Society of Pennsylvania; speech of the Oneidas relative to Louis Cook's annuity, June 8, 1805, Ayer 659, Newberry Library.

47. Dec. 11 entry, Journal of Samuel Kirkland, Oct. 16–Dec. 31, 1803, folio 1, Northern Missionary Society Papers, Rutgers University Library, New Brunswick, N.J.

48. July 22 entry, Journal of Samuel Kirkland, Apr. 1–Oct. 1, 1804, in ibid.; *Kirkland Journal*, 398–99; Oneidas to the Governor of New York State, Jan. 24, 1805, 235a, SKP.

49. *Whipple Report*, 259–63.

50. Kirkland to Alexander Miller, May 24, 1800, 211c, SKP; *Kirkland Journal*, 393, 419.

51. *Kirkland Journal*, 374.

52. Ibid., 385–86, 390–92.

53. Quoted in *Kirkland Journal*, 418–19; *The Spectator* (New York), Sept. 6, 1815, 3. Handsome Lake's proscription of alcohol was greeted with "extreme displeasure" by

some Oneidas. Journal of John Sergeant, Aug. 11, 1805, MS 48, box 3, folder 10, Society for Propagating the Gospel among the Indians and Others in North America records, Massachusetts Historical Society, Boston.

54. *Whipple Report*, 263–65; indenture between Cornelius and Jane Dockstader and Peter Smith, Oct. 10, 1807, bk. 16 of deeds, 111, Oneida County Courthouse, Utica, N.Y.

55. *Whipple Report*, 266–69; receipt, Angel de Ferrière to Daniel D. Tompkins; account, [Feb. 16, 1809], docket 301, box 2678, RG 279, NA; "An Act Relative to the Purchase of Part of the Reservations Belonging to the Christian and Pagan Parties of the Oneida Nation of Indians," Mar. 24, 1809, New York Session Laws, chap. 107. "Anthony" may refer to the treaty signatory Anthony Shonoghriyo. "Paulus" may refer to treaty signatory Paul Anenshontye.

56. Tompkins to Chauncy Humphrey, Jan. 14, 1809, in *Papers of Daniel D. Tompkins*, 2:420; receipts to Daniel D. Tompkins, Feb. 21, 1809, A0832, NYSA; Simeon DeWitt to New York State Assembly, Feb. 2, 1810, *Journal of the Assembly of the State of New York*, Feb. 26, 1810, 142–43; "An Act for the Payment of Certain Officers of Government and for Other Purposes," Apr. 5, 1810, New York Session Laws, chap. 193; Oneida petition to state legislature, Feb. 7, 1814, Newberry Library; Surveyor-General's Report, *Journal of the Senate of the State of New York*, Feb. 17, 1815, 104–8; Simeon DeWitt to New York State Legislature, Feb. 9, 1810, *IIDH*.

57. South [Pagan] Party to Tompkins, Jan. 30, 1810, Surveyor-General's Land Papers, ser. 2, A4016, 24:149, NYSA.

58. Chiefs and Warriors of That Part of the Oneida Nation Now Called Christian to Governor Tompkins, Surveyor-General's Land Papers, ser. 2, A4016, 24:165.

59. South Party to Tompkins, Jan. 30, 1810; *Report of the Directors of the Northern Missionary Society* (Albany, N.Y.: Websters and Skinners, 1813); James Dean to John Tayler, Jan. 31, 1810.

60. Dean to Tayler, Jan. 31, 1810, Surveyor-General's Land Papers, ser. 2, A4016, 24:146; Ripley, *The Bank of Faith and Works United* (Philadelphia: J. H. Cunningham, 1819), 69–71.

61. Joint Resolution of the Senate and Assembly of New York State, *Journal of the Senate of the State of New York*, Feb. 28, 1810, 71; *Whipple Report*, 272–74; "Memorandum relative to Indian Annuities," [after 1839], A0832, box 1, folder 1, NYSA; Hauptman, *Conspiracy of Interests*, 55–56; *Whipple Report*, 267–68; Clinton quoted in William W. Campbell, ed., *Life and Writings of DeWitt Clinton* (New York: Baker & Scribner, 1849), 191.

62. Campbell, *Life and Writings of DeWitt Clinton*, 186 ("plowing"), 188, 189 ("opposed"); *A Summary Account of the Measures Pursued by the Yearly Meeting of Friends of New York, for the Welfare and Civilization of the Indians Residing on the Frontiers of that State* (London: Phillips, 1813), 11, 14, 20–27; Christopher Densmore, "New York Quakers among the Brotherton, Stockbridge, Oneida, and Onondaga, 1795–1834," *Northeast Anthropology* 44 (1992): 85–86; NYYMIC Minute Book 1:103, 109, 131, 150, FHL; *Summary Account*, 20–21; Minutes of the Committee on the Indian Concern, Dec. 10, 1810, [70]; Alex F. Ricciardelli, "The Adoption of White Agriculture by the

Oneida Indians," in *The Emergent Native Americans: A Reader in Culture Contact*, ed. Deward E. Walker Jr. (Boston: Little, Brown, 1971), 334–36.

63. *Whipple Report*, 275.

64. Tompkins to Matthias Hildreth, Apr. 17, 1811, in *Papers of Daniel D. Tompkins*, 2:342–43; *Whipple Report*, 278. The Oneidas were given twelve hundred dollars.

65. Tompkins to Thomas Grosvenor, Feb. 12, 1812, in *Papers of Daniel D. Tompkins*, 2:480–84; Tompkins address to New York State Legislature, Jan. 1812, in ibid., 2:448; Erastus Granger to Henry Dearborn, Dec. 21, 1808, docket 301, box 2674, RG 279, NA.

66. Tompkins to Legislature, Feb. 20, 1813, in *Papers of Daniel D. Tompkins*, 3:260–61; "An Act Authorizing the Governor to Hold Treaties with the Indian Nations and Tribes within This State," Apr. 5, 1813, New York Session Laws, chap. 130.

67. Six Nations to the President of the United States, Sept. 29, 1812, in *Red and White on the New York Frontier*, ed. Charles M. Snyder (Harrison, N.Y.: Harbor Hill Books, 1978), 56–57.

68. General Smyth to the Soldiers of the Army of the Centre, broadside, Nov. 17, 1812, in Snyder, *Red and White*, 61; Carl Benn, *The Iroquois in the War of 1812* (Toronto: University of Toronto Press, 1998), 30, 150; *Public Speeches Delivered at the Village of Buffalo, on the 6th and 8th Days of July, 1812, by Hon. Erastus Granger . . .* ([Buffalo, N.Y.], 1812), 13–14.

69. *The Journal of Major John Norton, 1816*, ed. Carl F. Klinck and James J. Talman (Toronto: Champlain Society, 1970), 286.; Benn, *Iroquois*, 31; John Armstrong to Dearborn, Sept. 23, 1812, in *The Documentary History of the Campaign on the Niagara Frontier*, ed. Ernest A. Cruikshank ([1902?]; repr., New York: Arno, 1971), 1:291.

70. *Repository* (Canandaigua, N.Y.), Sept. 15, 1812, in Cruikshank, *Documentary History*, 1:262–63; Six Nations to the President, Sept. 29, 1812.

71. Anthony F. C. Wallace, *The Death and Rebirth of the Seneca* (New York: Alfred A. Knopf, 1970), 294–96; Armstrong to Dearborn, Sept. 23, 1812, *New York Evening Post*, June 2, 1813, in Cruikshank, *Documentary History*, 1:291; Certificates of Claims by War of 1812 Veterans, A3352, NYSA; Benn, *Iroquois*, 158.

72. Certificates of Claims by War of 1812 Veterans; Draper Manuscripts, 11U:214.

73. Cruikshank, *Documentary History*, 2:169, 262–63; Peter B. Porter to Six Nations, n.d., in ibid., 4:392–93; "List of Indians Who Delivered up Horses Taken of the Inhabitants of Canada," [1813], in Snyder, *Red and White*, 70; "Speech of Red Jacket at a Council Held at Buffalo, Oct. 21, 1813," in Cruikshank, *Documentary History*, 3:86 ("trifled with"); "Council Proceedings, Feb. 2, 1814," in Snyder, *Red and White*, 75.

74. John C. Fredriksen, *Green Coats and Glory: The U.S. Regiment of Riflemen, 1808–1821* (Youngstown, N.Y.: Fort Niagara Publications, 2000), 50–51; Porter to Brown, July 3, 1814, Porter to Brown, May 26, 1814, Porter to Brown, June 23, 1814, in Cruikshank, *Documentary History*, 4:26, 398, 406; Benn, *Iroquois*, 155–60, 163; Donald R. Hickey, *The War of 1812: A Forgotten Conflict* (Urbana: University of Illinois Press, 1995), 185; Six Nations petition to Secretary of War, Feb. 20, 1815, Ely Parker Papers, American Philosophical Society, Philadelphia, Pa.; George Drummond to George Prevost, July 10, 1814, A. Z. Orne, "Return of the killed, wounded, and prisoners of

the enemy," July 9, 1814, in Cruikshank, *Documentary History,* 4:35–36, 42; Draper Manuscripts, 11U:196, 200.

75. Peter B. Porter to Farmer's Brother, Young King, Captain Billy, Major Berry, Shongo, and Colonel Lewis, July 25, 1814, in Snyder, *Red and White,* 77–78; Jasper Parrish to Porter, July 27, 1814, and Aug. 15, 1814, and Maj.-Gen. Brown's Diary, July 5–25, 1814, in Cruikshank, *Documentary History,* 4:419, 433, 466.

76. *Journal of Major John Norton,* 353–54; quoted in Benn, *Iroquois,* 165.

77. Benn, *Iroquois,* 175–79.

Chapter 6. The Nation in Fragments

1. Southerners were well aware of the double standard. Ronald Satz, *American Indian Policy in the Jacksonian Era* (Lincoln: University of Nebraska Press, 1975), 24, 41; Laurence M. Hauptman and L. Gordon McLester III, *Chief Daniel Bread and the Oneida Nation of Indians of Wisconsin* (Norman: University of Oklahoma Press, 2002), 54.

2. Petition of First Christian Party, Feb. 21, 1814, CB503, box 1, William Leland Thompson Collection (F14), Albany Institute of History and Art, Albany, N.Y.; "Extracts from Rev. Wm. Jenkins' Journal," in *Report of the Directors of the Northern Missionary Society* (Albany, N.Y.: Websters and Skinners, 1815), 10–11; John Randel Jr. to Simeon DeWitt, Feb. 2, 1816, Surveyor-General's Land Papers, ser. 2, A4016, 1:101, NYSA.

3. Laurence M. Hauptman, *Conspiracy of Interests: Iroquois Dispossession and the Rise of the Empire State* (Syracuse, N.Y.: Syracuse University Press, 1999), 18–19, 44–45; Carol Sheriff, *The Artificial River: The Erie Canal and the Paradox of Progress, 1817–1862* (New York: Hill & Wang, 1996), 9, 115; Benjamin Wright, "Notes and Remarks on a Line Run for a Canal from Rome to Seneca River . . . in 1816," Benjamin Wright Papers, NYSL.

4. Anon., June–July 1821 diary, Joseph Downs Collection, Winterthur Library, Winterthur, Del.; *Autobiography of Thurlow Weed,* ed. Harriet A. Weed (New York: Da Capo, 1970), 1:148; Reginald Horsman, "The Origins of Oneida Removal to Wisconsin, 1815–1822," in *The Oneida Indian Journey: From New York to Wisconsin, 1784–1860,* ed. Laurence M. Hauptman and L. Gordon McLester III (Madison: University of Wisconsin Press, 1999), 53–69.

5. New York State Assembly report on Indian affairs, Mar. 4, 1819, *IIDH.*

6. Petition of the Oneida County Board of Supervisors to the New York state legislature, read in Assembly, Jan. 15, 1821, *IIDH;* petition concerning the state of trespassers on Oneida lands, Jan. 15, 1821, A1823, NYSA.

7. Carolyn Thomas Foreman, *Indians Abroad, 1493–1938* (Norman: University of Oklahoma Press, 1943), 121, 125; Matthew Dennis, *Seneca Possessed: Indians, Witchcraft, and Power in the Early American Republic* (Philadelphia: University of Pennsylvania Press, 2010), 194–99; George Hamell, personal communication, May 25, 1999; *The Times* (London), Jan. 25, 1819, 2, and Jan. 28, 1819, 3; *The Yankee* (Boston, Mass.), May 1, 1818, 2; *New York Columbian,* Aug. 24, 1818, 2.

8. *Baltimore Patriot,* July 19, 1819, 2; *Vermont Intelligencer and Bellows' Falls Advertiser,* Jan. 24, 1820, 3; Albert Gallatin to unidentified correspondent, Sept. 11, 1819; Gallatin to Angel de Ferrière, Sept. 11, 1819; De Ferrière statement, Oct. 27, 1819; Gallatin to John Quincy Adams, Oct. 27, 1819; Gallatin to Reuben Beardsley, Oct. 28, 1819; Thomas Taylor to Gallatin, Nov. 1, 1819, all Papers of Albert Gallatin, New-York Historical Society, New York. On Sagoyountha's age, see Draper Manuscripts, 11U:213–14, State Historical Society of Wisconsin, Madison.

9. Copy of remarks by T. L. Ogden to Bishop John Henry Hobart, Dec. 14, 1814, *IIDH;* Satz, *American Indian Policy,* 4–6; David A. Ogden to Peter B. Porter, May 21, 1821, docket 301, box 2674, RG 279, NA; Robert Troup and David A. Ogden to James Barbour, Dec. 20, 1827, M234, r. 832, NA.

10. Alexander Dallas to Daniel D. Tompkins, Aug. 5, 1815, Letters Sent, Indian Affairs, vol. C, Records of the Office of the Secretary of War, NA.

11. Lewis Cass to David A. Ogden, Jan. 29, 1818; Calhoun to Ogden, May 14, 1818, in *The Papers of John C. Calhoun,* ed. Robert Meriwether (Columbia: University of South Carolina Press, 1959–2003), 2:293–94; James W. Oberly, *A Nation of Statesmen: The Political Culture of the Stockbridge-Munsee Mohicans, 1815–1972* (Norman: University of Oklahoma Press, 2005), 27; Ogden to DeWitt Clinton, Mar. 12, 1818, *IIDH;* Ogden to Parrish, Apr. 26, 1818; Ogden to Calhoun, Aug. 4, 1818 ("fevers"), both Jasper Parrish Papers, Vassar College Library, Poughkeepsie, N.Y.; Troup to Parrish, Aug. 24, 1818, in Meriwether, *Papers of John C. Calhoun,* 2:293; David Ogden to Calhoun, Aug. 4, 1818, and Aug 19, 1818, Papers, Buffalo and Erie County Historical Society, Buffalo, N.Y.

12. David A. Ogden to Parrish, June 18[?], 1816, Parrish Papers, Vassar College Library; Troup to Parrish, Aug. 24, 1818.

13. Copy of the speech in answer to the Revd Doc Morse delivered by Peter Summer, Chief Orator of the Oneida nation, July 18, 1821, RG 107, M221, r. 93, NA; Timothy Dwight, *Travels in New England and New York* (London: William Baynes & Son, 1823), 3:185.

14. Message of the Governor, *Journal of the Assembly of the State of New York,* Jan. 27, 1818, 14.

15. Oneidas to James Monroe, Nov. 11, 1818, RG 107, M221, r. 182, NA; Oneidas to DeWitt Clinton, Nov. 11, 1818, A1818, NYSA.

16. John Anthony and Moses Skenandoah to Williams, Dec. 9, 1814, Eleazer Williams Papers, 2:394, State Historical Society of Wisconsin, Madison. Late in life, Williams wrote a biography of Louis Cook. Franklin B. Hough Papers, SC7009, box 91, NYSL.

17. John Demos, *The Unredeemed Captive: A Family Story from Early America* (New York: Knopf, 1994), 242–46; Evan Haefeli and Kevin Sweeney, eds., *Captive Histories: English, French, and Native Narratives of the 1704 Deerfield Raid* (Amherst: University of Massachusetts Press, 2006), 222–27; Geoffrey E. Buerger, "Eleazer Williams: Elitism and Multiple Identity on Two Frontiers," in *Being and Becoming Indian,* ed. James Clifton (Chicago: Dorsey, 1989), 117–18; Eleazer Williams, *Life of Te-ho-ra-gwa-ne-gen, alias Thomas Williams, a Chief of the Caughnawaga tribe of Indians in Canada,* ed. Franklin B. Hough (Albany, N.Y.: J. Munsell, 1859), 57–59.

18. Albert G. Ellis, Williams's disgruntled assistant at the Oneida mission, observed that Ellis wanted him "to read the theological works, but scarce ever touched one himself." Ellis, "Recollections of Rev. Eleazer Williams," *Report and Collections of the State Historical Society of Wisconsin* 8 (1877–79): 323.

19. Ellis, "Recollections," 325; Joseph O. Powless diary, typescript, 31, Green Bay Area Research Center, State Historical Society of Wisconsin.

20. Colin G. Calloway, *The American Revolution in Indian Country: Crisis and Diversity in Native American Communities* (New York: Cambridge University Press, 1995), 117–18; Ellis, "Some Account of the Advent of the New York Indians into Wisconsin," Wisconsin Historical Society *Collections* 2 (1856), 419.

21. Eleazer Williams, *Selections from the Psalms and Hymns According to the Use of the Protestant Episcopal Church in the United States of America* (New York: Protestant Episcopal Tract Society, 1853); Ellis, "Recollections," 323; Anon., June–July 1821 diary; *Journal of the Life, Labours, and Travels of Thomas Shillitoe in the Service of the Gospel of Jesus* (London: Harvey and Darton, 1839), 367.

22. Geoffrey E. Buerger, "Thomas Williams," in *Dictionary of Canadian Biography* (Toronto: University of Toronto / Québec: Université Laval, 1966–2005), 7:911–12; Barbara Graymont, "Atiatoharongwen," in ibid., 6:39–41; Philippe Sylvain, "Eleazer Williams," in ibid., 8:939–40; Carl Benn, *The Iroquois in the War of 1812* (Toronto: University of Toronto Press, 1998), 61; Buerger, "Eleazer Williams,"112–36; State of New York to Isaac Denniston, Jan. 14, 1815, A0832; State of New York to E. Patrick, Mar. 21, 1816, A0832; State of New York to Walter Allen, Sept. 10, 1816, A0832, all NYSA; *Whipple Report*, 369–72; Oneida chiefs to Parrish, n.d., 1816, MS 1246, NYSL; Philadelphia Yearly Meeting Indian Committee minute book, May 24, 1817, Quaker Collection, Haverford College Library, Haverford, Pa.; Erastus Granger to George Graham, Jan. 20, 1817, in *Red and White on the New York Frontier,* ed. Charles M. Snyder (Harrison, N.Y.: Harbor Hill Books, 1978), 85; "An Act for the Relief of the St. Regis, Oneida, Onondaga, and Seneca Indians," Feb. 12, 1817, New York Session Laws, chap. 34.

23. *Whipple Report,* 284–86. The building of a church may be evidence that Williams had yet to develop his interest in removal in 1819. Indeed, he wrote to a supporter in that year: "One thing that I had already seen, that to save the Oneidas there must be change either in the place of residence or their morals. As I had already been successful in the latter, so I [illegible] they may so still be improved as to prevent the necessity of the former." [Nov. 1819], Eleazer Williams Papers. Ellis, Williams's assistant, however, accused him of skimming substantially from the construction contracts, thereby providing a potential motive for supporting the construction of a church even if its use was to be of short duration. Ellis, "Recollections," 326.

24. Isaac Denniston payment to John Denny, July 8, 1817, and to Eleazer Williams, June 26, 1817, A0832, NYSA; *Whipple Report*, 284–87; John Randel Jr., "Field Book of Cowasselon Tract," Surveyor-General's Field Books, A4019, 13:189, NYSA.

25. DeWitt Clinton to John Pintard, Sept. 29, 1817, Ayer 3046, Newberry Library, Chicago.

26. Ellis, "Recollections," 331–32.

27. Amelia Cornelius, "Tribal Discord and the Road to Green Bay," in Hauptman and McLester, *Oneida Indian Journey,* 128; John Brandt et al. to Cass, Aug. 12, 1820, *IIDH;* Daniel Tegawatiron [Bread] to Cass, Aug. 12, 1820; same to William Woodbridge, Aug. 12, 1820; Calhoun to Williams, Feb. 9, 1820; Indians to William Woodbridge, Aug. 12, 1820; same to Cass, Aug. 12, 1820, all *IIDH; Petition and Appeal of the Six Nations* (Sangerfield, N.Y.: Joseph Tenny, 1829).

28. Ogden to Porter, May 21, 1821; Ogden to Cass, May 17, 1821 (included in former to Porter); Williams to unidentified recipient, Apr. 18, 1821, Eleazer Williams Papers; C. C. Trowbridge, "Journal of a Tour to Green Bay," July 1821, *IIDH.*

29. Thomas Christian's first documented appearance as a leader was in the 1817 request to the state for famine relief. If John Anthony Bradt was John Anthony (elsewhere Antony), as I believe he was, he was a signatory to the 1814 letter to Williams soliciting his ministry, the 1815 Christian Party treaty, and the 1818 petition against removal. It is impossible, however, to distinguish between John Skenandoah and his recently deceased father in previous appearances of the name.

30. Chiefs of the First Christian Party to John C. Calhoun, Mar. 14, 1822, M221, r. 93, NA; Ellis, "Recollections," 335–36. Ellis was present among the Oneidas and states clearly that the 1821 delegation was conferred some authority by the First Christian Party. His eagerness to expose all of Williams's faults and foibles suggests that he would have happily denied Williams the slightest shred of legitimacy if the situation were any different.

31. Robert W. Venables, "Victim versus Victim: The Irony of the New York Indians' Removal to Wisconsin," in *American Indian Environments: Ecological Issues in Native American History,* ed. Christopher Vecsey and Robert W. Venables (Syracuse, N.Y.: Syracuse University Press, 1980), 140–51. On the Menominees' bogus chief problem, see Robert E. Bieder, *Native American Communities in Wisconsin, 1600–1960: A Study of Tradition and Change* (Madison: University of Wisconsin Press, 1995), 139–43; petition of the Menominies, June 16, 1824, in *The Indian Removals* (New York: Arno, 1974), 536.

32. Trowbridge, "Journal"; Treaty between the New York Indians and Menominies and Winnebagos, Aug. 18, 1821, in *Petition and Appeal,* 15–17; Samuel Stambaugh to Cass, Aug. 4, 1831, in *Indian Removals,* 525–26.

33. C. C. Trowbridge to Cass, Sept. 7, 1821, RG 75, NA; Chiefs of the First Christian Party chiefs to Calhoun, Mar. 14, 1822; Oneidas to Monroe, n.d., r. 2, Eleazer Williams Papers; Stambaugh to Cass, Aug. 4, 1831; Venables, "Victim versus Victim," 148–49; Treaty between the New York Indians and Menominies, Sept. 3, 1822, in *Petition and Appeal,* 21–24; Williams to Calhoun, Dec. 27, 1822, *IIDH.*

34. Oneidas to Samuel Royce, Feb. 29, 1821, Ayer 663, Newberry Library.

35. Quoted in Oneidas to Monroe, Aug. 8, 1821, docket 301, box 2675, RG 279, NA; John Lawton to Calhoun, Aug. 16, 1821, in Meriwether, *Papers of John C. Calhoun,* 6:391–92. The Baptist minister who wrote a letter of introduction for these men noted that "the Onondago tribe consider themselves equally aggrieved with the . . . pretended agency" because Williams claimed to act on behalf of all "New York Indians."

36. Ellis, "Recollections," 328; Parrish to Calhoun, Aug. 21, 1821, Ontario County Historical Society, Canandaigua, N.Y.; quoted in Oneidas to Monroe, Aug. 8, 1821.

37. Oneidas to Monroe, Oct. 14, 1821, described in Meriwether, *Papers of John C. Calhoun,* 6:435–39; Ellis, "Recollections," 333; First and Second Christian Parties to Monroe, Jan. 22, 1822, RG 279, NA.

38. Statement of Solomon Davis, Feb. 19, 1835, A4016, 2:74, NYSA.

39. "A Copy of the Speech in Answer to the Revd Doc. Morse Delivered by Peter Summer," July 18, 1821, M221, r. 93, NA; Draper Manuscripts, 11U:263.

40. Justus Ingersoll to Thomas McKenney, Mar. 25, 1830, M234, r. 832, NA; Williams to Parrish, Apr. 10, 1824, *IIDH;* Simeon DeWitt, "Report on the Petition of Martin Denny," Feb. 1, 1822, A1820, 38:315, NYSA.

41. Alan S. Taylor, "Capt. Hendrick Aupaumut: The Dilemmas of an Intercultural Broker," *Ethnohistory* 43 (1996): 431–58; Rachel Wheeler, "Hendrick Aupaumut: Christian Mahican Prophet," *Journal of the Early Republic* 25 (2005): 187–220; Judy Cornelius, "Additional Notes on Eleazer Williams (1797–1858) and the Origins of the Episcopal Tradition among the Oneidas," in Hauptman and McLester, *Oneida Indian Journey,* 131; Amelia Cornelius, "Tribal Discord and the Road to Green Bay," in Hauptman and McLester, *Oneida Indian Journey,* 128; Oberly, *Nation of Statesmen,* 39.

42. Parrish to McKenney, Oct. 11, 1824, M234, r. 832, NA.

43. Calhoun to Parrish, May 14, 1818, in Meriwether, *Papers of John C. Calhoun,* 2:294; Philip Otto Geier III, "A Peculiar Status: A History of Oneida Indian Treaties and Claims: Jurisdictional Conflict Within the American Government, 1775–1920" (Ph.D. diss., Syracuse University, 1980), 171; *Whipple Report,* 287–90; petition of the chiefs and warriors of the First Christian Party, Dec. 30, 1829, A1823, NYSA.

44. Justus Ingersoll to Samuel Hamilton, Aug. 29, 1831, M234, r. 832, NA; Orlando Allen, "Personal Recollections of Captains Jones and Parrish and of the Payment of Indian Annuities in Buffalo," *Publications of the Buffalo Historical Society* 6 (1903): 538–40.

45. Geier, "Peculiar Status," 172–73.

46. Memorial of the Second Christian Party, Feb. 17, 1826, A1823, NYSA; *Whipple Report,* 298–300.

47. Petition of Second Christian Party to New York State, Jan. 25, 1826, A1823, NYSA.

48. Mary Doxtator affidavit, Second Christian Party to New York State Legislature, Feb. 17, 1826, A1823, NYSA; Richard G. Niemi, "The Interconnected Lives of Stockbridge Indians Mary (Peters) Doxtator and Peter Pohquonnoppeet" (paper presented to the Fourth Algonquian People's Conference, Albany, N.Y., Mar. 2003).

49. Second Christian Party petition to New York State Legislature, Feb. 24, 1826, A1823, NYSA.

50. John C. Spencer, "Report of the Standing Committee of the N.Y. State Legislature on Petition, Feb. 17–18, 1826," A1823, NYSA.

51. Mar. 6, 1834, New York State Senate doc. 88; *Whipple Report,* 301–3.

52. Donald B. Smith, *Sacred Feathers: The Rev. Peter Jones (Kahkewaquonaby) & the Mississauga Indians* (Lincoln: University of Nebraska Press, 1987); Jones, *Collec-*

tion of Hymns for the Use of Native Christians of the Iroquois (New York: A. Hoyt, 1827). Barclay names the Oneidas' preacher Daniel Adams. The diary kept by the clerk of the Oneida nation notes, however, that "Rev. [William] Doxtater [d. 1842] . . . was the first to be authorized to be in charge of Methodist Church in Oneida Castle . . . A.D. 1828. It was thru him that we accepted the Methodist Church, he is from Ohsweken [Grand River, Canada]." Adams was mentioned as a Methodist Mohawk who arrived in 1830 and removed to Duck Creek in 1832, where he resided until 1837. Jones preached to the Oneidas at the Thames. Wade Crawford Barclay, *Early American Methodism, 1769–1844* (New York: Board of Missions of the Methodist Church, 1950), 2:146; Powless diary, 9, 14, 17.

53. Draper Manuscripts, 11U:215; "Petition of the First Christian Party of the Oneida Indians for Further Compensation," Jan. 28, 1835, A4016, 11:75, NYSA; quoted in petition from the Christian Party of Oneida Indians, Feb. 24, 1834, New York State Senate doc. 74.

54. Peleg Gifford to DeWitt Clinton, July 7, 1826, A4016, 1:61; petition of Martin Denny et al., Jan. 7, 1830, A1823, NYSA; petition from the Christian Party of Oneida Indians, Feb. 24, 1834. See also "Petition of the First Christian Party," Jan. 28, 1835.

55. First Christian Party to State Legislature, Dec. 30, 1828, A1823, NYSA; Simeon DeWitt, "Report of the Surveyor-General," Mar. 6, 1834, New York State Senate doc. 88; *Whipple Report*, 291–93.

56. Justus Ingersoll to Samuel J. Huntington, Oct. 4, 1830, M234 r. 832, NA; *Whipple Report*, 303–5; "List of Orchard . . . Who Did Emigrate," 1830 (filed as "Onondaga Indians"), A0832, NYSA; Report of the Commission on Indian Affairs, Mar. 7, 1835, New York State Assembly doc. 260.

57. Patricia K. Ourada, *The Menominee Indians: A History* (Norman: University of Oklahoma Press, 1979), 79–88, 94; Venables, "Victim versus Victim," 145–49.

58. John H. Eaton, Instructions from the Secretary of War to Erastus Root James McCall and John T. Mason, in "M'Call's Journal of a Visit to Wisconsin in 1830," *Wisconsin Historical Collections* 12 (1892): 174–75.

59. "M'Call's Journal," 195–96, "Documents Illustrating M'Call's Journal," *Wisconsin Historical Collections* 12 (1892): 213.

60. In addition to Bread, the Oneida signers were John Anthony Brant, Henry Powless, Nathaniel Neddy, Cornelius Stevens, and Thomas Neddy, *Indian Affairs*, 2:382.

61. John F. Schermerhorn to Carey A. Harris, Nov. 24, 1837, M234, r. 583, NA; James Stryker to Cass, "Estimate of 1833," Mar. 13, 1834, M234, r. 832, NA; Oberly, *Nation of Statesmen*, 43–51; Hauptman and McLester, *Chief Daniel Bread*, 48–77.

62. Oneida chiefs to Cass, Dec. 15, 1831, M234, r. 832, NA.

63. Clayton Mau, ed., *The Development of Central and Western New York* (Danville, N.Y.: F. A. Owen, 1958), 298–301; John Nelson Davidson, *Proceedings of the State Historical Society of Wisconsin* 47 (1899): 181.

64. Jackson Kemper, "Journal of an Episcopal Missionary's Tour to Green Bay, 1834," *Wisconsin Historical Collections* 14 (1898): 432; Kemper, "Journal," 439–40; Fish

Cadle to George Boyd, Sept. 2, 1834, 489–90, and Boyd to S. Mason, Sept. 30, 1834, George Boyd Papers, State Historical Society of Wisconsin.

65. Samuel Stambaugh, "Report on the Quality and Condition of Wisconsin Territory, 1831," *Wisconsin Historical Collections* 15 (1900): 365, 406–7; Kemper, "Journal," 433; "Statement of the Number of Each Tribe of Indians within the Green Bay Sub Agency," Sept. 30, 1840, Boyd Papers; *Annual Report of the Commissioner of Indian Affairs to the Secretary of the Interior, 1844–1845* (Washington, D.C.: C. Alexander, 1844), 58–59, 130–31; Horsman, "Origins," 70–71.

66. Alfred A. Cope, "A Mission to the Menominee: Alfred Cope's Green Bay Diary," *Wisconsin Magazine of History* 50 (1967): 137.

67. Alex F. Ricciardelli, "The Adoption of White Agriculture by the Oneida Indians," in *The Emergent Native Americans: A Reader in Culture Contact*, ed. Deward E. Walker Jr. (Boston: Little, Brown, 1971), 336.

68. Henry R. Colman, "Recollections of the Oneida Indians," *Proceedings of the State Historical Society of Wisconsin* 59 (1912), 157; twentieth-century missionary J. K. Bloomfield, *The Oneidas* (New York: Alden Brothers, 1907), 242.

69. Cope, "Mission to Menominee," 136; Colman, "Recollections of the Oneida Indians," 155.

70. Cope, "Mission to Menominee," 144.

Chapter 7. Diaspora and Survival, 1836–1850

1. Charles J. Kappler, ed. and comp., *Indian Affairs Laws and Treaties* (Washington, D.C.: Government Printing Office, 1904), 2:439–49; Grant Foreman, *The Last Trek of the Indians* (Chicago: University of Chicago Press, 1946), 334. See Lewis Cass's instructions to John Schermerhorn in Cass to Schermerhorn, July 13, 1836, M21, r. 19, NA.

2. Mary H. Conable, "A Steady Enemy: The Ogden Land Company and the Seneca Indians" (Ph.D. diss., University of Rochester, 1994), 119; John Schermerhorn's report of his proceedings with New York Indians, Dec. 28, 1836, and Schermerhorn to Andrew Jackson, Aug. 29, 1836, M234, r. 583, NA.

3. John Schermerhorn to Elbert Herring, Nov. 12, 1833, M234, r. 832, NA; James Stryker to Lewis Cass, Mar. 21, 1834, M234, r. 832, NA; Schermerhorn to Cary Harris, Sept. 1, 1836, M234, r. 583, NA; Schermerhorn to Andrew Jackson; treaty with the New York Indians, Sept. 16, 1836, *IIDH;* Schermerhorn's report of his proceedings with the New York Indians, Dec. 28, 1836; Laurence M. Hauptman and L. Gordon McLester III, *Chief Daniel Bread and the Oneida Nation of Indians of Wisconsin* (Norman: University of Oklahoma Press, 2002), 92–94.

4. Schermerhorn to Harris, Nov. 27 (24?), 1837, M234, r. 583, NA; Elijah Schenandoah, Christian Beechtree, Jacob Powlis, Thomas Webster, and Henry Jordan to the President, Senate, and Secretary of War, Nov. 24, 1837, M234, r. 583; Ransom Gillet to Harris, Feb. 9, 1838 (Feb. 16, 1838), *IIDH.*

5. Elijah Skenandoah et al. to the President of the United States, Nov. 24, 1837, and Silas Wright to Harris, Mar. 15, 1837, M234, r. 583.

6. Schermerhorn to Harris, Nov. 27, 1837, M234, r. 583, NA; notes of Western Expedition conduct of Schermerhorn, box 3, folder 4, Boo-2 Indians, Buffalo and Erie County Historical Society, Buffalo, N.Y.

7. Oneidas to President Van Buren, Aug. 17, 1837, M234, r. 583, NA. Up to six Oneidas may have been part of the expedition. Memorial from Six Nations to President Van Buren, Oct. 2, 1837, Huntington Library, San Marino, Calif.

8. Schermerhorn to Harris, Nov. 22, 1837; Schermerhorn to J. R. Poinsett, Nov. 20, 1837; Gillet to Poinsett, Oct. 29, 1837, all M234. r. 583, NA.

9. Gillet to Harris, Nov. 26, 1837, M234, r. 583, NA; articles of agreement, Feb. 23, 1837, *IIDH* (see also additional or supplementary articles, Feb. 23, 1837); Conable, "Steady Enemy," 130–31; Laurence M. Hauptman, *Conspiracy of Interests: Iroquois Dispossession and the Rise of New York State* (Syracuse, N.Y.: Syracuse University Press, 1999), 180–81; Gillet quoted in n.d., Ransom Gillett Papers, box 1, folder 4, SC11329, NYSL.

10. Gillet to Harris, Nov. 26, 1837; Gillet to Harris, Dec. 27, 1837, M234, r. 583; Gillet to Harris, Mar. 26, 1838, M234, r. 583.

11. Kappler, *Indian Affairs*, 2:502–16; Francis Paul Prucha, *American Indian Treaties: The History of a Political Anomaly* (Berkeley: University of California Press, 1994), 202–7; Hauptman, *Conspiracy of Interests*, 175–90; Stephen J. Valone, "William Seward, Whig Politics, and the Compromised Indian Removal Policy in New York State, 1838–1843," *New York History* 82 (2001): 108–34.

12. Agreement between Heman Potter and Baptist Powless, Dec. 25, 1837; agreement between Potter and Jonathan Jourdan, Dec. 25, 1837; statement of Catharine Jourdan, May 28, 1840; Baptist Powless to John F. Schermerhorn, July 20, 1840/Sept. 28, 1840, all *IIDH*. On Oneidas present and their limited authority, see Ransom Gillet, report of treaty, Feb. 27, 1838, M234, r. 583.

13. John Anthony contract with Heman Potter, Dec. 27, 1837 (Eleazer Williams was the witness to this agreement); Honyost Smith contract with Potter, Dec. 27, 1837, both *IIDH*; Kappler, *Indian Affairs*, 2:517–18.

14. Gillet to Harris, Jan. 18, 1838, *IIDH*; Second Christian and Orchard Party, Feb. 22, 1818, M18, r. 11, Feb. 22, 1838, M18, r. 11, NA. (This document is missing; the only evidence of its existence and content is the notation in the Register of Letters) John Hadcock to H. L. Sumner, May 1, 1840, M234, r. 318, NA. Arlinda Locklear, "The Buffalo Creek Treaty of 1838 and Its Legal Implications for Oneida Land Claims," in *The Oneida Indian Journey*, ed. Laurence M. Hauptman and L. Gordon McLester III (Madison: University of Wisconsin Press, 1999), 85–89.

15. Gillet, report, Feb 27, 1838; Cary Harris, "Special Instructions as to the Oneidas & St. Regis," after Jan. 15, 1838, *IIDH* (Harris's qualification regarding the Oneidas was echoed in is draft instructions to Gillet: "~~the Oneidas~~ that portion of the Oneidas who signed the treaty at Buffalo"); Gillet to the Chiefs head men and warriors of the Oneida Indians in New York, Aug. 9, 1838; Gillet to Harris, Aug. 11, 1838; Gillet to Harris, Aug. 16, 1838, all M234, r. 583, NA. Since no Oneidas were compelled to adhere to the terms of the Buffalo Creek Treaty, fifteen Oneidas signed a statement accepting the treaty.

16. Second Christian Party to Seward, Jan. 7, 1839, William Henry Seward Papers, University of Rochester Library, Rochester, N.Y.; Second Christian Party to Martin Van Buren, Jan. 18, 1839, M234, r. 583, NA.

17. John Hadcock to H. L. Sumner, May 1, 1840, M234, r. 318, NA; Schermerhorn to J. R. Poinsett, Apr. 11, 1840, M234, r. 584, NA; Oneida sachems and warriors to Sir Charles Metcalfe, n.d., RG10, 441:843–46, National Archives of Canada, Ottawa; Donald B. Smith, *Sacred Feathers: The Reverend Peter Jones (Kahkewaquonaby) and the Mississauga Indians* (Lincoln: University of Nebraska Press, 1987), 174; officer quoted in S. P. Jarvis to S. B. Harrison, Sept. 25, 1840, RG10, vol. 504, C-13342, National Archives of Canada.

18. Oneida sachems and warriors to Sir Charles Metcalfe, n.d., RG10, vol. 441:843–46, National Archives of Canada; Joseph B. Clench to Moses Schuyler and his People at Oneida Castle, Jan. 1840, RG10, vol. 441, C-9636:7 (all Clench quotations); Oneidas to Poinsett, Feb. 6, 1840, M234, r. 584, NA; Hadcock to Sumner, May 1, 1840.

19. R. J. Surtees, "The Development of an Indian Reserve Policy in Canada," *Ontario History* 61 (1969): 87–98; quoted in Peter S. Schmalz, *The Ojibwa in Southern Ontario* (Toronto: University of Toronto Press, 1991), 165–70; Minute in Council, Aug. 14, 1840, RG1, E3, vol. 59, r. C-1197:199, National Archives of Canada.

20. Schermerhorn to Poinsett, Apr. 11, 1840; Oneidas to Seward, July 7, 1840, Seward Papers.

21. *Whipple Report,* 309–29; Nathan Burchard, "Field Book of the Survey and Allotment of the Oneida Purchase of 1840," Surveyor-General's Field Books, A4019, vol. 46, NYSA.

22. Copy of survey of land belonging to the First and Second Christian Parties, Nov. 30, 1840, *IIDH;* Oneidas to Seward, May 7, 1841, and "Stay Party" Oneidas to Seward, July 23, 1841, Seward Papers. "An Act in Relation to Certain Tribes of Indians," May 25, 1841, New York Session Laws, chap. 234, established a salary of one hundred dollars a year for the attorney "in lieu of all other compensation heretofore provided."

23. S. Walden to S. P. Jarvis, Mar. 16, 1841, RG10, 128:72193, r. C-11483, National Archives of Canada.

24. William H. Smith, *Smith's Canadian Gazetteer* (Toronto: H. Rasnell, 1846), 188–89; Jarvis to Robert Bruce, June 11, 1850, RG10, vol. 183, pt. 1, no. 4401–500, p. 105950–56, National Archives of Canada.

25. Alex Ricciardelli, "The Adoption of White Agriculture by the Oneida Indians," in *The Emergent Native Americans: A Reader in Culture Contact,* ed. Deward E. Walker Jr. (Boston, Mass.: Little, Brown, 1971), 318; copy of memorial from chiefs and warriors of Six Nations to the President of the United States, Oct. 2, 1837, *IIDH;* Clench quoted in Jack Campisi, "Ethnic Identity and Boundary Maintenance in Three Oneida Communities," (Ph.D. diss., SUNY-Albany, 1974), 270.

26. Green Bay Oneidas quoted in Cornelius Stevens et al. to Seward, July 27, 1840, Seward Papers; State of New York, Census of Indians for 1845; D. E. Sill to W. P. Dale, Nov. 8, 1861, M234, r. 589; A. Sherman to F. A. Walker, Jan. 4, 1873, M234, r. 591; D. Sherman to J. L. Smith, May 4, 1877, M234, r. 594, all NA; Robert W. Ven-

ables, ed., *The Six Nations of New York: The 1892 United States Extra Census Bulletin* (Ithaca, N.Y.: Cornell University Press, 1995); "Report Respecting Indians in New York by Thomas Wells," 1848, New York Yearly Meeting Indian Committee scrapbook, FHL; Nathaniel T. Strong, appendix to *Census of the State of New York for 1855* (Albany, N.Y.: Charles Van Benthuysen, 1857), 500–519 (quotation on 506).

27. Seward to Moses Schuyler, draft, May 1, 1841; same to same, n.d., r. 20, Seward Papers; "Report of the Committee to Visit the Onondaga Indians &c," New York Yearly Meeting Indian Committee minutes, 1840, FHL.

28. *Whipple Report*, 320 ("prudent"), 334, 348; Anthony Wonderley, *Oneida Iroquois Folklore, Myth, and History: New York Oral Narrative from the Notes of H. E. Allen and Others* (Syracuse, N.Y.: Syracuse University Press, 2004), 49–50, 193–96.

29. "An Act Relating to the Oneida Tribe of Indians," Mar. 8, 1839, New York Session Laws, chap. 58; New York Yearly Meeting Indian Committee Minutes, Nov. 1840 or after, FHL; Lewis Henry Morgan, *League of the Iroquois* (1851; repr., Secaucus, N.J.: Citadel Press, 1962), 119. Morgan also created a fraternal order based on Iroquois cultural elements. Ironically, he adopted the name "Skenandoah." Steven Conn, *History's Shadow: Native Americans and Historical Consciousness in the Nineteenth Century* (Chicago, Ill.: University of Chicago Press, 2004), 71–94.

30. "An Act to Enable Resident Aliens to Hold and Convey Real Estate," Apr. 10, 1843, New York Session Laws, chap. 87; "An Act Relative to the Oneida Indians," Apr. 18, 1843, ibid., chap. 185.

31. Deborah A. Rosen, *American Indians and State Law: Sovereignty, Race, and Citizenship, 1790–1880* (Lincoln: University of Nebraska Press, 2007), 23–38; Matthew Dennis, "Sorcery and Sovereignty: Senecas, Citizens, and the Contest for Power and Authority on the Frontiers of the Early American Republic" in *New World Orders: Violence, Sanction, and Authority in the Colonial Americas*, ed. John Smolenski and Thomas J. Humphrey (Philadelphia: University of Pennsylvania Press, 2005), 193–97; *Goodell v. Jackson*, N.Y. Lexis 36 (1823); *U.S. v. Elm*, 25 F. Cas. 1006, 1007–1008 (1877); "An Act in Relation to the Oneida Indians," Dec. 15, 1847, New York Session Laws, chap. 486; "An Act for the Relief of the Indian Owners of Lot Number 3 of the Oneida Purchase Made in the Year 1842," Apr. 11, 1849, New York Session Laws, chap. 420.

32. Wells, "Report Respecting Indians."

33. Thomas Donaldson, *Extra Census Bulletin. Indians. The Six Nations of New York* (Washington, D.C.: Government Printing Office, 1892), 25; *Free Church Circular* 4, no. 1 (Feb. 20, 1851): 7–8; Thomas Cornelius et al. to Hiram Jenkins, Nov. 25, 1863, M234, r. 590, NA.

34. Oneidas to Joel Poinsett, Feb. 8, 1840, and chiefs of the Seneca, Onondaga, Cayuga, Oneida, and Tuscarora tribes to Martin Van Buren, Nov. 25, 1840, M234, r. 584, NA; William Medill to Charles Cist, Oct. 5, 1847, M234, r. 597, NA; T. Hartley Crawford to John C. Spencer, Nov. 16, 1842, in *New American State Papers: Indian Affairs* (Wilmington, Del.: Scholarly Resources, 1972), 2:13–14.

35. Stephen Osborne to Crawford, Sept. 12, 1843; Osborne to Crawford, Oct. 13, 1847; Abraham Hogeboom to unidentified correspondent, Oct. 27, 1843; Osborne to

Crawford, Mar. 4, 1844, all M234, r. 597, NA; Crawford to William Wilkins, Nov. 25, 1844, in *New American State Papers,* 2:86.

36. Stephen Osborne to Crawford, June 5, 1845, Osborne to Medill, Dec. 24, 1845; Osborne to Crawford, Sept. 12, 1843; same to same, Oct. 13, 1843; same to same, Mar. 4, 1844; Osborne to Medill, Dec. 24, 1845; Hogeboom to unidentified correspondent, Oct. 27, 1843, all M234, r. 597, NA; Crawford to William Marcy, May 21, 1845, and Osborne to Crawford, June 5, 1845, both M234, r. 586, NA.

37. Thomas H. Harvey to T. Hartley Crawford, Sept. 6, 1845, M234, r. 597. Denny was referring primarily to Oneidas from Green Bay, where the bulk of whatever Oneida support for removal to Kansas existed was to be found; Six Nations Indians to the President, July 30, 1845, M234, r. 586, NA; George Fox, James Cusick, Baptist Powless, Thomas King, and John Denny to President of the United States, Sept. 11, 1845, M234, r. 596, NA. A letter was also sent by Oneidas at Duck Creek to Marcy, July 10, 1845, complaining of the influx of white settlers. M234, r. 596, NA.

38. Report of the commissioner of Indian Affairs, Nov. 24, 1845, in *New American State Papers* 2:119–49; James Cusick and Seneca White to Marcy, Oct. 6, 1845, M234, r. 597, NA; H. Price to the Secretary of the Interior, Feb. 9, 1883, U.S. House of Representatives, 47th Cong., 2d sess., report 2001; Osborne to Medill, Dec. 24, 1845, M234 r. 597, NA; Report of the commissioner of Indian affairs, Nov. 30, 1846, in *New American State Papers* 2:150–69.

39. George W. Clinton to Medill, May 28, 1846, M234, r. 597, NA; Medill to Marcy, Nov. 30, 1846, in *New American State Papers,* 2:150; Osborne to Medill, July 9, 1846, M234, r. 597, Hogeboom to Medill, Aug. 8, 1846, M234, r. 587; Hogeboom to Medill, Aug. 22, 1846; Medill to Marcy, Nov. 30, 1846; Medill to Cist, Oct. 5, 1847, M234, r. 597; W. P. Angel to Medill, June[?] 25, 1848, M234, r. 597, all NA.

40. George W. Clinton to Medill, May 28, 1846; Hogeboom to Medill, Aug. 22, 1846; James N. Cusick to Marcy, Aug. 4, 1846; John Havarty[?] to Medill, June 2, 1846; Richard W. Cummins to Thomas H. Harvey, Aug. 4, 1846, all M234, r. 597, NA ("left no funds").

41. Hogeboom to Medill, Aug. 22, 1846; Bela H. Colegrove, "List Containing the Names of Such New York Indians Now Residing in Kansas Territory, n.d" (this list consists of seventy names, twenty-eight of which were unconfirmed); W. P. Angel, "List of Indians," June 25, 1848, all M234, r. 597; Report of the Committee of Indian Affairs, New York State Senate, Mar. 24, 1847, no. 70; Resolution of the New York State Assembly and Senate, Feb. 16, 1847; John King to the President of the United States, Mar. 2, 1847, M234, r. 597, NA.

42. Richard G. Bremer, *Indian Agent and Wilderness Scholar: The Life of Henry Rowe Schoolcraft* (Mount Pleasant, Mich.: Clarke Historical Library, 1987), 271–83; Richard U. Shearman to Henry Rowe Schoolcraft, Oct. 4, 1845, r. 35, Henry Rowe Schoolcraft Papers, Library of Congress, Washington, D.C.

43. Schoolcraft to Nathaniel S. Benton, July 17, 1845, Schoolcraft Papers, r. 10; Richard U. Shearman to Schoolcraft, Oct. 4, 1845, Schoolcraft Papers, r. 35.

44. Donald H. Parkerson, *The Agricultural Transition in New York State: Markets and Migration in Mid-Nineteenth-Century America* (Ames: Iowa State University

Press, 1995), 90; Nancy Shoemaker, "The Census as Civilizer," *Historical Methods* 25 (1992): 4–11; Shoemaker, "From Longhouse to Loghouse: Household Structure among the Senecas in 1900," *American Indian Quarterly* 15 (1991): 331–32.

45. Neal Ferris, *Archaeology of Native-Lived Colonialism: Challenging History in the Great Lakes* (Tucson: University of Arizona Press, 2008), 141. Of course, if Shearman missed some, the total yield would be higher. But the production seems to have been close not only to Heidenreich's estimate but to the production of corn among the Tuscarora on the Six Nations reserve in 1861, as established by Ferris. For a description of the mortar and pestle, see T.C.M., "Among the Autochthons," *The Circular*, Nov. 2, 1868, 264.

46. Ferris, *Archaeology of Native-Lived Colonialism*, 149.

47. Richard U. Shearman to Schoolcraft, Oct. 4, 1845, Schoolcraft Papers, r. 35.

48. *Daily Journal of Oneida Community*, no. 51, Mar. 15, 1866, 1.

49. Strong, appendix, 506. The problem of obtaining accurate data arose again in 1865, complete with the enumerator's condescension: "It was with much difficulty that I got their report; . . . they were very reluctant . . . until they came together and talked over the matter, and the more intelligent explained it to them." *Census of the State of New York for 1865* (Albany, N.Y.: Charles van Benthuysen, 1867), 601.

50. Susan Fenimore Cooper, *Rural Hours, by a Lady* (New York: George P. Putnam, 1850), 175–82.

51. George R. Hamell, "The Iroquois and the World's Rim: Speculations on Color, Culture, and Contact," *American Indian Quarterly* 16 (1992): 451–69; Christopher L. Miller and Hamell, "A New Perspective on Indian-White Contact: Cultural Symbols and Colonial Trade," *Journal of American History* 73 (1986): 311–28; Beverly Gordon, "The Niagara Falls Whimsey: The Object as a Symbol of Cultural Interface" (Ph.D. diss., University of Wisconsin–Madison, 1984), 285–92; Wonderley, *Oneida Iroquois Folklore*, 188.

52. Constance Noyes Robinson, *The Oneida Community: An Autobiography, 1851–1876* (Syracuse, N.Y.: Syracuse University Press, 1970), 26; John Hadcock to Lyman C. Draper, May 6, 1872, Draper Manuscripts, 11U:264–65, State Historical Society of Wisconsin, Madison; quoted in "The Indian Gathering," *The Circular*, July 4, 1852, 134.

53. *The Circular*, Apr. 14, 1864, 20 ("stocked"); "The Indians at Oneida," *The Circular*, Aug. 20, 1866, 181 ("boudoir"); *Daily Journal of the Oneida Community*, June 21, 1867; *Daily Journal of the Oneida Community*, July 21, 1866. In 1868, Oneida women complained of "hard times" after being barred from selling beadwork on railway cars. *The Circular*, Feb. 24, 1868; "Indian Gathering," 134.

54. Miss Leslie, "Western New York: A Slight Sketch," *Godey's Lady's Book*, Nov. 1845; *The Circular*, Dec. 24, 1857, 195; *Utica Evening Telegraph*, July 27, 1857; *The Circular*, Sept. 11, 1865, 204; Wonderley, *Oneida Indian Folklore*, 190; Theodore Corbett, *The Making of American Resorts: Saratoga Springs, Ballston Spa, Lake George* (New Brunswick, N.J.: Rutgers University Press, 2001), 177–80; Gordon, "Niagara Falls Whimsey," 199–200; Karen Dubinsky, *The Second Greatest Disappointment: Honeymooning and Tourism at Niagara Falls* (Toronto: Between the Lines, 1999), 60–66;

Gerry Biron, "A Cherished Curiosity: The Niagara Floral-Style Beaded Bag in the Victorian Era," *American Indian Art Magazine* 35, no. 4 (2010): 42–51.

55. Cooper, *Rural Hours*, 175.

56. Margaret Hall, *The Aristocratic Journey, Being the Outspoken Letters of Mrs. Basil Hall Written during a Fourteen Months' Sojourn in America, 1827–1828*, ed. Una Pope-Hennessy (New York: G. P. Putnam's Sons, 1931), 59–61; *Rhode-Island American* (Newport, R.I.), July 13, 1827, 2.

57. "Indian Gathering," 134.

58. William S. Sturtevant, "Early Iroquois Realist Painting and Identity Marking," in *Three Centuries of Woodlands Indian Art: A Collection of Essays*, ed. J. C. H. King and Christian F. Feest (Altenstadt, Germany: ZKF Publishers, 2007), 129–43.

59. T.C.M., "Among the Autochthons."

Conclusion

1. Ray Halbritter and Steven Paul McSloy, "Empowerment or Dependence? The Practical Value and Meaning of Native American Sovereignty," *New York University Journal of International Law and Politics* 26 (1994): 567–68.

Index

Page numbers in italics refer to figures and tables.

A native of the Bronx, KARIM M. TIRO graduated from Drew University and the University of Pennsylvania. He is presently an associate professor of history at Xavier University in Cincinnati, Ohio. He is co-editor, with Cesare Marino, of *Along the Hudson and Mohawk: The 1790 Journey of Count Paolo Andreani*. His essays have appeared in *American Quarterly, American Indian Law Review, Journal of the Early Republic,* and elsewhere.